MW01200989

# ReVoLuTion, ShE WROTE

RED LETTER PRESS • SEATTLE

# CLARA FRASER

# SHE WROTE

INTRODUCTION BY JOANNA RUSS

© 1998 by Red Letter Press
409 Maynard Avenue South, Suite 201
Seattle, WA 98104 • (206)682-0990
RedLetterPress@juno.com
All rights reserved
Printed in the United States of America

First Edition. 1998

*Library of Congress Cataloging-in-Publication Data*
Fraser, Clara, 1923-
Revolution, she wrote / by Clara Fraser ;
introduction by Joanna Russ. —1st ed.
p. cm.
Includes bibliographical references and index.
ISBN 0-932323-04-9 (paperback)
1. Feminist theory.
2. Women and communism. 3. Socialism.
4. Lesbian feminism. I. Title.
HQ1190.F725 1998
305.42'01—DC21 97-43471

*Cover Design:* Bill Cumming
The portrait of Clara Fraser shown on
the cover and title page is a detail from
a 1959 painting by Bill Cumming.
The full-length portrait is
reproduced on page 103.
*Book Design:* Helen Gilbert

Articles in this book were first
published in the *Freedom Socialist*
newspaper unless other credit is given.
Photos courtesy of *Freedom Socialist*
newspaper and Clara Fraser.

1

*To the wonderful, communal world of
comrades and the intense sphere of co-workers
who taught me about life in this
paradoxical country and gave me
firm encouragement when I most needed it
in my jousting with the bad guys.*

*And to the historical pantheon of free-thinkers,
doers, and geniuses who impacted my mind
from my earliest years and
whose dynamic hold never let loose of me—
Clara Zetkin, Rosa Luxemburg,
Meridel LeSueur, Sojourner Truth,
Karl Marx, Frederick Engels,
Lenin, James P. Cannon
and, above all, Leon Trotsky.
Great feminists all of them, whose profound ideas are
always there to guide me out of thickets and
illuminate the road ahead.*

*From them I learned that the act of fighting injustice
is full of hope and joy when it is viewed,
and properly so, as a slice of an innate
historical tradition, an ancient reaching out
for universal human fulfillment.*

# Contents

## 4. Scoundrels, Sellouts, and Wimps

## 5. A Radical Yankee in King Capital's Courts

# Scenes from a Rebel Life
*Photographs*

# Introduction

**T**he logic of feminism is to expand inexorably into generalized radicalism.

I came to this conclusion only a few years ago, after 23 years of feminist activism, work and study. I came to a whole host of related conclusions, too: that single-issue activism is a dead end, that class, sexism and racism depend upon each other and that the feminism which doesn't understand this will inevitably decay into careers-for-well-to-do-white-ladies (who think that somehow they are representative of all the world's women), that no one must psychologically cut off parts of their own identity because these don't fit into the prescriptions of this or that particular group, that unjust behavior is exactly that and it's unacceptable, even when done by people in your own oppressed group, and that the famous "psychology of women" is no different from the psychology of other oppressed groups, i.e., that it's the psychology of oppression itself.

Clara Fraser came to these conclusions too—but long, long before I ever did. The edge she had over me wasn't an individual one. It wasn't her brilliance or her energy—though she *is* brilliant and energetic (and if anybody wants to call me brilliant, I certainly won't protest) but something a good deal more important. Clara's advantage over me is that she has always been a socialist revolutionary and that she has worked with others in Radical Women, a group she helped found, which has successfully combined feminism and socialism for 29 years. She is also one of the founders of the Freedom Socialist Party. Both organizations have branches in many cities in the United States and overseas. It was a shock to me when I read the manuscript for the book you now hold in your hands and realized how entirely her columns and speeches had anticipated what I thought was new. It wasn't; it was only new to me. That's why the first sentence of this introduction isn't mine. It's Clara's—and it was written in 1965!

How do you think I feel about that?

Well, you're wrong. I'm delighted. In fact it's a joy to find myself saying exactly what others have said before me and continue to say in a tradition that spans at least 150 years. In any politics worth the name, "I" can do infinitely less than "we."

Here are some more socialist feminist ideas from Clara. They controvert everything I was told about socialist feminism when I first became a feminist and a good deal that I have heard since.

> Never, never, never must male or female radicals counsel feminists to subordinate or table their demands in the interests of an abstract, isolationist "class" unity.
>
> (1978)

> [Their] contempt for women has carved a great gulf between leftists and feminists. Sexist revolutionaries have much to answer for.
>
> (1995)

> [Minority women] are destined for leadership of the entire human race.
>
> (1972)

> The single-issue is the dead-end issue. It always ends up

smack against the wall. True, it is large, but it is also, in-variably, diffuse, ambiguous, contradictory, deceptive and mercurial. . . It moves to the right, *not* to the left, and it moves radicals right along with it.

(1973)

In 1973 Clara also predicted:

Women's liberation, led and oriented towards the center, will turn into its opposite, women's *reformism*, which in turn always becomes an enemy of workingclass and mi-nority women.

Even more important, in the same year:

The capitalist system *cannot* grant working and minority women substantial reforms because these would seri-ously weaken the very pillars upon which the system itself rests.

Therefore:

Without [socialist feminist] leadership, the women's movement, like every other movement, will petrify, cor-rode, adapt and drown inside the Democratic Party or inane, single-issue liberalism. Or it will adopt an ultra-left, insanely sectarian and/or terroristic stance, born of desperation and bitterness.

I became a feminist as soon as I knew that such a movement existed, 27 years ago as of this writing. I have seen everything Clara predicted above come to pass. Only weeks ago in *The Nation* (of all places!) Gloria Steinem was quoted as saying that we had better vote for Clinton because Dole would be worse, a "wait until next time" that has an awfully familiar ring. Well, hey, as Steinem herself used to say about sudden insights, *Click!*, there is feminism either turning rightwards with a vengeance or (at the very least) drowning inside the Democratic Party ditto.

But if socialist feminism in general, and Radical Women and the Freedom Socialist Party in particular are so important, why didn't I understand all this in 1984, when I first got to know about them? The answer is all too simple.

Just as I used to think, many years ago, that radicals were little cartoon men who hid bombs under their coats (where they hid them in the summertime, when it was too hot to wear coats, I never did figure out), in the same way I had been taught an automatic and entirely unthinking response to a certain list of words, which included "workers," "Marx," "Marxism," "Marxism-Leninism," "the ruling class" and so on. Even after I had met socialist feminists in person and realized that they were on to something extremely important, I still couldn't quite eradicate that suspicion, inculcated most vigorously during the Cold War (when I was a teenager), that becoming a socialist meant I would have to (1) martyr myself, (2) give up thinking on my own, (3) give up my feminism, (4) lose my job, (5) associate with overbearing and nasty people, and (6) listen to the ghastliest, most boring kind of rhetoric you can imagine, which would kill me in two minutes max.

Just as meeting declared lesbians for the first time in 1970 scared me half to death because I knew the moment would come that they would do something horrible, sexual and— well, something *lesbian* that would scar me forever—in the same way, I couldn't quite believe that socialists wouldn't eventually reveal their basically evil nature. They would leap at me, tie me down in spite of my screams and struggles and administer some drug that would make me their will-less slave.

The name of this nonsense, of course, is propaganda. It's like the similar falsehood that the struggle against sexism and the struggle against racism are rivals and that you must choose one of them but never both. Similarly we are taught that socialists can't just be people, warts and all, but that every wart on a socialist face is a sign of deep, political evil while others' warts are merely personal imperfections and don't have political implications.

I've seen the movement that I joined in 1969 make terrible errors. I have seen feminism turn, all too often into an advancement club for middle-managerial, white, professional women. I've seen academic feminism become so jargon-ified and elaborate that even the theories in it that are useful can hardly be understood by anyone—including a good many academics—who's not already part of it.

Much feminism has moved steadily away from the radicalism that characterized it in the 1960s. Its fundamental error has been to ignore the interconnectedness of all oppression. Feminist theory can't explain every oppression. Not all women are "naturally" on the same side on other issues. The radical feminist view that women are the primary social issue of the ages irrespective of class, race, nation, etc., is paralleled by cultural nationalism in people of color and ethnic movements.

And as Clara says:

> Cultural nationalism is what the Black Panthers used to call "pork chop nationalism." It is where you make the cultural folkways. . .and lifestyles of your own group into a substitute for politics, philosophy and a strategy for change. It doesn't work. . . What it *can* do is destroy a movement. . .

> My father used to have a friend [whose sole interest was] "what's in it for the Jews?". . . The only thing he cared about was what might directly, narrowly, benefit the Jews. . . This type of attitude has produced the Palestinian uprising known as the *intifadeh*. If you're going to do the cultural nationalist trip, you end up being Jewish

Nazis shooting down Palestinian kids.

(1989)

Feminism is precious to me. That's why I hate seeing it become a new lifestyle for middleclass, career-minded couples or an improvement in certain men's public manners or an excuse for demanding that more women work a 90-hour week (and the mass media blame *feminism* for that!) or another way of blaming individual people for not being billionaires.

Clara knew all this all along. So read this book carefully. Have fun with it, too. Her writing is pointed and very funny. The very titles will make you chortle, from the name of the book itself to "Exit Stage Right" (Betty Friedan) or "Dr. Zhivago: Dixiecrat of the Steppes." To "The Love that Dare Not Speak its Name" she simply adds "in the Army." Her extended comparison of the employer who fired her (Seattle City Light) and its lawyers' defense when she sued, to Mount St. Helens and an imaginary defense of *it* against the charge of having erupted builds and builds. "Eruptions" she wrote "are a management prerogative of mountains," and "Anyone leveling such a charge obviously hates mountains and wants to level *them*." There are six more comparisons, each more accurate (and more purposely absurd) than the last. (The mountain, of course, *had* erupted. And Clara ultimately won her suit against her former employer.)

Clara is also *hopeful*. Her wit is her own, of course, but her hopefulness is hers *and* socialist. At a time when demonizing the poor or otherwise helpless has become an indoor sport in our United States, when the media offer us ever more trendy circuses and bread disappears, when human beings are treated as consumables, when we're told that wealth and style are the only things that matter (mall ethics, I call it), when the greed of the ruling class is so openly displayed that ever more logic-twisting and censorship are regularly employed in the hopes that we won't notice, in an election year in which it took a thorough-going bigot even to mention poverty as an issue, this book is hopeful. It has good reasons to be. Read it and find out what they are.

I could go on quoting Clara's words forever, but I won't. Like Spock's Vulcan father, Sarek, I submit to the logic of the situation.

Here's Clara.

JOANNA RUSS
Tucson, Arizona

# Cover Artist's Note to Readers

Forty years ago, I walked away from ideology and back to art. But I did not walk away from friends who remained. So I was pleased to be asked to help design a cover for Clara's book, which is, of course, highly ideological.

I can only say that I am happy to be able to use my skills to pay tribute to Clara's courage and particularly to her refusal to accomodate to the willful blindness of men in their obtuse failure to recognize the personhood of women.

BILL CUMMING
Seattle, Washington

# 1

## Toward *Human* Beingness

# Of Hermits, Hedonists and Related Narcissists

1979

In the melting pot ghetto of East Los Angeles where I grew up during the Great Depression, everybody seemed to know that the only way to keep things from getting worse was to organize to make them better.

Everyone was involved in some group bent on improving some facet of social arrangements. What outfit you belonged to was your badge of distinction, the mark of your individuality and the guidepost to your relations with others. And the kind of life that gravitated around causes was full of meaning and stimulation. Social activists found satisfaction, ideological understanding, humor, and companionship as the fringe benefits of commitment, and it was an exciting way to rise to the call of *human* beingness. The political *was* the personal.

That's right, back in those olden times working people cared about the world, and everybody had a pet panacea, especially in that golden Southern California clime of sects and movements where anything seemed possible and the improbable was institutionalized. And to the adolescents growing up optimistic, athletic, and reflexively welded to our clubs and teams and schools and neighborhoods, the symbol of high craziness was the *hermit*, the barefoot weirdo who wandered through the Hollywood hills and fled if people approached. We laughed 'til we fell down, teenage-style, at a man who chose solitude instead of the human comedy.

Our heroes, naturally, were the freedom fighters and rebels. One day in 1938, a group of wounded Spanish Civil War veterans visited our high school, and classrooms emptied as students and teachers alike rushed to welcome the Abraham Lincoln Brigaders and to gaze, star-struck, at the glamorous figures. One of them, praise be, lived on my street and offered to walk me home. He walked and I floated, Cinderella at the ball. *That* was prestige!

We were poor, with nothing but prospects, but filled with hope and idealism and the enormous capacity for enjoyment. We never had any money; everything we earned went for clothing, school supplies, streetcar fare, movies and dance halls—the basics. Daddies were periodically unemployed and mamas slaved in the garment shops or in somebody's kitchen or store, and we hung on every tale of our parents matching wits and fists with the bosses. We helped neighbors in need, fed the beggars who came to the door if they asked *nicely*, and went to all the mass meetings against the mass of injustices. We had a wonderful time applauding the speakers, booing the bad guys, and kidding around with the buddies we ran into. We were a *community*, and that was invigorating.

How good it was to be young and alive and turned on and tuned in and doing something that mattered.

Quiet as it's kept, it still is. While nothing is too good for the working class, and no labor-saving household device should ever be sneered at, when the sole purpose of living is to luxuriate in the "good life," in "personal life," in the panoply of "self-discovery" lures and hoaxes—irrespective of what's happening in the world and to whom—then it is clear that many people are simply losing their *Homo sapient* bearings. So I welcome the current dissection of this phenomenon of narcissism because it focuses the spotlight on the follies of the resigned, the fashionably cynical, the boringly self-absorbed, and the yearners for private contentment amid public chaos.

As if individual satisfaction can be achieved by political

withdrawal in a society sick unto death and crying out for more, not less, collective responsibility and intervention!

The "Me Generation" is the inexorable outcome of the official, anti-humanitarian, anti-work, racist, sexist, bourgeois culture. Some of these shallow eat, drink and be merryites, frantic to get it on before the sky falls down, can get real nasty, and radicals are being mau-mau'd by these me-me's. But others are unaware of the option of creating stunning progress, unexposed to the exhilarating benefits of collective politics. Still others passively await a new giant movement to supply safety and comfort in numbers.

In any event, the tables will turn, and the new crop of self-pamperers will become as extinct as their predecessors, the hermits. For a new upsurge, a new uplift, is in the air, and the cultural cycle will soon reflect the upbeat connectedness of the '30s and the '60s instead of the disengagement of the '50s.

The culture always reflects the socio-economic times. But this doesn't excuse a surrender to alien class pressures, and we must let consciousness be our guide in dealing with the privatists. Time is on our side—for they will soon discover that they're not really having any *fun*.

# 2

# The Amazon Arsenal

# Thelma and Louise "R" Us

1992

Ever since feminists organized the modern movement in the '60s, we have been harangued from all sides for being insane, unfulfilled, petty-bourgeois, narcissistic, frivolous, home-wreckers, strident bitches, dykes, man-haters, and enemies of civility and civilization.

And we purportedly derail organizations by elevating secondary questions.

The right wing said we should be jailed; the left wing said we'd gone overboard on this women's lib trip. Black leaders said we were destroying race solidarity. Union bureaucrats said discrimination wasn't a bread and butter issue. The man in the street said all we needed was a good fuck.

Not that it's funny, but who's got the last laugh now?

Just read the papers, folks, and note what the headlines are screaming about.

Rape. Job discrimination and sexual harassment. Differential education and training. Violence against women. The "proper" or "improper" role of political wives. Birth control and abortion. Health care. Childcare and child abuse. Granny dumping. Wife/girlfriend murder. Outrageously unequal legal treatment à la Anita Hill, Patricia Bowman, Desiree Washington, Leona Helmsly, Zsa Zsa Gabor, ad nauseam.

Even the marital relations of politicians are under the

microscope, and while much of this is puerile, prudish, puritanical and irrelevant, it's a sign of the new times.

If we must use a yardstick and measure afflictions to discern who are the most affronted people in the U.S. *or* internationally—and I know that people hate these comparative-agony calculations—the mathematical answer is overwhelming. Women of color, women of age, women of youth, women of marriage, women of divorce, women on welfare, women who are prostitutes, women of accomplishment, women of minority sexual persuasion, women who organize at the workplace, women who organize revolution—*females* win the endangered species contest.

Women are slaughtered because their dowries aren't adequate, because they were born without penises, or because they dare to rebel against slavery. But we rarely realize that while the price for assertiveness in the USA may not be *physical* execution, it is execution in every other sense.

American women, whether they exemplify success or struggle desperately to survive, are *all* subjected to merciless hatred, resentment, fear, denunciation, excoriation, retaliation, intimidation, deprivation and inquisition.

Women are the permanent unrecognized undercaste of U.S. society. And the *proof* of that transparent fact is that almost nobody recognizes it! The condition of women dominates the news, but no political conclusions are drawn.

*We are just as ignored when our issues are in the limelight as when we're invisible!*

In 1967 my closest comrades and I stunned the radical movement by launching a faction fight against my then-husband. He had violated every socialist standard of conduct by denying me the right to an uncontested divorce and child custody. He had provoked a courtroom scandal, accusing me of bad motherhood, over-attention to politics, bad wifery, adultery, and the usual crimes of my gender.

Because I labeled his behavior as political treachery, my ex became a martyred hero to most of the Left. But phallocentric public opinion couldn't change the facts, and that well-known leader was not a leader much longer.

That should tell you where I stand on the question of whether Senator Brock Adams, so-called liberal Democrat, should continue in office even though practically everybody seems to know he's an utterly unscrupulous, conniving sex oppressor. It should tell you where I stand on the matter of whether Mike Tyson, because he is a Black man, should be excused for behaving like a demented monster.

I am sick and tired of Rights, Lefts, and Centerites apologizing for men who brutalize women on the grounds that these men are otherwise politically effective and inspirational. Inspired by a male who is a vile abuser of women, I ain't.

**B**ut feminists, take heart. There is going to be a new global upsurge of women like you have never seen, one that will engulf every economic relationship, every institution, every government. The second sex can no longer tolerate, whether they know it or not, the shackles and brainwashing and outrages visited upon them by the male establishment and its yuppie or scaredy-cat female enablers.

It is time for swift-striking gender insurgency. Time for women guerrillas, 20th century Amazons, mad shrieks of protest, and careful mobilization of political battalions. Goddammit, sisters: Let's *get* revolutionary. Let's understand that the private profit system is at the bottom of all this horror, and let's catapult ourselves on to the mainstage of history. The world is waiting for the sunrise.

# Revenge of the Dykes, Choicers, Witches, Ghettoites and Single/Working/Welfare Moms

1992

Any time some unctuous hypocrite pontificates about the absolute morality of the traditional family, reach for your pocketbook, look around for lurking fascists in government, and cling like mad to your personal integrity.

Male politicians, dutifully echoed by wife-robots, are trying to make you, the *victims* of their horrible anarchy, into the reason for economic disaster and social dysfunction. How dare they!

How dare these extollers of a system that starves and exploits and crucifies untold billions blame the underpaid and the destitute for the poverty, miserable education and training, crime, dope, cynicism, domestic turmoil, and rejection of obsolete middleclass values *that the profit system itself generates?*

The sinister self-righteousness flown under the "family values" banner at the '92 Republican convention powered a thinly veiled, proto-Nazi blitzkrieg against the way enormous numbers of people live their lives. Feminists were damned, single moms denounced, working mothers scolded, any and all abortions reviled, lesbians and gays excoriated. The problems of racial minorities were totally ignored—but every reference to welfare abusers and criminals was a coded allusion to persons with dark skin.

Nor did President-Elect Charming and the Democrat brat pack defuse the incendiary call-to-arms against us lifestyle criminals. They knocked themselves out to parade their own mom and pop orthodoxy. The Clintons schlepped their teenage daughter to every photo opportunity imaginable, while Gore made his accident-victim son the subject of unbearably schmaltzy oratory.

But all those macho office-holders with carefully coiffured, mostly-blond wives and beautifully garbed children cannot speak for the U.S. majority, who do not live or think like them or own checkbooks like theirs.

We've come a long way, baby, since antiquity, when property was communal, relations between men and women democratic, and females revered and central to the matriarchy—not only as the mothers, but as chief providers of food, medicine and political decisions.

When private property landed in male hands—*accidentally*, because men controlled the herds that became the first money commodity—women lost their economic equality. Their work became *private*, no longer public. Men became a ruling *class*, and women—after centuries of resistance—became virtual slaves.

Ever since, the male unconscious has carried within it this memory of original guilt, of their world overthrow of the female sex, of a primal *mea culpa*, and men deny or justify this historical abomination by asserting male supremacy.

The family has no eternal or holy or cosmic values of its own. Family values reflect and express the conditions of production of a given period. A certain set of economic relations requires a certain kind of kinship structure. And the patriarchal, male-dominated, monogamous family came into being for the purpose of transmitting inheritance of property through the male line.

As with the family, so with the state, which also exists to

promote the ruling class. The state ends up *decreeing* a specific type of family to perpetuate the system it guards. The capitalist state needs women to be subordinate; taken to its outer limits, this means *kinder, kirche, küche*—"children, church, kitchen"—the slogan of Hitler, the Quayles, shorthaired preachers, and, I fear, the muzzled Hillary.

So anybody who thinks that the Democrats are going to vanquish the New Nazis is suicidally naive. The U.S. today is Weimar Germany after World War I, facing the same choice between fascism and socialism. And the U.S. today will set the pace for the rest of the world—Germany, Japan, France—in deciding what to do about Hitler's heirs. That is why militant activism by anti-fascists is vital.

Feminists, people of color, lesbians and gays, all workers: wake up! Social revolution is the only viable alternative to the concentration camps—and the only answer to vanishing jobs. With a technology geared to produce goods without producing jobs, high-tech capitalism is becoming an oxymoron, a contradiction in terms. Socialism is computers plus justice.

The global order of competitive trade and multi-currencies is absurd. It cries out to be replaced with production for use, not for greed, so as to eliminate the endless wars and hatreds spawned by dwindling markets and poverty.

A rational analysis for the mess can provide a rational solution—but *never* while the reason for the worldwide crisis is massively attributed to women, gays, ethnics, and unions. The family values brouhaha is a depraved and insulting attempt to deflect our attention from the basic problems of the world economy onto the usual scapegoat suspects.

Don't let this happen! Give the looters-with-license hell. Tell 'em to take their bourgeois values and shove 'em. And once we have created a revolution in the way we deal with wealth, this proper Jewish mother promises you that family values will take care of themselves. As always.

# Forward to the Past:
# The New Puritanism

1997

**R**epent, all ye sinners. The age of neo-prudery is upon us and fire and brimstone await.

The scarlet letter, that shameful badge of Adultery, has returned to berate us.

The media wallows these days in news of people "cheating" on their state-approved significant others. Dick Morris confesses, Bill Cosby apologizes, Madonna announces a turn to virtue, and talk show hosts and counselors moralize about betrayal and deceit, as if departure from monogamy is high treason.

Just why is adultery the number one Thou Shalt Not?

Here's a clue. Cheating is a financial term, and it can only be applied to sexual relationships if female and male bodies are seen as personal property—which, in this commodity-ruled patriarchy, they are, since paternity still dictates who inherits what. In today's climate of economic anxiety and blind narcissism, the noxious idea that *people can own people* (as in slavery) erupts like a beanstalk.

But crass reality must be dressed up if medieval mores are to sell. So here comes GOD to ordain fidelity to be Right and fornication (extracurricular) Wrong.

For the nonbelievers, pop culture takes over. Jealousy is not even depicted as mercenary or egomaniacal or super-possessive any more. It's currently *noble*. The good wife who uses any bloody means necessary to ward off interlopers, à la *Fatal Attraction,* is a movie cliché.

What's more, celibacy is the prescription du jour even for singles, especially females, teenagers, and the poor. The new welfare destruction bill allots not one penny for jobs, but provides millions to push abstinence!

The flight from the more relaxed practices of many people is part of a larger retrenchment. Renewed sexual conservatism is rooted in and nurtures the general regression. And nowhere is the backsliding more pronounced than in the mass movements of the '60s, which have all shape-shifted into their veritable opposites.

For instance. When feminists first proclaimed "the personal is political," we hardly expected that the personal would *replace* the political, with tawdry gossip about officials' bedroom peccadilloes substituting for discussion of their policies and becoming the basis for measuring their "character"! Certainly, we condemn sex harassment, but truly consenting behavior is nobody else's business, and rarely reveals much about someone's integrity or worth.

Our point back then was that the oppression of women is not accidental or isolated, but a symptom of a universal second-class role that the whole dismal for-profit system depends on. This fact, however, has been stood on its head in the recent welfare laws, which blame individual women for broad social ills. And the National Organization for Women's top strata failed to robustly resist this monstrous "reform" because they support Bill Clinton, despite his treachery on the issues.

Likewise, when street queers and drag queens revolted at the Stonewall Inn in 1969, the upsurge they set off prioritized sexual liberation as a matter of principle. They correctly identified homophobia as key to deification of the traditional family. But now the movement focuses on sexual self-policing and respectability mongering.

Gay pacesetters demand entrance into the heavenly domain of bourgeois wedded bliss, as gay couples plead they are straighter than straights—less inclined to "stray" or (gasp) divorce. Granted, the right of gays to marry is legitimate, but how foolish to elevate it to First Cause—and how ironic, at a time when old-school marriage is exiting the stage of history.

The civil rights movement, for its part, started out fired up to abolish the color line and gain total integration—not assimilation, but access to every civic benefit.

Yet, after decades of backlash, the African American cause has largely subsided into cultural nationalism, which stresses differences with other races and with Jews rather than human similarities. It glamorized separatism and unrealistically champions Black business as the solution to ghetto poverty. This ideology is disastrous, because when people of color remove themselves from their workingclass sisters and brothers, they remove an essential *leadership* sector from the common struggle of all the have-nots.

Nationalism, moreover, is infused inevitably with sexist baggage, relegating women to inferior status and outdoing the white establishment in condemning homosexuality.

All right, you've heard it from me before. Reform must grow into revolution or twist into reaction. It's an immutable law of nature—things go forward or backward. At the moment, society is headed cataclysmically in the wrong direction.

To a socialist, personal relations should be symbolized by openness, *not* a chastity belt. To a socialist, it's not the market that should be free but love.

# The Emancipation of Women

1965

This is an excerpt from a larger work, a Political Resolution originally presented at the 1965 convention of the Socialist Workers Party by what was then the Seattle branch of the SWP. When the branch broke away to form the Freedom Socialist Party, the resolution constituted the programmatic foundation of the new party. The complete resolution, *Crisis and Leadership*, is being re-issued by Red Letter Press.

T he defiance of one woman, Rosa Parks, sparked the Montgomery Bus Boycott and inaugurated a new era in American politics. It was no accident that a Black woman worker played this role. Two hundred years of history and two revolutions conditioned and tempered her for leadership of the Third American Revolution. The mass movement for civil rights in Mississippi is becoming more consciously revolutionary every day, and the leaders of this movement are predominately women.

They have the support of an important section of southern white women, even though this support is characteristically quiet and even secret. For many decades, hundreds of southern white women have worked clandestinely on the "Problem" in the crevices of the police state, and on behalf of their Black sisters in bondage. (See the works of Lillian Smith, particularly *Killers of the Dream.*) They had come to realize the unmentionable fact that southern white males were the lordly beneficiaries of a two-edged oppression: they robbed the Black woman of any acknowledged paternity for her child, and they hypocritically degraded the white woman into a truly segregated, dependent, chattel status. The myth of "sacred" white womanhood is one of the focal points of the ideology of white supremacy and ties the struggle for the emancipation of women directly to the Black liberation struggle.

This heritage of the economics of color slavery was restored to the South after the Ku Klux Klan destroyed the Reconstruction and established the police state, sharecropping and the chivalric code to insure segregation. But the revival of female lineage in the Black community ironically conferred a real benefit upon the Black woman, for the matriarchal conditions that emerged molded her into a figure of independence, self-reliance, responsibility and resourcefulness. Always engaged in social production, she was integral to the economy, to the community and to the family.

Accordingly, as a worker, a Black person, and a woman, she represented the three strands of American repressive culture; every prejudice focused on her and she felt deeply the three-fold nature of the fight for freedom. She was destined objectively for her function today as the vanguard of political consciousness, spirit and vitality; in Mississippi she runs for Congress, organizes farm labor unions and schools, confronts—and confounds—the Black men of her own movement with her initiative and firm resistance to all their attempts to subordinate and subdue her. For every Gloria Richardson who retires into domesticity, scores of Black women leaders are becoming professionals for the movement.*

They face thorny problems. Indeed, they face a double problem, for the nature of both the "race question" and the

---

* In the period since this was written, Black women have been consciously forced out of positions of leadership in the liberation movement. This represents a retreat for the movement. There is little that is revolutionary in the fight against "emasculation" and for male supremacy. Such a struggle can only represent the interests of a nascent Black bourgeoisie, trying to incorporate itself into the existing social order—at the expense of the great mass of Black Americans, male and female.

"woman question" is analogous. Each has a *dual* nature: exploitation on the job connects them each to the class struggle, while generalized political, legal and cultural oppression against them as a special "inferior" group confer an *independent* character to their struggle.

All dark-skinned people are victims of color prejudice. Similarly, what Lenin called "an entire sex," regardless of class distinction and regardless of whether they are wage-earners, is the victim of social prejudice. Women's "inferiority" derives from the condition of the *majority* of women, who are excluded by economics and tradition from participating in public social production and are confined to private domestic labor, leading lives of personal service to isolated families.

A man engages in social production, and thereby serves society; a woman essentially serves her man. Since the majority of women are peripheral to public industry and objectively dependent, all women are stereotyped as secondary. All come to represent an undifferentiated domestic function as a sex.

While the ruling class imposes a generally parasitic existence upon its wives, the wives and families of the working man are absolutely essential to the preservation of the capitalist system. The wife delivers and nurtures children, the future labor power of society, and her labor helps reproduce the daily labor power of her husband; yet both these functions are carried out with the smallest possible cost to the capitalist, who has providently arranged for the worker to bear economic responsibility for his family. A wife assures his domestic needs in the cheapest manner. Accordingly, the family as the economic unit of society constitutes a permanent source of proletarian conservatism and the basis for capitalist super-exploitation. Lord Delaware, requesting women for the American colonies, happily looked forward to "honest laborers burthened with children."

Wage slavery is the basic means of exploitation under capitalism, but it is also the foundation of "equality" in this society. In a market economy, human equality is established through the exchange of commodities by their owners, and however depressed the wages and conditions of the proletarian, he still appears in the marketplace as the owner and seller of that most precious of all commodities—labor-power. Through ownership of this commodity and through its exchange for wages, the mark of socially necessary human labor-power under capitalism, he not only asserts his social relationship and equality with others, he also establishes his political and economic strength—his ability to bargain and change the conditions of his life.

The housewife, however, does not appear in the marketplace as a seller of commodities, and however necessary her domestic labor may be to the maintenance of the family, she does not sell her labor power. In a society whose distinctive feature is the social character of labor and the wage system, the labor of women is private, personal and unpaid—hence, *slave labor*. Where a man sells his labor-power for a limited time, the wife sells *all* of herself to him. The formerly social and public productive labor of women has been reduced by bourgeois monogamy to the degradation of slave labor, dignified only by its modern-dress label—Occupation Housewife. Housework is simply secondary to "the acquisition of the necessities of life by the man; the latter was everything, the former an unimportant extra." (Frederick Engels, *The Origin of the Family, Private Property and the State.*)

But man is fundamentally a producing and a creative animal; dependency and parasitism, even more than slavery, are degenerative to the mind and body. The rebellion against this condition therefore transcends all classes of society.

> While upon the woman of the working class the cross of capitalist society rests heaviest in all ways, not one of her sisters in all the upper ranks but bears some share of the burden, or, to be plainer, of the smudge—and what is

more to the point, they are aware of it. Accordingly, the invocation of the "Rights of Woman" not only rouses the spirit of the heaviest sufferers under capitalist society, and thereby adds swing to the blows of the male militants in their efforts to overthrow the existing order, it also lames the adversary by raising sympathizers in his own camp, and inciting sedition among his own retinue.

—Daniel DeLeon, Preface to August Bebel's
*Woman Under Socialism* (1883)

Moreover, the capitalist system itself creates the conditions for the emancipation of women.

However terrible and disgusting the dissolution, under the capitalist system, of the old family ties may appear, nevertheless, modern industry, by assigning as it does an important part in the process of production, outside the domestic sphere, to women, to young persons, and to children of both sexes, creates a new economic foundation for a higher form of the family and the relations between the sexes.

—Karl Marx, *Capital* (1867)

It is therefore "plain," writes Engels, "that the first condition for the liberation of the wife is to bring the whole female sex back into public industry." However, the modern family is still "founded on the open or concealed domestic slavery of the wife" and within the family, the man "is the bourgeois and the wife represents the proletariat." The process of achieving "higher" relations is made demonstrably tortuous by the psychology of superiority induced in men as a concomitant of their privileged "bourgeois" status.

The Black movement for emancipation, like the labor movement before it, is running up against obstacles imposed by these ancient prejudices. The doctrine and practice of male supremacy has a long history of corrosive effect on the solidarity, momentum and morale of the movement.

## The masculine mystique

Racial emancipation often becomes associated with a fetish of male supremacy—"Be a *Man!*" The secondary role played by Black men for so long in society, the economy and the family is frequently over-compensated for as they press for civil rights.

Women are an available outlet for their self-assertion, and there ensues either a paterfamilias despotism, as endorsed by the Muslims, or a more subtle and sophisticated assumption of male supremacy derived from campus sociology, orthodox Freudianism, and general practice. The male leadership is frequently insensitive to the drive of Black women for acknowledged equality within the movement, for their right to do the work they are qualified and ready to do.

An added complication ensues when the intersection of chronic male chauvinism with the relatively advanced inter-raciality of the movement leads to the Black women identifying the chauvinism of the men with the relatively advanced sexual code characteristic of many of the young white women working in SNCC (Student Non-Violent Coordinating Committee). The frank rejection of middleclass puritanism by these northern women represents a partial break with the feminine mystique. They want to live as entire human beings, on all levels of life, acting directly on society as men do. Yet they are not prepared to contend for equality with men, for such a stance means a fight. Like most U.S. women, they are conditioned to be "feminine," i.e., softer and nobler creatures by virtue of their non-competitiveness. The potentially disastrous corollary of this submissiveness is their indisposition to support the Black women who are contending and competing because their leadership role is jeopardized by the regressive ideology of the men. The Black women find themselves isolated and defensively tend to adopt an objectively retrogressive moral code which deepens the gulf between the women still further.

The solution lies in the very process of working together, which offers promise of their ultimate convergence and alliance on the basis of their mutual oppression by men and by society. In order to endure and develop, the Black liberation movement, North and South, is going to have to rise to heights unachieved by any existing labor or political organization: it is going to have to *come to grips with the woman question.*

White women will have to develop consciousness and militancy on this question, and learn to bolster the course of Black women towards equality and leadership. Black women will have to see through the hypocrisy of the white middleclass norms of family stability and propriety. Black and white men will have to learn to subordinate subjective prejudices to a program and practice that incorporates appreciation of the woman question as an objective social issue that cannot be separated from civil rights. Equality and emancipation are indivisible.

The woman question will then be elevated from the back room into a proudly raised public issue of the liberation movement. Black and white women, exerting their strength through solidarity, will soon persuade Black and white men to cease and desist from the habits and outlook of the slaveholder and the movement will soar to new levels.

The murkiness of the subject of women's oppression is due to unconsciousness or denial of it among the majority of women. But as women begin to move in instinctive defense of civil rights, they will discern the similarity between the two struggles; the Black struggle becomes the training ground for the movement of women's emancipation, and each strengthens the other.

The overpowering social and cultural influence of the southern system upon the rest of the country has produced a twin oppression in every walk of life: race and sex discrimination go hand in hand, and one cannot survive without the other.

Concomitantly, the militancy of an ideologically emancipated woman can have far-reaching effects in any sphere where she finds herself; this is particularly true in the labor movement.

## Women and labor

The isolated home cannot possibly organize the woman at the point of her production; instead, it disorganizes and alienates her. Entry into public production transfers her from outer space into a socialized arena of struggle for both the class and her sex.

The logic of feminism is to expand inexorably into generalized radicalism, and women become doubly mistrusted and disliked by the labor bureaucracy, which prefers to leave workers unorganized and wages unequalized rather than absorb new women militants into the union and into the leadership. The woman question runs like a red thread through the problems of organizing the unorganized, industrial unionism in the North and South, the gap between skilled and unskilled labor, unemployment and marginal employment, and the determination of union policy, especially in strikes. (The movie *Salt of the Earth* vividly depicted the *decisive* importance of respecting and utilizing the advanced militancy of women.)

As the ratio of blue to white-collar workers continues its reversal, women workers are becoming predominantly white-collar, and the labor force of key industries is becoming increasingly white-collar. Yet because these new jobs are filled mostly by women, they remain outside union jurisdiction, and the organized sections of American labor dwindle. The current impasse of the telephone union, among others, is a result of the tradition of second-class economic and leadership status for women even when they form the *bulk* of the ranks. This paternalism is duplicated in virtually every existing union—garment, auto and aircraft, printing trades, electric, laundry clerks, building service, etc. Even waitresses and stenographers are usually represented by male officials.

To make matters worse, the failure of the labor movement to recognize the special problems and talents of the woman worker, to build a woman leadership, and to overcome its historic drag in this field, tends to be more or less duplicated in the mass movements of the present day, jeopardizing their future, as illustrated in the civil rights organizations. But as Black insurgency in the South intensifies militancy in the northern civil rights and labor movements, the advanced nature of the drive for sex equality in Mississippi and Alabama will spread to the women in the labor movement and in political organizations elsewhere, spurring them to greater efforts and their organizations to higher development.

The intimate connection between the woman question and the future of American labor—a connection today provided not only through women in industry but through women in the Black struggle—must not be underestimated.

# Which Road Towards Women's Liberation: A Radical Vanguard or a Single-Issue Coalition?

### 1973

Originally published as a Radical Women position paper

I t was enough for opportunism to speak out to prove it had nothing to say."

This was Rosa Luxemburg's judgment of Eduard Bernstein's attempt to dilute the theory and program of the German revolutionary party in the late 1800s by emphasizing *reform* over *revolution, mass action* over *theory,* the *number* of supporters over the *quality* of support, and militant *liberalism* (petty-bourgeois radicalism) over *intransigence* on goal and methods.

"The final goal, no matter what it is, is nothing," said Bernstein, "the movement is everything."

It is a sad commentary on our own supposedly sophisticated times that today it is not enough for opportunism to speak to be exposed and discredited; the proponents of popularity at any cost are all around us, espousing their shopworn doctrine that the mass movement is everything and the program a secondary consideration. Action for action's sake, unprincipled coalitions for the sake of bigness or status, and capitulation to the lowest ideological common denominator of the movement have all resulted in a tragic, unnecessary and extremely dangerous backwardness and pragmatism in the general movement for social change.

The worst manifestation of this pathetic need to be loved

instead of respected, to be a multi-class spokesperson for everybody instead of a revolutionary tribunal for the oppressed masses, is the horrific notion of the "single-issue movement."

This theoretic excrescence was born out of too-painful isolation, nurtured during a prolonged vacuum of real revolutionary leadership, and perpetuated by the tremendous reactionary pressures of capitalism bearing down hard upon a student/middleclass radicalism that remains basically disconnected from the proletariat and the super-oppressed minorities and working women.

"Single-issueism" is the process of crossing class lines and watering program down to a broadly acceptable minimum plank in order to construct an all-inclusive coalition that can achieve a particular demand or reform. "Single-issueism" is the highroad to reformism and invariably ends up in the most crass revisionism of revolutionary thought. Single-issue socialists in the peace movement announced five years ago that the Vietnam War *could* be ended by coalition between radicals and liberals, pacifists and revolutionaries, politicians and hippies, generals and privates, etc. Instead of building a radical antiwar movement and constantly striving to raise its level of consciousness and revolutionary thrust, the single-issue-ites transformed themselves from radicals into organizers of liberals, and switched from the previous goal of socialism to the new utopian illusion of "peace" under imperialism. To their vast shock and surprise, they had to witness the incredible spectacle of the movement growing up and over and past them, eventually outflanking them on the left and coming to view them as latter-day prototypes of the old Stalinist/reformist mold.

A similar current is still extremely strong within the movement for Black liberation. Based on the thesis that American Blacks are an oppressed nation rather than a super-exploited and oppressed race-class, the "porkchop" nationalists, as the Panthers dubbed them, call for all-Black unity in a struggle for "our piece of the pie," i.e., Black capitalism and Black affluence within the capitalist structure. The single-issue "Black Experience" agitators furiously denounce alliances based on class and on common grievances, and vie desperately for support from the system. Meanwhile, except for the Black Panthers, no vanguard exists to elevate the awareness and level of the movement.

The single-issue is the dead-end issue. It always ends up smack against the wall. True, it is large, but it is also, invariably, diffuse, ambiguous, contradictory, deceptive—and mercurial. Like CORE (Congress of Racial Equality) and Democratic presidential candidate Eugene McCarthy, it moves to the right, *not* to the left, and it moves radicals right along with it, especially those radicals who are busiest assuring us that this is the only way to fly and that the enemy is being outsmarted by being joined.

"By any means necessary," which used to mean that any needed and effective means would be used, now translates into "any means whatever are necessary," whether or not they really are. So expediency, safety and opportunism come to be labeled as "necessary," and all's well with the world.

Single-issueism is an inevitable violation of revolutionary clarity, integrity and responsibility, yet it persists because the ruling class confers respectability upon it.

Is it any wonder then, that the embryonic women's movement is retracing these barren pathways in its search for direction and character?

Every regional conference seems to place the question of "Reform or Revolution" at the top of the agenda, but every regional conference seems to leave the question unresolved. Indeed, we are definitely informed at some of these conferences that a "hardened position" on this issue will "alienate and drive away our newer supporters—and besides, a lot of older members don't believe in socialism anyway!"— as if this answer to the question had one iota of theoretic or strategic integrity.

The burning question remains, despite endlessly sophomoric attempts to evade or postpone it: Is women's emancipation a single-issue reform that can be won by a mass, all-inclusive, coalition of indignant and perplexed women? Or is it, by virtue of the nature of capitalism and the economic role of the family, a revolutionary question that demands a vanguard organization of ideologically developed women whose mandate is to radicalize the affinity-group coalitions, organize workingclass women, constantly enrich and update the theory of the movement, and call regularly for the united front when specific events demand massive intervention and demonstration?

Is women's emancipation a matter for liberals or radicals, and in what order? Is it a matter of psychology or politics? Is it, in other words, separate from or integrally connected to the questions of caste, race, and class?

Radical Women, as an organization, studied and answered these questions for itself *before* it proceeded to organize, and clarified and strengthened its answers in the course of its first stormy year of existence, a year marked by differences, factions and finally splits over these very issues.

Unlike any other women's organization in the country, Radical Women theorized first and organized later, understanding full well, as a result of long experience and observation, that the "medium" is not the "message," that form is not content, that the movement itself is not "everything." Instead, *theory* remains, as always, the *guide* to action, and without a revolutionary *program* there is no effective and consistent organization and activity.

Radical Women, then, started with program and developed authentic *radicals*, radical about capitalism and about women's rights. Radical Women is self-mandated to build a mass radical liberation organization composed of serious women who mean business when it comes to male chauvinism, class and race oppression, and revolutionary political power.

Still, we realize that the tens of thousands of women new to the movement must find their own way, on their own terms, to the deeper grasp of the essential nature of the movement. We confidently expect that the persistent and patient exposition of our viewpoint will continue to be highly effective in raising the general level of consciousness among women militants and that our principles will soon prevail as the characteristic instead of the atypical outlook of women's liberation.

Our stated beliefs on matters of program, structure and tactics are essentially as follows:

*1. Women's liberation can only be attained by a movement of radical women.*

It was the radical women, socialist women, who kept feminism alive during the '40s and '50s and introduced it into the New Left, long before woman's "place" became a practical problem in the organizational life of Students for a Democratic Society, Student Non-Violent Coordinating Committee, and the peace movement.

Socialist women, reared on Engels' *Origin of the Family, Private Property and the State*, Bebel's *Woman Under Socialism*, and *Lenin on the Woman Question*, greatly influenced Simone de Beauvoir and Betty Friedan (notwithstanding the ungracious lack of acknowledgment!). Those socialist women on the campuses, studying economics, history, literature, sociology, anthropology and psychology, forced the issue into academic life. Only a handful of women, *socialist* women, offered political support to the hard-pressed Black women "matriarchs" of the freedom movement, soon to be consigned to ignominy and defeat by the brutal new cult of Black male supremacy.

Socialist women initiated the mass actions on behalf of legalized abortion, comprehensive childcare, and legal reform, and socialist women unionists led the fight for on-the-job equality and the upgrading of woman's work. Every woman's issue that the liberals, independents, professionals and the government have since supported and adopted as goals was originally catalyzed into prominence by women radicals and radicalized women who know that what is most sorely needed in the movement is *leadership*.

Given the existence of a leadership core that organizes, plans and organizes, *the mass will materialize* and fight heroically for clear goals. Some reforms will and can be won; other issues are purely transitional and can be achieved only under socialism. But through every mobilization and on *every* issue, radical women steadily work to radicalize the *entire movement* and expand the vanguard itself.

Without such leadership, the women's movement, like every other movement, will petrify, corrode, adapt and drown inside the Democratic Party or inane single-issue liberalism. Or, it will adopt an ultra-left, insanely sectarian and/or terroristic stance, born of desperation and bitterness (much like SDS), and become consumed in its own hysteria. This ultra-left sector already exists, and only theory and logic—the lessons of history and experience—can persuade it into strategic sanity and the passion of revolutionary politics.

Women's liberation, led and oriented towards the center, will turn into its opposite, women's *reformism*, which in turn always becomes an enemy of workingclass and minority women. The capitalist system *cannot* grant working and minority women substantial reforms because these would seriously weaken the very pillars upon which the system itself rests: the super-exploitation of minorities and women for super-profits; the cultural oppression of minorities and women as a psychological sop to the male workers who derive unique privileges from their second-class status; and the bourgeois-monogamous family as the transmission belt for the continuity of private property, wage labor, and social alienation. Intrinsic change for working, poor, and minority women means intrinsic socio-economic change and the absolute elimination of the institutions of family, property, state, law, and popular culture in their present form.

Women's liberation, then, is a revolutionary question, and must be, first and foremost, a movement of women revolutionaries. Large, amorphous, petty-bourgeois organizations will continue to exist, and feed their best into the radical vanguard. But radicals must not lead these clubs and take administrative responsibility for them; radicals must win them over to a mass radical women's movement.

*2. The woman question has a dual and triple nature, and is therefore a multi-issue question.* I discussed this analysis in an article written in 1965:

> As a worker, a Black person, and a woman, [the Black woman] represented the three strands of American repressive culture; every prejudice focused on her and she felt deeply the three-fold nature of the fight for freedom...

> [The oppression of women] has a *dual* nature: exploitation on the job connects them to the class struggle, while generalized political, legal and cultural oppression against them as a special "inferior" group confer an *independent* character to their struggle.

> All dark-skinned people are victims of color prejudice. Similarly, what Lenin called "an entire sex," regardless of class distinction and regardless of whether they are wage-earners, is the victim of social prejudice...

> Since the majority of women are peripheral to public industry and objectively dependent, all women are stereotyped as secondary. All come to represent an undifferentiated domestic function as a sex...

When those words were written, the very idea that American women were oppressed *as a sex* was usually greeted with hoots of derision. Today, it is abundantly clear to most radicals (and even to liberals) that women are the second sex, subject to a virulence of prejudice, discrimination and oppression, not only unsurpassed today by white racism against Blacks, but assiduously practiced inside the Black freedom movement itself. Working women are exploited as workers and doubly exploited as female workers, since their special oppression as a sex permits extra exploitation of them in their capacity as workers, and for minority women, racial oppression adds a third focus of suffering.

So the "woman question," by its very nature, is both a class question and a special sex question, a race question and a special sex question, or simply a special sex question (where the woman is neither wage earner nor an ethnic minority). But like the race issue, the "woman question" is the product of a particular type of society organized in a particular way at a particular conjuncture of history, and is therefore a question of social fundamentals and great political significance. *The subjugation of women is the oldest form of oppression and affects a majority of the world's population.* Women, indeed, are the only oppressed majority.

Women's liberation is ideologically both independent and interconnected. To regard it as single issue is to deny its integral interrelationships with technological development, property relationships, and the class structure of society.

The burning problems of women, like the burning problems of Blacks, Jews, workers, or rebellious youth, are rooted in the very economic structure of capitalism, and can only be structurally eliminated by the overthrow of capitalism and the creation of a socialist communal society.

Women's liberation, therefore, demands socialism and a special, dynamic role for women in the general movement for socialism. Women, like Blacks, will play a special vanguard role in the general revolutionary movement, for they are specially oppressed and doubly driven by the urgency of their needs for swift socio-economic change. But this special and dual role of women is severely underestimated or completely misunderstood by sections of the general radical movement and sections of the women's movement itself. The women's movement is either castigated for not subordinating itself to the "important and basic" questions of the "people" or the "workers," or it is condemned for "selling out" to other people's struggles.

If we adopted the posture of listing ourselves 17th in the scheme of social priorities, we would reveal a theoretical ignorance of the very nature of our struggle—its *special, unique and massive* character which renders it strategically decisive in any mobilization of revolutionary forces.

If we concentrated only on showing how "political" and other-oriented we are, we would be playing the time-dishonored, traditional women's role of self-sacrifice and self-abnegation, traits never known to engender long-lasting revolutionaries.

On the other hand, if we ignored everything else and worked only for women's rights, we would be flying in the face of our own understanding of the causes of women's subordination and the real solution to our dilemma. We would become "nationalists" and "separatists" in another blind alley, and again we would be downgrading our mandate for accepting responsibility to the overall movement and its direction.

The correct course lies in a synthesis of the two poles of the women's movement—its special nature and its general nature—and in always making the *interrelationship* clear. We are independent and connected; we have an equal and dual responsibility—to ourselves and to others. The *interpenetration itself is more important* than either the separateness of our oppression as women *or* the togetherness of our role as political radicals. We refuse to be forced to choose sides in a game of false contradictions. Logically, historically and politically, we are able to reconcile what is at one and the same time identical and different. Through dialectic instead of formal, mechanistic reasoning, we can chart our own course.

*3. Our tactic for mass action is the united front.*

As a vanguard group, we do not worship smallness or purity or advancedness. We aim at a mass radical woman's movement, and at mass radical support for our movement. We call for alliances on a principled basis whenever particular issues arise on which many divergent groups can agree, and we promote the concept of the united front as a key lever of building massive actions and raising mass consciousness. But, we refuse to dilute the united front into a classless, counterrevolutionary peoples front which hands power over to the liberal bourgeoisie and glorifies reformism as preferable to revolutionary solutions. We *do* engage in the united front as long as it is productive and remain ever ready to go it alone should its programmatic integrity and methods become compromised.

Radical Women is a women's organization and a political organization that maintains its programmatic clarity on many issues while it engages in broad-scale actions with others on specific issues.

We anticipate an eventual permanent united front of radical women, and simultaneous with this, a permanent nationwide regroupment of radicals in a new and vigorous revolutionary party.

*4. The supportive or affinity-group character of a woman's liberation organization should be a result and effect of its primarily political nature, rather than its central reason for existence.*

All the sympathy and empathy and sexual solidarity in the world cannot together substitute for a clear-headed ideological understanding of the causes of oppression and the psychological reflex within ourselves. "Friendship is friendship, but politics is politics," says an old Russian proverb—and *program* is decisive in summoning our powers of resisting, coping, and changing.

The contention of some women that special soul dialogues and intimate group interchanges are energizing and crucial to expanded awareness is highly doubtful and perpetuates the image of women as inner-oriented, subjective and psychological in viewpoint, as opposed to the objective, outer-oriented and sociological perspective of men.

Naturally, there is some truth to this stereotype because it is nurtured by the culture, but it can easily be overcome and changed, precisely through the expedience of acting politically and objectively, and women can learn to do this with amazing ease if given half a chance.

This question is important as it bears on the single-issue versus multi-issue differentiation, for singularity and subjectivity mutually reinforce each other, as do generality and objectivity. The rap group that never develops into an organization, for instance, perpetuates both subjectiveness and unconcern for related social issues, and organizations that deliberately restrict themselves to a single woman's issue, or women's rights alone, perpetuate the feminine, self-oriented mystique. A general political group, however, engenders a mature, objective and international approach which is the only basis for the passion that creates revolutionary change.

Our mutual aid and mutual supportiveness grow naturally out of our common experiences and joint actions, and we do not need to "organize" or "schedule" solidarity. Our fundamental mission is to politically define and then play our role in society; our *relations* with each other will be conditioned by our success in our basic political mission and also by the very limitations imposed by this perverted society on all human relations.

Our task is to retain and continue to clarify our character

and role, never allowing ourselves to become invisible parts of a homogenized blur of everybody and anybody "interested" in women's rights. Our identity as politically radical women is central to our continued existence and impact. We are an organization with a program, with a structure, with a policy, and with a goal, and without these we would be derelict in our responsibility to the mass of humankind.

# Woman as Leader:
# Double Jeopardy on Account of Sex

Speech presented to Group Without a Name (Psychiatric
Research Society), September 8-10, 1972, Seattle, Washington

The preposterous distinctions of rank. . .corrupt, almost
equally, every class of people. . . Still there are some
loopholes out of which a man may creep, and dare to
think and act for himself, but for a woman it is a
herculean task, because she has difficulties peculiar to
her sex to overcome which require almost superhuman
powers.

—Mary Wollstonecraft (1791)

*Famulus* means domestic slave, and *familia* is the total
number of slaves belonging to one man. . . The term was
invented by the Romans to denote a new social organism
whose head ruled over wife and children and a number
of slaves, and was invested under Roman paternal power
with rights of life and death over them all.

—Frederick Engels (1884)

In the beginning, in the matriarchate, woman *was leader.*\*
Because descent was reckoned in the female line, mother-
right prevailed. Because property was communally owned
and distributed, social equality prevailed. And because the
labor of managing the communistic household was as much a
public and a socially necessary industry as the procuring of

---

\* I use the term "leadership" in the political, rather than the professional
or business-tycoon sense. Leadership connotes a *relationship* between

food, political equality prevailed—everyone's labor was equally needed, respected, and equitably recompensed.

In a society of equals, woman was mother, producer and political policy-maker.

Then came the deluge. As wealth and exchange increased, and money evolved, the sexual division of labor caused a funny trick to be played on women. The first surplus, and therefore the first commodity—a use-value deliberately produced for the purpose of exchange—was cattle. And the men owned the herds! An inequality of ownership developed, and a new phenomenon—private property—emerged, snugly in the hands of the males. The primitive collective was destroyed, wrecked by the steamrolling power of the new private property relations.

"Household management lost its public character," says Engels in *The Origin of the Family, Private Property and the State*. "It became a *private service*; the wife became the head servant, excluded from all participation in social production."

The destruction of the primitive commune and the matriarchal system involved a titanic cataclysm, lasting for centuries, and ranging around the world. The democratic matriarchate was smashed, and in its place was substituted patriarchy, monogamy (to insure the proper inheritance of the private property), classes, slavery and the state.

"The overthrow of the mother-right was the *world historical defeat* of the female sex," Engels writes. "The man took command in the home also; the woman was degraded and reduced to servitude. . .this degraded position of the woman. . .has gradually been palliated and glossed over, and

---

a movement, group or bloc, and its vanguard. The vanguard is composed of a cadre that is voluntary and is democratically selected. The boss or general who hires or drafts a staff is not a "leader," nor is an expert in some field who does not create a movement. A leader *leads* others, expresses and influences the ideas and feelings of others, and acts in concert with others to change the social and cultural climate.

sometimes clothed in a milder form; in no sense has it been abolished."

This is the historical career of woman—from leadership of a society marked by liberty, humanity, and equality to the degradation and ignominy of chattel status. Defeated, enslaved, and freely killed for transgressions in the world of Rome and then western Europe, her lot gradually improved until she was only exploited, oppressed and tormented under capitalism.

Hers is a story of slavery and serfdom, of double exploitation on the job and oppression as an entire sex, of prostitution legal and otherwise, of decreed inferiority because of biological destiny and intellectual deficiency. The designation of women as inferior results from the status of the *mass* of women, who are barred by economics and culture from involvement in public industry and are limited instead to private, isolated, household labor.

As long as most women are outside the labor force and are dependent on men for support, the female sex is viewed as second-rate and expected to play an exclusive role of domestic service.

From such a social position and backdrop, few leaders can emerge. Queens, witches and upstarts, yes—but no modern leaders.

"Now, just a minute, you fanatic feminists," we are told at this point. "Male labor is also exploited by the capitalist."

True, brother—but at 40% higher wages than woman receives, and 99% higher wages than the welfare mother and the unemployed woman worker. And 100% higher wages than the unpaid housewife.

"But everybody is oppressed by a cruel world," claim the pundits.

Not as an *entire sex*, they're not. Not as the second sex, judged to be biologically, emotionally, mentally and temperamentally inferior to men.

"Baloney! Who ever stopped you from being equal? You have been educated and you have freely chosen the domestic over the social leadership role!"

Thanks a lot, fellas, but no thanks. What you really did was miseducate us, brainwash us, and channel us like a herd of sheep into the corral you had ready and waiting.

And to add insult to injury, you did it all in the name of "Science," alluding to the entrenched authority of Freud, that great sexual equalitarian; Talcott Parsons, the functional (what?) sociologist; Margaret Mead, of Super-earth-mother fame; the entire educational establishment; and Madison Avenue's motivational research (*whose* motives?). You "educated" us just enough to intimidate us with your phony, reactionary authorities.

Cultural prejudice, vested interests, political expediency and sheer misanthropy were paraded before women students as science—irrefutable and unchallengeable.

In the dehumanizing process of being inculcated with this second-class education for second-class folks, women lost all historical memory of their once proud and heroic role. Whether they were poor or rich, workingclass militant or respectable colonel's lady, they were forced to choose slavery, and then forced to pretend to like it, and then "educated" to fiercely resist any personal tendency to economic and political status in their own right. Female ambition was the sign of the devil, the dybbuk in all women, the acting out of penis envy, and the childish refusal to grow up and have the proper kind of orgasm.

Psychoanalytic therapy mushroomed into Big Business, because it served the needs of Big Business and forced women back into their place—the place of unpaid and cheap labor, an enormous source of profits for the capitalist class.

Yet, after centuries of domestic retreat or silent death in the factories and the streets, women erupted and roared out their rage and defiance; the psychoanalysts were aghast. This novel manifestation of pussy-power in the context of *political action* was abhorrent to them. So they sneered.

"Well, young lady, where are your leaders? What do you do besides talk? If you're so liberated, why aren't you equal?"

## "We aren't leaders because we aren't yet equal"

The jailers always deride us for our lack of freedom. Our executioners condemn us because we died. Our seducers sneer at our gullibility.

We live under a system of capitalist patriarchy, ruled by a class composed of old, white, male scions and their hired bureaucrats. Capitalist political economy and the bourgeois culture it disseminates super-exploit women and ruthlessly suppress our protests. We are the objects of a universal contempt, paternalism, fear and hatred.

Like all victims of idiotic prejudice and institutionalized discrimination, women became what you said they were— inferior. Men defined us, and men were the authorities. Women did, and continue to do, all the things that oppressed races, exploited classes, or tyrannized colonies did—women grew to hate themselves, to denigrate themselves, to be so consumed with alternating guilt and resentment that they paralyzed themselves. Women courted favors from their overseers and further demeaned and humiliated themselves in the process. Women perpetuated their own prolonged adolescence because men found this attractive and reassuring. Women employed guile and cunning, shuck and jive, manipulating and maneuvering to gain position. And women competed fiercely with each other for the available goodies— security, jobs, status, marriage, and men.

Trained rigorously to be followers, to be "feminine" (frothy and dependent and illogical), to be private and sentimental and narcissistic, to be weak and charmingly ambivalent and contradictory—how in hell are we now supposed to blossom forth as instant marvels of maturity and responsibility—as leaders??? How in hell can we suddenly metamorphose ourselves into the strong, self-reliant, consistent, stable and authoritative ilk from whence leadership derives?

We can't. Not en masse, and not overnight. So long as all women are specially oppressed as a sex, few women leaders can emerge, and those who do will reflect and express this general oppression of their sex. To be a women is to be afflicted. To escape the general affliction is a rarity, but some women leaders seem to have so escaped. The majority of woman leaders, however, have grown out of the struggle itself. To protest and mobilize against the general affliction of women, and its source in the socio-economic system, is a much more prevalent reflex than individual separation from the sex and the struggle. From out of the milieu of protest and confrontation, scores of women leaders are emerging.

When solidarity supplanted middleclass, individual careerism and singular stardom, at that moment in the late '60s, a female leadership began to be born, a leadership buoyed by the tremendous currents and tides of a living mass movement.

Still, for every leader who skyrockets into prominence or consistently carries through vanguard responsibilities, three leaders drop by the wayside. For to be a woman leader —a leader *of* women, or of women and men—is to face a double jeopardy on account of sex, a double danger and a double cost.

## The woman leader as a social abnormality

All the qualities classically necessary for leadership have been specifically prohibited, denied or abridged for women.

The woman leader consequently faces not only the ordinary and expected pitfalls and prices of an up-in-front role, but extremely unusual penalties as well, for she is "different"—atypical, strange, mysterious.

Unless she is a widow performing the proper tribute to

the deceased by "carrying on his great and noble work" (the contemporary form of suttee), she is usually regarded as insane, sick, distorted, childless, lesbian, unsexed or consumed with flaming sexual frustration. Even those who admire her allude frequently to her uniqueness as a human type—a mutant on the evolutionary tree.

She copes with this nervous response to her in one of three ways:

*1. The super-feminine compensation game*

To look at this adorable, petite, melting-eyed doll, you would never dream she's a community mover and shaker and a demon organizer. Easily half of her energy is expended in negating her identity as a leader, and indeed, her game does effectively subdue the wrath and deflect the hostility of the sexists.

Eventually, however, one or the other identity has to go, and if the leadership role doesn't come to predominate, she will lapse into mediocrity and become petrified in a rut. Her super-femininity compromises her feminism and reinforces sex role-playing. Her credibility suffers, and then her performance declines.

*2. The grand sacrifice syndrome*

Hounded on all sides by overwhelming pressures, she relinquishes her role and steps back into obscurity "for the good of the movement" or to retain her "sanity."

This is especially prevalent among Black and minority women, who are mercilessly intimidated by their own race/ ethnic movements for their out-front status. The rhetoric of "Black manhood," "machismo," and "get behind your man" widely expresses Stokely Carmichael's famed pronunciamiento, "The proper position of women in the movement is prone."

But self-sacrifice to a false god is not only blasphemous, it boomerangs. Which is why minority women comprise the most explosive and dynamic sector of the feminist movement, even if they are largely underground. Oppressed as a race, as a class, and as a sex, they are destined for leadership of the entire human race. The Angela Davises point the way.

*3. Keep on truckin'*

That so many women leaders actually manage to keep going is a remarkable tribute to the intensity of the oppression against women. The whip of the counterrevolution never stops, and the very turbulence of the struggle creates a centripetal force that fixes the leadership firmly in the center of the political cauldron.

In this variant of response to pressure, the double jeopardy serves as a spur, as double reason and justification for carrying on the struggle. Indignation, outrage and compassion can be extremely energizing, and a dual oppression often redoubles the responsive energy. This is the remarkable dialectic of women's leadership, wherein her motion and drive are resultants of the fierce contradictions involved in her position.

## The woman leader as political radical

Woman is nigger. Woman is dybbuk. Woman is cheap labor. Woman is unpaid domestic labor. Woman is bitch. Woman is whore. Woman is cunt. Woman is no lady.

Woman is the lowest item on the social totem pole. The political alternatives for her are consequently polarized.

Because of the integral relation between women's rights, monogamy, and private property, the movement for woman's emancipation is an equivalent to, and a corollary of, the class struggle. Woman is either a part of, or ideologically and spiritually aligned with, the proletariat. Life forces her to the left, or into the far right.

The logical extension of the feminine mystique is fascism *(kinder, kirche, küche)*, which explains the large numbers of middleclass women in the John Birch Society, anti-abortion and Fascinating Womanhood groups (both church-inspired), and anti-ERA formations (corporate-financed). But the woman in the feminist movement turns left, for Marxist philosophy corresponds to her actual, objective place in the sun—outside, underneath, and seething.

The role of the liberal moderate is virtually excluded for women leaders (as distinct from women politicians in the two-party system, who do not lead but follow the polls and the whims of voters). The logic of woman's situation in life, added to her personal experiences within the system, impels her to a radicalization that is truly remarkable in scope and intensity.

The woman leader accordingly tends to become a political radical. And if straight political life is one of routine jeopardy, radical politics is jeopardy compounded. She is not only a female libber, she's a goddam commie who refuses to go back where she didn't come from. She exults in taking on the power structure, and the populace, with a multi-issue, revolutionary double-barreled blast.

Then, after being recognized and sometimes even respected by the media and the public as an outspoken and intransigent feminist and radical, she finds herself half torn to shreds by her own movement—a New Left still fraught with lingering sexism and a ferocious anti-leadership mystique. Born of ideological anarchism, the current network of collectives, "alternative institutions" and free service projects deplore and detest organization and leadership, which they label as anti-human, Leninist-machine, imperialistic constructs.

The New Left still supplants program and leadership with the cult of "human relations," "relating to people," and following after the spontaneity and given level of consciousness of the masses. The functions of leadership—to guide, coordinate, supervise, initiate, advise, teach, organize—is anathema to them. The woman leader is double anathema. She has a program, operates within a structure, views the world sociologically and objectively. The New Left pontificates that "lifestyle is our politics" and "lifestyle humanism means no leaders."

The coping mechanisms of the woman leader as she confronts her floundering comrades are similar to the three options previously indicated.

She can pretend *not* to be a leader, and lead—that is, assume responsibility quietly, clandestinely, and with super modesty, as indicated for women. Or she can give up in disgust or be broken down. Or she can wait them out, knowing that the lessons of history and the inevitable growing up process of the New Left itself are on her side.

## Leadership and privation

Assuming our woman leader has survived the first two instances of double jeopardy—social abnormality and political radicalism—how does she survive economically?

Neither the woman's movement nor the radical movement can, as a rule, support her. With the exception of a tiny handful of publicly supported or liberal-establishment/church-subsidized feminist centers and academic-research projects, no outlets exist that will pay her a living wage for her talents and expertise.

The regular workaday world is terrified of her. Business and industry, government on all levels, academia and social agencies shudder and turn faint when she appears at the personnel departments. ("Our funders, our Board, our clients, the media—what would they think?")

Where she is able to locate a niche—on a campus, in the anti-poverty program, in social agencies—she will be ruthlessly exploited, underpaid and overworked, as the price paid by a feminist and a radical for that coveted "meaningful" job. Her energy will be thoroughly sapped; her availability for community, regional or national leadership is harshly restricted, both by apprehensive executive directors and by her own exhausting work schedule.

In order to get a job, she must usually lie—underplay her qualifications and skills and job history. But the employment agencies are skittish of her anyway, and it is difficult to be the quiet secretary or new factory hand or cheerful waitress when her name is turning up in the papers, or the boss's wife catches her on television, or the CIA, FBI, Civil Service investigators, etc., grill the neighbors. So she's always getting fired, or "laid off," and the endless job-hunting drains her energy and nerves even more.

Women professionals with their own businesses, or women who are supported or assisted by husbands and boyfriends, are few and far between in the roster of women leaders. In the United States, radicals are rarely crucified, shot or systematically tortured, give or take a few police raids and mass arrests. Instead, dissidents and rebels are systematically blacklisted and half-starved to death. Welfare is rarely a solution for women leaders, because the privation involved is so enervating and so demoralizing, and the brunt of this grinding poverty is borne by the children.

The survival mechanisms, then? Again, these are similar to the previously indicated options.

She may suddenly, or gradually, change her ideology and social concepts. She may capitulate utterly to social acceptability—or just move over a bit to allowable limits of non-conformity. Sometimes unemployment will serve as the trigger, and at other times, affluence and a good job will do it. The hunger of the establishment to co-opt, to buy off militants, is truly insatiable.

She may elect to retain her theory and her ideas as an individual, while dropping her public role and organizational/ group affiliations. She retires to private, wage-earning life.

If she's lucky, or gifted, or indomitable and dedicated, or just ornery—and if she can count on a little help from her friends and her sisters—she will manage to keep it all going, somehow: the movements and the struggles, external and internal, the job, the family, the personal study, the house, and maybe even the yard. Endowed with health, humor and a horror of injustice, the woman leader persists, galvanized daily by the mounting outrages of a decadent and putrefying society.

## Special oppression creates a bold new leadership

The bondage of women crippled them, but it also, finally, motivated women to rebel, to expose, to resist and to organize.

Helpless anguish and rage at the plight of their sisters in poverty, in despair, in desperation, animated women to rise out of passivity and ambivalence, to raise the eternal cry of the unrepresented and unenfranchised—*power!*

Women leaders created a brand new movement, and the movement in turn engendered more women leaders, up from slavery, up from demoralization, up from the lower depths.

Women leaders shouldn't be here, but they are. Women leaders really can't exist, but they do. Women leaders cannot conceivably survive, but they will.

Women leaders will prevail because it is historically and sociologically necessary they do so. Women's leadership and the women's movement will survive precisely because the jeopardy facing them is so great. All women, and some men, recognize clearly the difficulty of maintaining a consistent assault on the bastions of American capitalism; yet the very difficulty of the task creates a heightened radicalization and an expanding revolutionary orientation.

For when any system becomes so repressive to advocates and spokespeople and organizers for the oppressed, that system has already placed *itself* into deep jeopardy. It is hated, resented, despised—and it will be tumbled onto the ash bin of history. Its callousness and depravity are its own gravediggers; the system itself creates its nemesis.

The very issue of female leadership, then, is a *revolutionary* question. The double and triple burdens borne by women leaders are a product of a dysfunctional and sadistic society, and women are learning once again how to relieve their burdens by means of involvement in the enormously liberating process of social struggle. The end result will be revolutionary mass action, revolutionary political action that will transform the power structure in this country and usher in a new epoch of socialist economic relations and democratic human relations.

And at the forefront of this international army of humanists will march a huge phalanx of women—women of all colors, all ages, all nations, and even all classes—because women as a sex have been brutalized for too long and are becoming the ultimate revolutionaries.

We are so far down on the bottom, we have nowhere to go but up. And as we move upward, because we are principled and not opportunists, because we have never been rich or powerful enough to learn corruption, we shall push everyone up with us as we go. Because we live in double jeopardy, we shall eliminate all jeopardy from human relations. In our surge to survive, we shall speak for all the oppressed.

This is the timeless essence of true leadership. This is the principle and the practice of the matriarchy—where it all began.

# Response to "Notes on Leadership"

1975

In the following article, Fraser critiques "Notes on Leadership," a
discussion paper issued by Lexington Socialist Feminists in 1975. These
Kentucky women were dissatisfied with both the "traditional
conception of leadership" and the New Left "radical democracy" pattern
because both pushed women into auxiliary roles. Rather than examining
the politics behind these organizational forms, the Lexington group
implied that leadership itself might be an oppressive concept.
Nevertheless, the writers were also concerned that feminists, like the
New Left, were having "difficulty building viable, long-term
organizations," and they judged that "a major part of our dilemma
revolves around our ability/inability to come to grips with collective
leadership in practice."

**N**otes on Leadership," in my opinion, raises the right
issues and places them squarely in the proper
context—the historical one. So I find myself in
agreement with the approach, and with many of the particular
formulations. However, I am not exactly sure just what the
conclusions are, i.e., the *solutions* offered, and there seems to
be—again, I am not sure!—a lingering aroma of what I call New
Left Organizational Anarchism, which I do disagree with.
Perhaps your intent was to be tentative and suggestive, rather
than definitive, in order to better stimulate discussion; in any
case, let me indicate the shape of my reflexes to what I think
you are proposing.

You describe concepts of leadership as being polarized
between traditional bourgeois structures, based on hierarchical
power, and the relatively recent New Left rejection of all
organizational forms in favor of collective decision-making and
constant re-examination of policy. You imply that both poles

are deficient, and that a new leadership model must be constructed.

A deeper thrust into political history would soon reveal that another model does exist, one that has proven its feasibility. I refer to the Leninist-Bolshevik practice of *democratic centralism*, which, in its undefiled (by Stalinism) form, is a marvelously flexible and practical process. In its real form, utilized honestly to serve revolutionary politics, it is never static, mechanical, rigid or mysticized. Instead, it is dynamic, sensitive, adaptive, and clearly designated as a tool, a means, a method for achieving goals and serving programs, and, moreover, a method which demands total participation and involvement in decision-making as well as operations.

Democratic centralism simply means that decisions are made by the total body, and that after decisions are made, the body acts in a centralized, united, uniform manner to achieve the agreed-upon goal. Disputes are suspended while the action is underway; afterwards, a free-wheeling and deep-going post-mortem is in order, as a check upon the action and policy, and a basis for further decision-making.

As regards internal-vertical organizational forms, democratic centralism provides for levels of leadership, divisions of labor, and clear-cut area and project accountability; yet every leadership level—organizer, executive committee, subcommittees, boards, commissions, officers and staffs—is conclusively subordinate to the total membership, meeting in convention, or general meeting, or plenary session. And disagreements, rather than being squelched, are encouraged and even organized; groupings, tendencies, and factions are not only permitted but provided equal access to party publications and distribution resources, and organized, official discussion periods and voting periods are a regular part of the organization's calendar of events.

I have worked under conditions of democratic centralism for most of 35 years, and it works! It provides brilliantly for collective thought and conclusion, vastly democratic processes, ample opportunity for questioning, challenging, debating and just plain reflection—at the same time that it insures effective and efficient administrative procedures. It offers both stability and change, both proven leadership and developing leadership, both self-discipline and a flowering of ability, talent and personality.

It should be apparent, by now, that I do not seem to have the same vibrations about certain concepts as you seem to! For instance, I am not opposed to Structure or Hierarchy or Dominance or Power or Organizational Methods—*as such*. These are things, processes, connoting no absolute right or wrong in themselves. It is actually the combination, the interrelations, the synthesis of these phenomena that counts. Hierarchy, Dominance, etc., are not bad, not masculine, not capitalist—they may or may not be, depending on who uses them how and for what purpose and to what effect. What's wrong with "non-debatable goals," "persuasion skills," "technical know-how," personal style/personality/charisma, energy, rugged individualism??? Nothing is wrong, if these are used democratically, collectively, thoughtfully, considerately, and in a fashion guaranteed to protect individuality and human dignity.

The New Left's rejection of these no-no's in favor of endless touchy-feelie probes and shudders only led, as we know, to mutual suspicion, subjectivism as holy writ, clique politics, alienation, paralysis and finally collapse and even self-imposed, elitist death. Yet the antipathy to serious, well-delineated organization complete with a definitive leadership function lingers on, and I think this is too bad, because it is counterproductive.

In the feminist movement, we saw the convulsions of New Leftism running riot, rampant with emotionality for its own sake and irrationality for its own sake. Why is the human ability to rationally persuade, deal in abstractions (i.e., political theory), debate concepts, master technical skills and impress others relegated to the dustbin of "masculine" characteristics? This actually demeans women, who, in mixed organizations, easily equaled and often surpassed males in these capacities. The problem was not our inability to compete, but the entrenched *sexism* that caused a lack of recognition and a lack of respect for the skills and abilities of the women. So women, rebelling at the discrimination, seized on the forms of organization instead of the theory, program and political practices of mixed groups as the culprit, and committed the disastrous error of inventing a new ideology which *began* with organization theory or rather, anti-organization theory.

Now this, I submit, was irrational, if understandable and to a certain degree inevitable. This was illogical, ass-backwards, because organizational form must flow from program, must serve it, and not vice versa. If your goal is simply self-expression, free of constraints, then endless rap-sessions are fine, but if social revolution is your bag, then leadership style and structure must be very different indeed.

When feminists enthroned "consciousness" as queen, they assassinated sociology, which is definitely objective, i.e., dealing with classes, races, sexes, ages, institutions, conditions, mass practices, and so on. In life and in politics, neither awareness nor social processes can exist independently of each other, and each takes on meaning and identity only in relation with the other.

Just as democratic centralism combines and reconciles authority with democracy, a viable leadership theory can absorb the interpenetration of hierarchy with equality, and provide for both at the expense of neither in a truly dialectical flow. Authority and collectivity need not be poles at either end of a linear continuum, need not be mutually exclusive contradictions; they can also be gradations on a spiral, reinforcing each other in a constant movement from lower to higher levels of functioning. And while our discussion here addresses a political rather than a philosophical issue, our *method of thought* is pertinent to our conclusions, and revolutionary, dialectical logic should prove far more helpful to us than the narrow constrictions of formal, academic logic still based on Aristotle's limp old syllogisms.

I believe, in short, that what you want—freedom from bureaucratic high-handedness—and what I want—a disciplined combat organization capable of overthrowing capitalism, taking power, and building workers' democracy on a global plane—can be achieved through the *same* organizational/leadership constructs. If I truly believed that one had to be sacrificed to achieve the other, I would promptly become a Stalinist or shoot myself.

I have another problem with your paper. You do announce one "non-negotiable item": you reject dominating patterns of relationships. And this you call the keystone of your "ideology."

But what do you mean by "domination"? If it means refusal to be intimidated and silenced by superior brute force or fear of angering a leader, fine. But if it means refusal to recognize and respect manifestly superior logic, special experience, analytic consistency, firm programmatic grasp, proven proficiency—if it means, in effect, a rejection of everything we mean by *Leadership* (with a capital L!)—then you are again espousing not a new concept of leadership, but that tired old warhorse of anti-leadership. You want a leadership, in effect, that does not *lead*. A true leadership never dominates in the sense of behaving oppressively or relegating all leadership functions to itself; but it does dominate in the sense that it makes the rules as actions are implemented and it is a key watchdog of the doctrine and the principles of practice.

And isn't this what we want women to be?

I appreciate that you aspire toward a cogent definition of leadership, but you simultaneously shy away from it, as in your plea for "situational" leadership, which always exists, but doesn't resolve the problem you pose. Because who decides which approach and which people are best for which situations? We're right back where we started.

I believe the most horrendous chapter of the women's movement was that incredible period when anybody even remotely resembling a leader or spokeswoman, especially if they were recognized by the media, was viciously condemned, slandered, attacked and pilloried by other feminists. The movement has really never recovered from this blood bath, this excrescence of orgiastic matricide. We played the bosses' game, the males' game, in that reverse-macho exercise. We generated a sinister, *Suddenly Last Summer* cannibalism that graphically revealed the shocking, subterranean depths of our mass self-hatred, self-contempt and fiercely competitive "femininity." And this is our real problem, I suspect, not the difficulty of creating a sensible and fair and meaningful and non-threatening leadership process.

Without leadership, there is no movement, no organization, no development of consistent theory, no division of labor, no refinement of practice, no stability, no training and demonstration, no growth. Without leadership, nothing guarantees that the program will be implemented, for everybody cannot do everything at the same time. We desperately need strong, rational, logical, persuasive, effective, energetic, rugged female individuals as leaders, just as we need ranks with the same qualities who love and admire and support and criticize their leaders as they themselves learn to develop and perfect leadership qualities. Nobody has to be dominated, or repressed, or intimidated, but everybody has to learn to take criticism and evaluation. Real leadership welcomes and organizes debate, criticism, hard looks at policy and practice; real leadership is nothing to fear, and something to tenderly nourish!

Yet feminists, socialist feminists, continue to *fear* being "dominated by abstraction or personalities."

Permit me to indulge in a "masculine" epithet. I think this is ridiculous. Tragic. Blind. Women still *fear* other women. We want, I assume, to storm the barricades against sexism, racism, imperialism—and yet we're afraid of each other.

But fear is not a program, much less an "ideology." And fear is negotiable, i.e., discussible, analyzable, changeable. Neither men nor lack of organizational principles are the enemies here—*we* are the enemy, the enemy at home, the enemy within. We are divided, split, uncertain within our own minds on the *propriety* of women being leaders, and we can easily end up hoisted on the petard of our own role-schizophrenia, our own unconscious acting out of the feminine mystique.

I say to socialist feminists: please, enough already, let's stop the carnage against ourselves. Leadership is a reality and an even greater potential; it is a burning need and we can never, never produce enough leaders. Let's meet the paralyzing fear head-on, and say what we really know: the fear was a wish, and when we stop wishing to be dominated, we will stop fearing ourselves, and others, and we will welcome the leadership of other women, which is our only road to *muscular mass action* and fundamental social change.

One final comment, or elaboration on a previous point:

In the final analysis, discussions of leadership cannot productively occur in a vacuum, cannot be separated out of the context of *program*. If you decide to go underground, and resort to guerrilla tactics, you would have to adopt stringent military organizational forms. If you opt for revolutionary politics, it follows as the night the day that you must build mass combat organisms marked by a bold and forceful cadre. If you accept this reasoning, then strong leadership must be built, but strong leaders may well display tendencies toward personal domination. Indeed, if they didn't, they probably wouldn't be strong leaders. And this is where everybody else, the collective, comes in: the *control* function is squarely in the hands of the total group precisely in order to curtail bureaucratic and oppressive feints. This means the collective may not resort to "rejecting" dominating patterns by eliminating leadership, but is obligated, is responsible for exercising its muscle (so to speak!) to hold leadership in rein where indicated. And in this collective enterprise lies the ultimate leadership, the real heroines. This was Marx and Engels' concept and it is mine. And I think it should be yours, because it is neither male nor female, bourgeois nor New Left, military nor anarchist. It is simply *objectively true.*

I sincerely hope I haven't misinterpreted you, or overstated what I tend to see as your position. I'm in complete accord with your view that the women's movement has an "important leadership role to play in regard to left politics." Indeed, I believe we are destined to *be* the leadership of the radical movement, and that is why I feel so strongly and carry on so vociferously on the subject. Thanks again for asking me to contribute to the discussion.

# Male Marxists with a Freudian Hangover

1977

Sigmund Freud once groaned that he would never understand women.

Well, Siggy, likewise, I'm sure. There are some men—and I speak particularly about radical men—whom I cannot for the life of me fathom.

I cannot understand men who live in the very midst of—but ignore—a giant-sized, worldwide and historic new movement that bids fair to attain revolutionary dimensions from its earliest beginnings.

I cannot understand men whose only advice to an army of militants enraged by irrational and brutal treatment is: save your hot breath and wait around for the final stage of communism before you presume to raise any grievances.

I cannot understand men who react with derision to the curses and cries of sorely pressed and scorned workers who are exploited beyond belief on the job and oppressed almost past caring when away from it.

I cannot understand men who rigidly limit the definition of "worker" to those who look like men.

I cannot understand men who view leaders in the class struggle—worker vanguards in the fight against bosses, conservative labor fakers, phony government arbitrators, and hypocrites of every stripe—as provocateurs disrupting workingclass unity.

I cannot understand men who loftily announce that they are for Freedom Now, Equal Rights Now, and Non-Discrimination Now—except for one stratum of untouchables.

I cannot understand men who continue to uphold the discredited fetish of last-hired, first-fired.

I cannot understand men who advise active unionists not to raise vital political matters which might "turn off" workers.

I cannot understand men who coldly gaze upon the process of subjugated people emerging out of the depths into political awareness and organization, and brand this process as divisive.

I cannot understand men who are literate and knowledgeable but never bother to read anything from a vast new source of political literature created by extremely talented analysts of the socioeconomic and cultural scenes.

I cannot understand men who inflict upon suffering and despised toilers a peevish scolding to the effect that the just demands of these ancient lowly are secondary or tertiary or quadruciary in comparison with the demands of some other segment of toilers.

I cannot understand men who garrulously address every minor and obscure question engendered by life under capitalism but have zilch to say about a major and explosive issue that has absorbed the country for ten long years.

I cannot understand men who are accustomed to making their own decisions on every aspect of their physical and medical welfare, who stand idly by as the bourgeois state continues to nationalize the bodies of an entire segment of the population, designating these bodies as state property under government control.

I cannot understand men who respond with alacrity and huzzahs to the demands of an oppressed minority, but remain blind to the bitter fate of a majority of the human race.

I cannot—but why go on? The list is endless, which is

unfortunate for all the prospects of socialist democracy in our time. The list, after all, is only one more infuriating reflection of the chronic subjection of women by men through the long, dark centuries since the tragic eclipse of the matriarchal gens.

Radical men hail every hint and hope among anybody, anywhere, of upsurge, ferment, rebellion, protest, outbreak, eruption, dissension, mutiny and insurgency. But they urge only farewell and dissolution as the proper tactics for the women's emancipation struggle.

Millions of radical men around the world stand convicted of a century of politically criminal underestimation of woman and her plight and her work and her worth. The sex-centric lack of any respect from these men for the human, ideological and strategic values of the dynamic women's movement adds up to nothing less than political rape and doctrinal counterrevolution.

Radical men too often expect radical women to be not leaders but brides of the revolution, not comrades-in-arms but comrades in straitjackets.

"But—but—but," you sputter. "What about women radicals who also downplay socialist feminism?"

Women? Women revolutionaries who reject and insult their own beleaguered sex?

*I cannot understand them, either.*

# How Long, Oh Lords, How Long?

### 1978

**M**y favorite candidate for downer-of-the week award is the patronizing radical who tells us "you people are too impatient—Rome wasn't built in a day."

Well, we people have a lot to be impatient about, and rebuilding imperial Rome isn't exactly what we had in mind.

Patience is undoubtedly a virtue for radicals. Our grasp of the long view, of the contradictions in the historical process, lends us buoyancy in a sea of troubled waters.

But when a socialist coolly informs some of the most wretched of the earth that they must wait *until* the revolution, *throughout* the revolution, and *long after* the revolution before their oppression is significantly relieved—at that point, patience-and-fortitude turns from virtue into vice.

Why do men tell women to wait for civil rights? Why do whites say it to national and racial minorities and majorities? Why do straights say it to gays, oldsters to youth, the non-handicapped to the walking wounded?

We've heard a million times how the remnants of bourgeois culture and discrimination will linger on and on. . .how the evils rooted in class society will not disappear immediately. . .how anyone oppressed in any other way than on-the-job and by-the-boss will have to cool their heels and prepare for virtual centuries of degenerated, chauvinistic workers states unready to guarantee full legal, political, economic and lifestyle equality to those most subjugated under capitalism.

How inspiring. How sensitive. What creative use of the vast power of workers' democracy for a shining new culture. So we tourist-class folks don't rate first-class accommodations on the ship of socialism.

**A**re we supposed to forget the impossible dream?

No way. These prophets of the theory of increasing misery under socialism don't know their dialectics from the hole in the ground they are digging for themselves.

The patience-mongers have a blueprint for structural change that ignores modern times. Their schema for socialist development, after bourgeois state power and capitalist property relations are abolished, is ass-backward. Their fixed notion about the sequence of revolutionary stages is a theoretical error of the gravest magnitude, betraying a mechanical, Menshevist ignorance of the anatomy of a revolution and the psychology of a revolutionary.

All "you people" born to jeopardy as workers and compounded jeopardy on account of minor characteristics— take heart. *You* are the locomotive of the revolutionary train. You will decide the priorities of reconstructing the economy and the ideological superstructure. You will see to it that no worker-wallflowers are left waiting and miserable at the socialist ball.

You, the multi-vanguard of the proletariat, are the real "new mass vanguard," and you have already taken to the drawing boards to design a socialist future that will insure the fact that you and your kind are never again consigned to the back burners of the political agenda. This prospect is no misty utopia, but the living, growing future under construction today.

**T**he mañana-mouthers should have a little faith in

human nature. Millions of people are learning to shed regressive biases and ideas. Surely, hard-core pessimists can bother to learn something about the techniques of de-programming worker bigots and undertake educational campaigns to advance this process *today*.

The "Marxist realist" who thinks the attainment of elementary civil rights is out-of-sight even under socialism speaks for nobody but the white male minority—and he will soon speak for a minority of *them*. And shortly thereafter he won't be speaking at all, for his voice—the last voice you heard before leaving the leagues of irrelevant radicals—was the refracted voice of the oppressor.

# Socialist Feminism: Where the Battle of the Sexes Resolves Itself

1978

First published as an International Discussion Bulletin for the Committee for a Revolutionary Socialist Party.

*Co-authored with Susan Williams, M.D.*

How many radical scholars recall that Marx ends *The Poverty of Philosophy* with these ringing words: ". . .the last word of social science will always be: 'Combat or death: bloody struggle or extinction. It is thus that the question is inexorably put.'" And the author is? Madame George Sand, no less, feminist extraordinaire.

Feminism, the struggle for women's equal rights, is always a powder keg of the class struggle.

As both an ideology and a living mass movement, feminism has always arisen from and flourished in concert with the general movement for radical social change. And the social philosophy of feminism was first formulated by radicals.

The first ardent spokeswomen for their sex in the Western world, geniuses like Mary Wollstonecraft and Susan B. Anthony, were political revolutionaries who probed deeply into the close theoretical and practical ties between sex oppression and the exploitation of labor. All the great, early, feminist theorists and practitioners were eloquent tribunes or staunch supporters of the working class, and courageous fighters for socialism.

From its inception, feminism was a passionate cry for total, fundamental, revolutionary social change, and a demand for justice for all the underprivileged.

## Woman and socialism

Socialists inherit a long and proud tradition as exponents of the emancipation of women.

The greatest revolutionaries and advanced thinkers have always been acutely sensitive to wrongs inflicted on the most oppressed sectors of society, and the great Marxists of the 19th century helped to pioneer in dangerous territory when they took up the cudgel for the liberation of the second sex.

In the first two decades of the 20th century, the Socialist Party, the Socialist Labor Party, the Industrial Workers of the World, and the anarchists boasted scores of brilliant women leaders—speakers, writers, organizers and labor activists (including Emma Goldman, Elizabeth Gurley Flynn, Rose Pesotta, and many more). Thousands of women flocked to the Communist Party, and no account of the social history of the 1920s and 1930s is complete without the documentation of their enormous contribution to labor, socialism, and the radical-cultural scene of literature, theatre, and art.

Throughout the late 1940s and the '50s, when women were herded back to *kinder, kirche and küche*, the woman question was kept alive by a handful of Trotskyist women in the SWP, many of whom are today in the leadership of the radical pole of the women's movement (and obviously out of the SWP!). These are the women who coined the term "socialist feminism" to distinguish their advanced politics from single-issue, civil rights feminism, and from the anti-communist sector of the "radical feminists." And these are the women who sparked not only revolutionary feminism but contemporary revolutionary *socialism* as well.

## Revolutionary feminism

We proudly call ourselves feminists because we recognize that this accepted word for the struggle for women's equality lies at the heart of the class struggle in the western world today—and at the same time reaches out to women of all classes and races, beckoning them to the banner of workingclass revolution.

Real, consistent feminism is intrinsically related to basic economic change and to revolutionary politics. And vice versa.

Socialist feminists sharply differentiate themselves from the political opportunism and delusions of the reformist sector of the movement, and are recognized exponents of the radical alternative. Socialist feminism is the philosophy of an extremely broad sector of women, and a growing number of men, who arrived at this position from opposite but complementary poles.

Some Old Left socialist women either initiated contemporary feminism (as in Seattle, where the nucleus of Radical Women pre-dates NOW), or joined up with it. Young women radicals from the New Left exploded into feminism in a sudden reflex after years of pent-up fury against male chauvinism and the easy machismo of the charismatic, antiwar superstars. (New Left women merged with Old Left women, for instance, to form Radical Women in 1967-68).

"Non-political" feminists moved swiftly to generalized radical politics, impelled by the inexorable logic of their own transitional demands for nothing less than a total upheaval and transformation of family, economic, cultural and political relations. Affected by and acutely concerned about Vietnam, the Black rebellion, and academic freedom, feminism was the bridge that carried them to socialism.

Thousands of women found it intellectually and ethically impossible to embrace feminism *unless* it were overtly linked to socialism, and an even larger complement of women rejected the male-dominated Left unless and until it embraced feminism and female leadership in life.

## Dual nature of sexism

Hence, the woman question has historically been indissolubly linked to the class struggle. But at the same time, the founders of the feminist movement always highlighted the *dual nature* of women's oppression.

All women, *regardless of class*, are subjected to political, legal, cultural and economic discrimination, and this subjugation *as an entire sex* confers *an independent character* to women's struggle.

The patriarchal capitalist class relies on women for the extraction of unpaid domestic labor, and simultaneously exploits women in still another way—as a vast pool of cheap labor. The bosses reap their super-profits from the hides of females. That is why the bourgeoisie can no more eradicate sexism than it can eliminate racism, which provides similar economic super-benefits to capital: all wage exploitation would have to go in the bargain.

The terrible survival problems of women, therefore, can be solved only by fundamental change, and feminist demands lead logically and irresistibly toward the clear necessity for socialist revolution.

The great socialist thinkers and organizers, utopian and scientific, vigorously championed women's liberation. They brilliantly illuminated the double-edged—sex and class—character of women's oppression, that propels women to rebellion.

As August Bebel says in *Woman Under Socialism*:

> All women, without difference of social standing, have an interest—as the sex that in the course of social development has been oppressed, and ruled, and defiled by man—in removing such a state of things, and must exert themselves to change it, in so far as it can be changed by changes in the laws and institutions within the framework of the present social order. But the enormous majority of women is furthermore interested in the most lively manner in that the existing State and social order be radically transformed, to the end that both wage-slavery, under

which the working-women deeply pine, and sex slavery, which is intimately connected with our property and industrial systems, be wiped out.

Feminism, like the struggle against racism, is at once *independent of* and dialectically *interwoven with* the class struggle.

## The colossal role of revolutionary women

Lenin recognized that the dynamism of women's struggle lay in its twofold nature, conferring upon woman the tremendous potential for unifying all the allies of the working class.

In his conversations with Clara Zetkin, Lenin insists that the woman question be examined *"as part of the social, working-class question,"* and be firmly bound with proletarian class struggle and revolution:

> The communist women's movement itself must be a mass movement, a part of the general mass movements; and not only of the proletarians, but of all the exploited and oppressed, of all victims of capitalism or of the dominant class. Therein, too, lies the significance of the women's movement for the class struggle of the proletariat and its historic mission, the creation of a communist society.

Woman in modern capitalist society occupies a unique place. She is oppressed in the home and super-exploited at the workplace. The woman of color is triply subjugated, on account of sex, class, *and* her race. Since the bourgeoisie uses both race and sex antagonisms to divide and weaken the entire working class, women, especially minority women, become the focal point around which all workers and all the oppressed can coalesce and act in solidarity.

Women, in Daniel DeLeon's words, the "heaviest sufferers under capitalism," represent, symbolize, and express *all* the victims of the dominant class, because half of all the afflicted are female. Women are accordingly central to the creation and the culture of communism.

Leon Trotsky's appreciation of the explosive, "colossal" force of women and his call to all revolutionists to value and respect it, hardly derived from an anti-materialistic "mystique" about women—or from a desperate search for a new messiah. His conclusion was based on a keen analytic dissection of the contradictory currents and strata within the working class, and the analysis revealed which elements of the class were politically decisive. Revolutionary leadership, he knew, stems from precisely those social strata that are historically, economically and politically conditioned for it and prepared to accept it.

## Turn to the woman worker

Almost 40 years ago, Trotsky foresaw that woman's unique economic and social position would sharpen in intensity as capitalism accelerated its dizzy downhill slide.

He exhorted the Fourth International—the world organizing force of revolutionary socialists—to work among the most exploited layers of the proletariat—to "turn to the woman worker" who suffers the most brutal blows of capitalism and thus is destined to provide "inexhaustible stores" of revolutionary commitment.

His prediction has been amply confirmed by current history. In the U.S., where the contradictions of decaying capital are most sharply posed, the doubly exploited working woman is a consistently fierce fighter within the labor movement, more often than not putting male militants in the shade.

The Socialist Workers Party, once the prime Trotskyist party in this country, rejects this contention, but they are hardly close students of the contemporary labor scene. Women workers are shaking up widespread sectors of the union movement and spearheading the organization of the unorganized and the creation of independent unions. Women are organizing thousands of previously non-unionized workers, particularly office, bank and public service employees. And women entering the non-traditional, skilled trades are proving to be a terror to the stodgy bureaucrats.

To anyone with open eyes and open mind, the picture is clear: female workers are already assuming leadership roles in the house of labor.

Turn to the woman worker! In women of all ethnic/national/racial groupings lies a vast capacity for revolutionary leadership—at a time in history when their strength and skills and energy are desperately needed.

## Triple jeopardy

Minority working women, representing the three great strands of oppression in this racist and sexist class society, are situated directly in the vortex of the revolutionary tornado destined to sweep away capitalism.

Women of color are in the forefront of all the civil rights struggles; the men usually make the speeches, but the women do the major organizing that sustains the minority freedom movements.

Because their situation urgently demands radical change, the mass of minority women are repelled by the petty-bourgeois, moderate pole of the feminist movement and propelled toward revolutionary feminism and socialism. Chicanas, Black, Puerto Rican, Asian and Native American women daily demonstrate their inexhaustible and incorruptible militance on the job, and if unionized, within the labor movement.

The minority woman worker, fighting daily on every front for her full democratic rights, represents *the radical pole of every movement for social change.*

She further represents the political *synthesis* of race, class, and sex struggles that takes form in the revolutionary movement, the political arm of the working class and its allies.

According to the *Freedom Socialist* newspaper, Summer 1978:

> When the working class speaks with the voice of minority women, its power is impressive. Hospital strikes, the Farah boycott, and the 15-year struggle with the J.P. Stevens company are prime examples of the linkage of issues accomplished by minority women unionists. Their struggles have become labor rights and civil rights battles of national significance—precursors of the coming radical change in the race/sex ratios among the labor leadership.

## Going-too-far department

Socialist feminism should be a marriage of equals working in an equal partnership, a happy coupling of two titanic forces made for each other and caring for each other in sickness and in health 'til the transition from capitalism is concluded. So to speak. But if sickness rather than health predominates in the uneasy, suspicious and acrimonious political battle-of-the-sexes today, that is the historical and ideological and characterological fault of the men.

What?! You're not to blame, poor dears, 'cause you're conditioned? Acculturated? Socialized? Channelized? Blah, blah, blah?

There is a point where sociology turns into psychobabble, and too many leftists indulge in it, take eager refuge in it, and nourish, flourish and luxuriate in it.

Can one imagine Engels, Lenin, and Trotsky *excusing* male supremacy on the grounds of its deeply entrenched nature? No, because they didn't. They were historical materialists, and dialecticians, and proponents of correct revolutionary expediency—and they excoriated male chauvinists, particularly *communist chauvinists*. Their hardest blows fell on their closest comrades, as well they might, because what mattered terribly to them was the consciousness and behavior of the vanguard, the party, the political leadership.

How can the teachers teach, and the role-models model, and the heroes be heroic unless they *are* advanced, unless they *are* self-liberated from all the old crap, unless they bravely wrench the last vestiges of penis-privilege from their behavior?!

And please spare us the admonition that civil rights is one thing but women's *leadership* another; that equality is ducky but autonomous women's groups are the work of the devil; that of course sexism exists, but to accuse any radical of it is to viciously malign and emasculate him.

This is vintage conservatism, what Lenin called philistinism and "platonic lip service" in regard to women, reminiscent of the pontificating of worried souls who tell us equal pay for equal work is only fair but bra-burning is appalling.

There will be no legal equality for women unless women lead the fight for it. They have to; men won't. To lead such a fight, they must organize—independently, or they'll be subsumed. And it is the Bolshevik, bounden duty of any revolutionary to note and define sexism (and racism and homophobia and all elitism) wherever and whenever they are excreted—and that is frequently. To call the beast by name is not terrorism; it is education, it is basic political expediency, it is the only avenue of self-defense for the oppressed.

And what's wrong with burning bras, anyway?

### The unity question

The hard-core sectarians of the Left who deplore the battle of the sexes as "divisive" to the battle of the classes will promote neither battle. Only those Marxist-Leninist-Trotskyists who respect and understand the social sex conflict, and incorporate it directly into the program, strategy, tactics and culture of the labor movement, are capable of meeting the job description qualifications for the noble work of American Revolutionist.

All communists, male as well as female, must take seriously the tasks of organizing the most exploited sectors of the class, and forging unity, in both the revolutionary and the mass movements, among working people, women, racial minorities, gays, and all the oppressed.

Radicals must recognize clearly that unity can only come about if it is based solidly on the demands of oppressed strata. Never, never, never must male or female radicals counsel feminists to subordinate or table their demands in the interests of an abstract, isolationist "class" unity. We do *not* concede one iota to the chauvinisms and bigotries of backward workers; our job is to enlighten and liberate labor from its own hang-ups, not rationalize, entrench and enshrine them.

Women have had quite enough of self-sacrifice, turning the other cheek and exuding nobility from the pedestal. It's chilly up there, and lonely, and the wages are terrible. In this era of women's liberation, unity means a deal, a quid pro quo, an agreement, a bond of mutual respect and *endorsement*. It does not mean capitulation of the women in return for nothing but "honor"; women today will take the cash and let the credit go. Women don't sell themselves cheaply anymore; as a matter of fact, they don't sell themselves at all. Unity is a two-way street—or a dead end.

## The century of the communist woman

Comrades should heed Lenin's admonition that "developing and leading a mass movement [of working women under communist leadership] is an important part of all Party activity, as much as half of all the Party work." Or more! But who's counting. This work takes *time!* And thought. And study. And respect. And allocation of resources. By both sexes.

Communist women must continue to work with care and tact in socialist and potentially socialist women's organizations, always strengthening their ties to revolutionary politics.

And communist men must learn what feminism is all about—read the literature, attend the meetings and demonstrations, practice equality in political life, relish the leadership of women, and appreciate the criticism they will receive. They should demand comment and criticism on their bad habits, and nourish their historic new opportunity for male liberation from the crippling bonds of the masculine mystique.

For the old decrepit highways of radical politics are obsolete. Socialist feminism is the swift-moving freeway to world revolution, and the road ahead promises new and higher relations between the sexes based on the triumph of human intelligence, generosity, and comradeship.

# Scenes from a Rebel Life

*Samuel H. Goodman,
Teamster and anarchist.*

*Young Clara Goodman with father
Samuel and mother Emma at the
Japanese Garden in Hollywood.*

*Emma Goodman, Business
Agent, International Ladies
Garment Workers Union.*

*Clara in the mid-1920s.*

*Clara with younger sister Flory, circa 1935.*

*With brother-in-law Bennie Adler and sister Flory Adler near Bellingham, Washington, July 1984.*

*20-year old UCLA graduate with B.A. in Literature and Education, 1944.*

*New arrival in Seattle, circa 1946.*

*With eldest son Marc Krasnowsky and mother Emma, circa 1953.*

MARY ANN CURTIS

*Journalist Marc Krasnowsky, 1996.*

*Jazz musician Jon Fraser, early 1980s.*

*Son Jon Fraser, 1960.*

*Public meeting, circa 1956, of the Committee for Socialist Education, a post-Khrushchev Revelations regroupment effort. From left: committee founder Dr. Jay Friedman; Terry Pettus, editor of* People's World; *Clara Fraser, Socialist Workers Party; radical activist Paul Bowen.*

*Gathering for a Socialist Workers Party retreat.*

*Portrait of Clara Fraser (1959) by acclaimed Northwest artist Bill Cumming.*

*First demonstration attended by the newly formed*
*Freedom Socialist Party: a 1966 antiwar protest at the*
*Peace Arch on the U.S./Canada border.*

*Radical Women founding mothers: Fraser, Melba Windoffer*
*(center), a veteran of the SWP split, and Gloria Martin,*
*commemorated by Clara in "Valedictory for a Free Spirit."*

*Coordinator of Community Relations during the late 1960s at Seattle Opportunities and Industrialization Center, a job training school associated with the anti-poverty program.*

*1973 May Day speech at Freeway Hall, FSP headquarters.*

*Protest against grand jury abuses, May 1972, Federal Courthouse, Seattle.*

*Interviewing Ramona Bennett, then chair of the Puyallup Tribe, during the tribe's audacious and successful 7-day occupation to reclaim Cascadia Juvenile Center, formerly Cushman Indian Hospital, in October 1976.*

ED RADER

*Testifying in Olympia, Washington at a March 1973 hearing on the groundbreaking Divorce Reform Bill co-authored by Fraser.*

*Clara leads the Bread and Roses Chorus in an uproarious rendition of "Rebel Girl," in the original FSP musical extravaganza, "A Day in the Life of a Woman Organizer."*

*Fraser at a November 1977 forum with radical feminist theoretician Ti-Grace Atkinson (left), and Rosa Morales, Chicana activist who waged a courageous sex discrimination case against the University of Washington Chicano Studies Department.*

*Rousing the masses at Radical Women's 10th Anniversary Conference, January 1978, Port Ludlow, Washington.*

*Fraser inspires a 1980 strike rally of the Inlandboatmen's Union.*

*Organizing for free speech from coast to coast: Fraser keynotes the June 1977 Practical Conference for Union and Working Women sponsored by the Feminist Coordinating Council in Seattle (right). Below, a December 1981 New York City forum on Fraser's case, chaired by Marxist literary historian Annette Rubinstein.*

LENORE NORRGARD

**Free Speech in the Workplace**

**Clara Fraser**

**vs.**

**Se tle Cit ight**

DOUG BARNES

*The courtroom at King County Superior Court erupts in jubilation at Fraser's victory against Seattle City Light on August 9, 1982.*

*Murry Weiss (center), a founder of U.S. Trotskyism and brilliant Marxist scholar, talks with Fraser and New York FSP Organizer Stephen Durham at the July 1980 National Plenum of Committee for a Revolutionary Socialist Party.*

*Myra Tanner Weiss, former leader of the SWP and a founder of Committee for a Revolutionary Socialist Party, at the Radical Women 10th Anniversary Conference, January 1978.*

DOUG BARNES

*On returning to City Light, Fraser helped found the Employee Committee for Equal Rights at City Light (CERCL) which exposed life-threatening harassment of tradeswomen and workers of color at a community rally in May 1983.*

*Clara was among a group of women, comprised mainly of African Americans, who were arrested at the South African consulate in Seattle during a March 1985 anti-apartheid rally to honor both Harriet Tubman Day and International Women's Day.*

KATHLEEN MERRIGAN

DOUG BARNES

*Freeway Hall Case defendants, 1988. Left to right, beginning with back row: Fred Hyde, Doug Barnes, Guerry Hoddersen and Valerie Carlson; Eldon Durham and Clara Fraser; Gloria Martin; Yolanda Alaniz. Not shown, Sam Deaderick.*

*Addressing the September 1988 Freedom Socialist Party Convention in Bremerton, Washington.*

JONATHAN FOE

JIM COLEY

*A pointed response to arch-sexist Spartacist League which went ballistic over Clara's 1992 column "Thelma and Louise 'R' Us."*

*Relaxing at a back yard barbecue in 1992, one of many memorable parties hosted by Clara and her collective household over the years.*

## clara's corner

"We're going to have a double
Editor. "And we need a column. Who
"Oh, I can," I said airily.
Omigawd.

*1976*

### Clara's Column

SIGMUND FREUD once groaned
that he would never understand women.
    Siggy, likewise, I'm sure.
some men—and I speak par-
bout radical men—whom I
the life of me fathom.
ive in the very midst of—b
d historic new movement that

*1977*

## Clara Fraser

### Media Revi

*1977*

## Clara Fraser

*1978*

## Clara Fraser

*1978*

## Clara Fraser

### LaRouche:
### Sex Maniac & Demagogue

*1986*

*Clara Fraser*

*A touch of C*

*1989*

*Clara Fraser*

### Lenin & Libera
### Seattle Style

*1997*

*Clara Fraser*

### A half-century o
### struggle at Boei

*1990*

*Two decades as a columnist for the FREEDOM SOCIALIST newspaper.*

# 3

# Linked in Common Class Bondage

# Oppressions: The Capitalist Connection and the Socialist Solution

Keynote speech to the "Parallels and Intersections Conference,"
Iowa City, Iowa, April 6-9, 1989

I like the title of this conference, "Parallels and Intersections: Racism and Other Forms of Oppression." It hints at what I believe: that since we have many forms of oppression, there must be a shared cause and reason for them all—an underlying, cardinal reality, some hidden essence and inner connection between all these various manifestations. What is that common link?

## Chains forged by history

All the many brands of oppression—racism, sexism, heterosexism, ageism, classism—are historical; they have not been always with us. It was not ever thus. And it's not going to be this way, come the revolution!

Whenever I say that, somebody always objects: "Oh yeah? You can't change human nature." Wrong! My business as a socialist *is* changing human nature away from the distortion that capitalism has made of it.

Human nature, by itself, is fine. If you've raised children, you know babies don't come into the world nasty and exploitative—they're nice people! They want support and help and solidarity. And they give love and gratitude. They're cheerful; they like life. It's what happens to them as they grow up that turns them into the kind of people you hate to meet.

So the problem doesn't start with human nature but with

historical categories.

Oppressions grew. They developed—not out of somebody's evil mind, but out of material reality. Given certain economic conditions, levels of technology, and the particular development of the forces of production, assorted varieties of subjugation *had* to happen.

When production of "commodities"—goods for sale— became widespread, private ownership arose and with it came new family structures and relations among people. Classes emerged. And to entrench these new classes, new forms of rule developed. The state was born; laws came on the scene. The culture changed.

New forms of oppression and exploitation are created depending upon the needs of the economy. There's constant interaction and change among economic institutions, the state, and the culture.

We live in an epoch in which there coexists class oppression, racism and sexism, heterosexism, ageism, ableism, anti-Semitism, et cetera, et cetera. There's a name for this kind of society and it's called capitalism. In its most developed expansionist form, it's known as imperialism. It's got everything. It is a shopping mall of oppressions and exploitations. It relishes and thrives on oppression.

All these manifold types of oppression sprung up at different times in history. Slavery, for instance, was originally a system of forced labor that had nothing to do with racism. Spartacus, the Roman gladiator and organizer of the great slave revolt, was white. The Jews were slaves in Egypt, but most Egyptians were darker-skinned than most Jews. Racism only came later—when American cotton producers needed to rationalize the enslavement of laborers from Africa. It was the conditions of the large-scale plantation economy of the U.S. South that created racism.

So all these bad "isms" didn't have a common historical origin. But they sure had a common destiny—capitalism.

# Divided we fall

By capitalism, I mean the system that exists on the basis of your unpaid labor. You as a worker produce commodities to be exchanged on the market. You produce not only enough to pay your own wage, but also an *added* value, a *surplus value*, over and above the cost of your maintenance. Surplus labor is your unpaid wage. In polite circles it is called "profit." And that's what capitalism is all about.

Capitalism is the all-embracing social context, the all-embracing social content, the all-embracing social cause and beneficiary of every form of oppression and exploitation today. This common context creates the parallels and the similarities between all of us despite our superficial differences of color and sex and age and sexuality. Capitalism is the core that engenders the intersections of all of our struggles, and all of our lives, and all of our problems.

But we do more than intersect.

Intersection as a concept makes me nervous. It makes me nervous when I'm driving, and makes me nervous in ordinary social life. Because at intersections we meet and then we go away. I don't like that. I prefer the Hegelian term of interpenetration. When we make contact, we become part of each other. We draw from each other. We reflect each other; we affect each other, without losing our identities. Our oppressions interpenetrate, interact, intersect and meet.

Indeed, each of us is composed of a myriad of intersections, making it impossible to separate ourselves out into special categories. How do I say about myself, "Okay, I'm Jewish: here's my Jewish part. And there's my Woman part over there." Where's my human part? God only knows.

It's important for us psychologically, in terms of wholeness and Gestalt, not to rip ourselves asunder and try to be one single-issue entity, and tell all the other aspects of our identity to go to hell. We deny our basic humanity that way, because so many of us represent and honor so many different things.

We are all afflicted—commonly afflicted—by a ruthless system, a cruel, vicious, remorseless, callous system. The same enemy holds us in bondage. That enemy has the same reasons for torturing all of us.

The ruling class wants to preserve its privileges, its interests, its power, its wealth, its dominion. And so it engages in a very interesting psychological technology called divide and conquer. It's a weapon designed to make us all hate and resent and compete with each other. And so many of us buy it.

We can't let ourselves do that! We have to make change! We have to make broad, revolutionary, social, economic and cultural change.

And we can do it through unity.

We are the people. We are the majority. We are the dynamic mass. If we go out and organize, we will change this world, and we must.

## Fusion versus collusion

Some people try to escape the system. They try to ignore it, whitewash it, pretend it doesn't effect them. They tell me, "Oh, you go out and organize, Clara. That's *your* thing. I'm of a finer ilk, a more delicate soul. I want to devote my life to beauty and kindness and gentleness, and having exciting relations with people. But you keep doing what you're doing— and work faster!"

I don't want to make fun of anybody who feels like that. It's always a temptation to want to avoid trouble. But although you may try to escape the system, the system won't escape you. You may try to ignore it, but it won't ignore you.

Sooner or later life and the system are going to put you in a struggle stance. Sooner or later you're going to find yourselves in a battle. And suddenly you'll find you need help and solidarity.

When people realize the system has turned against them,

they go through a heavy politicization. And a very, very quick consciousness-raising. When it hits you, when it hurts you, you can begin to generalize, to see that everybody is affected.

So we've got to have solidarity. We've got to stick together if we're going to create change. But this cohesiveness is the hardest thing in the world to achieve, as you all know if you've tried to organize and work in coalitions and united fronts. Unless coalitions and united fronts have a program based on class consciousness, they're not going to exist very long.

## Class—the key link

What is class? Class is simply a sociological standard that describes where a person stands vis-à-vis wealth. Marxists call it your relation to the means of production. What end of the commodity production process are you on? Are you a producer of goods, or are you an appropriator of profits? Are you a worker employed by somebody else, or are you the owner who reaps surplus value from the labor of your workers? Are you the one who does the work or are you managing workers on behalf of the bosses?

Workers are all the people who don't own their own means of production. By this I don't mean tools—I don't mean your guitar if you're in a band—I mean the whole, big factory, the site, the production operation.

So who are workers today? Who isn't? Movie stars, artists, musicians, government workers, professionals of all kinds, teachers, professors—almost everybody is a worker today.

Workers aren't just blue collar; there are very few of those as automation and cybernation take over and everything becomes computerized. We do different kinds of work these days. We work with our minds more and we sit on our behinds more. But we're still workers.

We are the class. We are the mass. We are the overwhelming majority. And taken together, the workers of color, the lesbians, the gays, the women, the young, the aged, and the handicapped are the majority of that majority class. That's what too many of us lose sight of. We really have some power if only we would use it. And that's why we should stop sniping at each other and start organizing.

Our lovely revolts—Black, Chicano, feminist, Asian American, Native American, lesbian/gay—were these upsurges merely for the purpose of changing the race, sex and sexuality of our oppressors? But isn't this what has happened?

I fought for affirmative action, and now I am affirmatively exploited. I am affirmatively oppressed by the woman lawyer opposing my discrimination case. I am affirmatively fired by my boss who is a person of color or a lesbian or gay man. We will end up slaughtering each other if we don't get down to a class program and an orientation toward fundamental social change.

There's a big class struggle going on out there, you know. And the question is, what side are you on?

To me, a workingclass program is a program that is anti-capitalist, anti-imperialist, internationalist, and frankly and boldly revolutionary, make no bones about it. To me there can be no liberation without socialism. And conversely, there can be no socialism without liberation for everybody. This system cannot grant freedom to Blacks, period. To Chicanos, period. To women, period. You can't have liberation for one group and nobody else. You can't be liberated as an individual if you suffer oppression on some other level of your existence.

## The natural solution

I've talked about socialism—what is socialism?

Socialism is not production for profit. It is production for use. It is not production for private ownership and the private ownership of resources. It is public ownership, common ownership of the wealth. It is not inequality and misery and persecution and discrimination; it is equality and fairness. It is not poverty and want; it is freedom from want. It is freedom from war. It is freedom from ugliness and squalor.

It is just the opposite of what exists today and it expresses what people need and dearly want and would love to see. Socialism is a humanistic culture, a celebration of life, not of absorption into the engines of death.

Socialism is also the opposite of cultural nationalism. And what is that? Cultural nationalism is what the Black Panthers used to call "pork chop nationalism." It is where you make the cultural folkways and pathways and lifestyles of your own group into a substitute for politics, philosophy, and a strategy for change. It doesn't work. It never works, because it's too superficial. What it *can* do is destroy a movement. It's very good at mangling interracialism and pro-workingclass solidarity, but it doesn't work to build anything.

My father used to have a friend who would come over to talk every week. My father was very interested in science and philosophy, and he would explain some exciting idea or discovery to Mr. Glover, and Glover would look at my father and say, "But what's in it for the Jews?"

That's the essence of cultural nationalism. The only thing he cared about was what might directly, narrowly, benefit the Jews. Isn't that a great outcome of centuries of Jewish culture and intellectual leadership? Thanks a lot, Mr. Glover.

This type of attitude has produced the Palestinian uprising known as the *intifadeh*. If you're going to do the cultural nationalist trip, you end up being Jewish Nazis shooting down Palestinian kids.

A terrible, terrible phenomenon is going on in Israel today. I'm ashamed of the Israelis. I'm on the Palestinian side and on the side of the radical Jews who want a socialist homeland in Israel in common with its other original inhabitants, its only permanent inhabitants, the Palestinians. There isn't any way to end the conflict in the Middle East except by establishing a bilateral, secular, socialist democracy.

Like the Zionists, too many cultural nationalists in the U.S. are missing the main struggle because their self-centeredness blinds them to the key principle we must not break: the principle of *class*. Nobody wants war within their sex or ethnic group, but you have to take sides against injustice even if it's coming from someone who looks like you. You have to recognize class—who's the boss, who's the worker, who's right and who's wrong. Class is the line we don't cross.

## A design for unity and change

My organizations, Radical Women and the Freedom Socialist Party, are multi-issue, anti-capitalist, socialist feminists. Most of our members are lesbians or gays, many of them are people of color, almost all are workers, some are students, a few are retired, some are disabled, some are parents. And all of them are leaders and theoreticians and practitioners and activists. All of them.

We fight on all fronts. We see the interconnections of all the different struggles. We see the intersections and we see the interpenetrations and we see the context and we see the common essence, and we have a vision of the future. We don't have a blueprint, but we do have a theory. And we believe our theory is inspiring enough to guide us to a consistent practice. We have a good time, and we also work hard. We've got a nice, global type of political buffet going.

Ours is the theory of the multiply-oppressed. If you're doubly exploited or triply oppressed, if you're in quadruple jeopardy, you're going to be that much more motivated. You've got that many more reasons to go out and hit the system. And you've got a lot of determination and energy and conviction and anger that will sustain you in tough times.

It is the multiply-oppressed who will be the first to rise, who will give the impetus and the direction and the push to revolutionary change. And we are the harbinger of that movement of the future.

# A Touch of Class

1989

**M**y mama told me there were certain words you didn't use because they weren't nice.

My daddy went even further—you couldn't even say "Shut up!" around him. That was garbage-can language.

Not until the '60s did Americans get to say the forbidden "F" and "S" words. Speech was so exuberantly free in that liberationist epoch that we could even talk in public about oppression, exploitation, imperialism, and—take a deep breath—capitalism.

Everybody today prattles about the unmentionables of yesterday: abortion, prostitution, masturbation, oral, anal, name it. The AIDS epidemic has at least vanquished Puritanism in everyday conversation; safe sex is definitely in.

**B**ut I'll tell you what's still out, what is still not nice, annoying, gauche. I'll tell you which two words rarely fail to elicit groans, snores, befuddlement, glazed expressions, or ruffled feathers from most people: "Working Class."

Trade union bureaucrats, and workers climbing the career ladder to Business Agenthood, are loath to use the phrase.

Gorbachev never refers to it. He's too absorbed in peaceful co-investment with ruling classes.

Upwardly mobile professional ladies and gentlemen of all colors and sexual preferences tend to squirm and glare when they hear the offending term. The greed generation considers it a 19th century vestigial hangover, an appendix slated for surgery because nowadays, of course, everybody is middleclass.

Cultural nationalists airily dismiss the concept: it's irrelevant and immaterial to their agenda, which relies solely on group worship of traditional folkways and/or skin color. True delights like soul food or blintzes or guacamole or sashimi become the political cement of a small sector of some ethnic groups, and class be damned.

Some leaders of Native American nations get really nasty about proletarian power. Russell Means, formerly of the American Indian Movement and presently of the Libertarian Party, views class and socialism as artificial constructs devised by Karl Marx and interesting only to "white Europeans."

The Greens (whole earth anarchists) say that class exists all right, but it's obsolete: capitalism and socialism are really the same thing because both deal with who shall own and control production. They claim we shouldn't produce at all because production is hazardous to health and environment.

Some lesbians and gay men can be absurd, too—white gays who genuflect on the establishment altar and hate Reds of whatever sexual persuasion, and separatist lesbians who scorn all males except their bosses.

**A**nd then we come to feminists. What do they think about radical politics and labor solidarity and workingclass-principled personal behavior? Well, here it seems some fresh breezes are blowing. For instance, feminists around the country have started inviting yours truly to explore this formerly no-no topic.

I recently spoke on socialist feminism to a conference on Women and Power at the University of Washington in Seattle. My remarks on the connections of race, sex and class elicited interest, some agreement, and some vehement opposition.

On March 31, in Oakland, California, I was the keynote speaker before 1,000 women at the 20th National Conference on Women and the Law. My talk was "A Call to Activism: Reviving the Tradition of the Rebel Lawyer." I was honored to be introduced by Merle Woo, a sister in class struggle. Freeway Hall Case attorney Valerie Carlson and several Bay Area socialist feminist colleagues also espoused a radical class viewpoint in their workshop speeches. Again, a mixed reaction, but at least our presence was noted!

On April 6, I addressed a national conference at the University of Iowa attended by 2,000. The subject was "Parallels and Intersections: Racism and Other Forms of Oppression." My lecture was on "Oppressions: The Capitalist Connection and the Socialist Solution." Nancy Reiko Kato also hit on the issue with a fine talk on the revolutionary feminist approach to race and class.

April 18 found me at the University of Nebraska in Lincoln, where the Women's Resource Center invited me to talk on "Using the Power of Class to Combat Racism and Sexism." I think they liked me in Lincoln.

Yes, indeed, the single-issueism of post-Vietnam War days is happily dead. Feminists today are considering alliances—radical, multi-racial coalitions of lesbians and straights to confront injustice. The attention paid to female workers and trade unionists is still not enough, but openness to a dynamic feminism wedded to a class-based internationalism is surging.

Most thrilling to me was the swift emergence of a Socialist Caucus in Iowa, composed of women and men, people of color and uncolor, gays and not-gays, from various countries.

We said the bad words out loud, over and over: working class, *working class*, WORKING CLASS, *WORKING CLASS!* We demanded that respect be paid to this decisive class that alone creates unity out of diversity and separates the fighters from those who do the bosses' dirty work.

As Linda Ellerbee, the columnist and television anchor, said to a *USA Today* interviewer, "Just because it's a rat race doesn't mean it's OK to be a rat."

This here mama done told you.

# A Half-Century of Struggle at Boeing

1990

**M**y heart leaps up anytime workers win a strike.

And when 43,000 Boeing employees in Washington State won their 48-day walkout just before Thanksgiving last year, I felt exhilarated.

I was "made whole" again, as the courts say—because 41 years ago I was part of a wonderful and tragic Boeing strike that lost. The 1948 action, the first Boeing strike, turned out to be a six-month-long losing battle against a vast array of enemies:

The labor-hating, union-busting, scabherding, strikebreaking Teamsters head, Dave Beck, who colluded with the company to raid and smash the Aero-Mechanics Union (Industrial District Lodge 751 of the International Association of Machinists).

The AFL bureaucracy, abetted by the Seattle Central Labor Council, which cheered Beck's nationwide recruitment of finkers and stinkers.

The anti-union Taft-Hartley Act, delaying tactics by the National Labor Relations Board, and local court injunctions against mass picketing.

Press hostility.

Irritation and timidity of the International officials (who delayed strike sanction and strike benefits until the company's refusal to negotiate scandalized them into it).

Nineteen forty-eight was a time of labor retreat, like the past period of the '80s. The postwar tidal wave of strikes was receding in the wake of the Mohawk Valley Formula, a blueprint for strikebashing crafted by the craftiest captains of industry and their lieutenants like President Truman and Congress.

Nonetheless, the majority of Boeing strikers bravely held out. Who couldn't stand the gaff were the union officials.

IAM paid staff weren't allowed to collect their pay during a strike. The slippery NLRB, moreover, promised that if the strike were ended, all strikers would be rehired and allowed to vote in a representational election between Machinists and Teamsters.

Terrified of Beck, the International and the Aero-Mechanics officials stampeded the demoralized unionists back to work.

Naturally, not all the strikers were permitted to return. Hundreds of the most devoted activists were barred from the gates by police; a blacklist was in full effect. I, of course, was on it.

The NLRB later let some of us back in but ruled against many for no stated reason. They demurred at calling us radicals or communists, but that was generally their dividing line between the acceptables and the pariahs.

I never did get back to Boeing, where I had been an "A" electrician heading a crew on the final assembly line producing Stratofreighters, Stratocruisers, and the B-52s that carried the atomic bomb. And Beck along with the FBI got me fired from a dozen subsequent jobs.

But we all got even in a way.

The IAM won the jurisdictional election in 1949 and Beck and his minions ignominiously departed the scene.

Weary of being spied on, pestered by FBI jerks, and suddenly cast out of jobs like a leper, I got a job driving for

Yellow Cab and won full membership in the belly of beast Beck's Teamsters Local 451. When the bosses and Beck finally discovered me there six months later, they were so apoplectic that they handed me, along with my final paycheck, a refund of the hundreds of dollars I had paid in union initiation fees and dues.

They expunged me from Teamster history—no record exists that I was ever a member in good standing!

So when the International Association of Machinists and Aerospace Workers waged a popular strike and returned to work last November 22 with an improved contract, my spirits soared.

I congratulate them, even though I feel that they could have stayed out longer and won a lot more, given the changes in political climate and widespread sympathy for their plight. The International this time was more militant than the local officials, and many Teamsters respected the picket lines.

I also should warn the union.

Scabs have still not been dealt with—fined, expelled, or put on probation. And recent massive layoffs—clearly retaliatory and punitive—are not being adequately protested.

Boeing management today is the same Boeing management as 41 years ago—unreconstructed foes of laboring women and men of all hues, ethnic and political. Boeing is also rife with corruption and extortion.

Beating Boeing demands tight organization, strong community outreach, full internal union democracy, and the guts and gall that stem from commitment to trade union principles.

The union makes us strong—but we must resist and change all the inner negatives that weaken the union.

It is no crime to be defeated in an unfair match; another day will dawn. It *is* irresponsible to follow nervous misleaders and surrender to their cynicism and expediency and super-caution.

History has a way of catching up with the villains. Our job as workers is to give history a hand.

# Interview with a Native Woman Warrior

1976

On the evening of October 23, 1976, a small but daring group of Pacific Northwest Indians, the Puyallup Tribe, electrified the nation by suddenly and efficiently taking control of Cascadia Juvenile Reception and Diagnostic Center, located just outside the city of Tacoma, Washington. The land and massive building had been stolen from the tribe by federal and state governments. Though once an Indian hospital, it was now a notorious juvenile jail. For seven eventful days, the entire region held its breath. Hundreds of Indians from tribes around the country and supporters of all races from neighboring cities came to help defend the tribe against potential government attack and bolster their negotiations with nervous federal and state bureaucrats. The uprising resulted in a substantial victory for the Puyallups. An agreement was hammered out at the eleventh hour, guaranteeing the return of Cascadia as a medical and social welfare center for the tribe, which it still remains.

Two days into the siege, Ramona Bennett, Chairwoman of the Puyallup Tribe and chief organizer of the takeover, granted an hour-long interview to Clara Fraser. Below is an abridged version of the interview published in the Fall 1976 *Freedom Socialist* newspaper.

F*raser:* I'm not going to ask you to "explain" your action here at Cascadia. I am familiar with the background of broken promises by the federal and state authorities and you know that the Freedom Socialist Party and Radical Women strongly endorse your taking back what is yours. When your leaders asked for our assistance, we were happy to help and to furnish personnel and supplies.

What needs to be said about the meaning of what you're doing that the press isn't reporting?

*Bennett:* There are two very important things that are not being adequately explained. One is that we have for the past several years objected to the program that has been called Cascadia Diagnostic Service. We have believed for a long time that this is a real Dark Ages program.

The kids who are already in trauma are being further traumatized by that sudden rip, the jolt of losing what little they've got in their home communities. And that hurts.

It really hurts the kids who are already in trouble, that sense of removal.

To me, it's like taking a little wild mouse that lives in the woods, that has its little nest, that gathers food, that does its little things for amusement. You take that little mouse and you put it in an aquarium with a concrete floor and you watch it bounce off the floor and you say, gee, that's a defective mouse! Look how crazy it is, running around hurting itself.

To me, that's what this program is like. It's inhumane.

*Fraser:* American capitalism seems to hate children in general, and delinquent or dependent kids are lost in our correction systems. It's barbaric.

*Bennett:* Now the other main problem is I don't think any of the regular press understands how critical our social needs really are. We have the highest arrest rate, the highest teenage suicide rates, the highest unemployment rates, the highest infant mortality rates. Our elders have the highest rate of tuberculosis, diabetes, disease.

The press also repeatedly makes the removal of the kids at Cascadia the main issue, when the real issue is the property question and the illegal action of the state in denying us our property. The issue is that the state knows they have been operating here on stolen property for 17 years and they haven't done a damn thing about it.

*Fraser:* As a socialist feminist, I am excited about the high quality and participation of Puyallup women in tribal affairs, about the strong and skillful leadership of the women. How do you see the relationship of feminism with the Native American struggle?

*Bennett:* I have quite a few feelings on the subject. I don't believe any women can be totally liberated until their society is liberated, until their families are liberated, and we have no liberated citizens so long as my people are suffering and dying. We are moving for the liberation of our whole community. We are moving for economic and social liberation.

We have four women on a tribal council of five, and the reason I see for our success is that we are a non-drinking council, and we also have a very high level of awareness of the needs of our people. So our tribe is advancing more rapidly than other tribes.

*Fraser:* Women generally are more aware then men of social needs because we're closer to them. And your women are very strong to be able to resist alcohol and alcoholism. But how do you explain the fact that so many women actually came to constitute the tribal council leadership?

*Bennett:* Well, our societies were always matriarchal and women were always important. Our men built the longhouses and the canoes, did the fishing, and controlled many of the social aspects of our society. But the women were involved with medicine, justice, education, decisions. Now the male occupations have been removed from our community and the men are deprived of their traditional work. The women have been able to retain many of their roles, so the women have stayed strong. It used to be that all of our people were strong, but the women had an advantage. The women have managed to remain strong.

*Fraser:* And your goal is to rebuild total strength?

*Bennett:* Yes. Where the men have been knocked down, the women give a helping hand. We want those men to learn from us what a community is and what mutual help is because we'll be looking to them for leadership in the future. We need them side by side with us, working as our partners.

We'll keep this land and this building, too. *It's all ours, and you fight for what's yours.*

# The Raw Courage
# of a Black Woman Writer

1979

**B**lack Macho & the Myth of the Super-Woman, by Michele Wallace, delivers a knock-out punch to the Moynihan-Eldridge Cleaver garbage that Black matriarchs—rather than capitalism—caused second-class citizenship and second-class egos for Black men.

"And when the Black man went as far as the adoration of his own genitals could carry him," writes this brave, 26-year-old rebel, "his revolution stopped. A big Afro, a rifle, and a penis in good working order were not enough to lick the white man's world after all."

It is good to hear the scathing voice of Black feminism. Wallace not only excoriates the Imamu Barakas and Stokely Carmichaels—and their muling mentor, Norman Mailer —for misogyny against Black women, she also recounts, compassionately but boldly, how Angela Davis and poet Nikki Giovanni, each in her own way, surrendered to the epidemic of masculine mystique that fatally poisoned the Black movement of the '60s.

". . .The single most important reason the Black Movement did not work," she writes, "was that black men did not realize they could not wage struggle without the full involvement of women. . . By negating the importance of [women's] role, the efficiency of the Black Movement was obliterated."

The appalling confusion of racial emancipation with *manhood* was addressed 14 years ago in a paper I wrote on "The Emancipation of Women."*

What happened, I said then, was "a paterfamilias despotism, as endorsed by the Muslims, or a more subtle and sophisticated assumption of male supremacy, derived from campus sociology, orthodox Freudianism, and general practice. . . To endure and develop, the Black liberation movement. . .is going to have to rise to heights unachieved by any existing labor or political organization: it is going to have to *come to grips with the woman question.*"

You bet. And Wallace is one of the tribunes speaking for a new generation of women of color who have cast out the devils of confusion and self-abnegation, defied the black-bitch slander, and shouldered public responsibility for racial and human progress. Right on, sister.

---

* See page 38.

# Ebony and Ivory—
# the Paradox and the Promise

1993

**W**hoopi Goldberg was interviewing a rising Black actor, and they were comparing experiences in Africa.

Goldberg was deeply troubled. She had expected to undergo a dramatic rapport with her roots, she said, but instead she felt like an outsider.

Her guest laughed sympathetically and replied, in effect, "We *all* feel like that when we visit Africa! Let's face it, we're Americans now—we changed the damn country and it changed us."

"African"-Americans are treated as colonized enemies in their own land. Even so, the vast majority do not want to go back to Africa. What they *do* want is fair play in the country whose politics, economics and culture were changed radically by their very presence here.

So why are many Blacks nationalists?

**T**hey cite a profound sense of shared origin and destiny. "Nationalism" is their operative word to connote militancy, pride of color, disgust with the status quo, and connectedness to one another and to a movement. And it expresses desire for the liberty to *choose* when to relax with the sisters and brothers and when to mingle with "the others" and suffer the stresses of interaction and the stings of prejudice.

Black nationalism, then, functions as a code word for racial affinity, self-esteem and social protest. Militants who have no intention of trying to establish a Black state, who would never dream of moving to Africa, and who fight like hell for justice in the USA, still think of themselves as nationalists.

Nationalism can be the outgrowth of a despairing belief that separation may be the only answer. Nationalism can stem from the fear of losing identity in the assimilationist melting pot. It can result from the lure of the siren song of "Self-Determination"—an extension of the right of *nations* to secession to a racial group that is not a nation.

But whatever else it's attributable to, the impulse toward nationalism often conceals a *revolutionary ideology*. Blacks joke that it's hard enough to be Black, so why be Red too? The nationalist tag is easier to live with than the M-word—Marxist.

And therein lies the rub, because Blackness cannot overcome *without* being Red. A society based on private ownership is *never* going to surrender the enormously profitable, and hence institutionalized, practice of racism.

Like all other near-radicals, Blacks grapple with the dilemma of endorsing a depraved and depriving system or embracing a political philosophy that will thrust them out of the mainstream and impede their chances for decent work and community acceptance. The nationalist posture sidesteps the conflict by being fiery yet unthreatening to the ruling class.

But sometimes the shortest route to winning majority support for a cause is exactly to move to the nether regions of unpopularity. The shock effect of a woman or man of color who stands tall and confident and insists on fundamental change is especially galvanizing, to self and to the world.

Black fighters lead the way for whites. Yes, most Blacks are weary of teaching and helping whites, but most whites can't help themselves. White are screwy (perhaps you've noticed); overburdened by guilt and denial and uncertainty, they won't mobilize for progress on their own behalf—but they will for others. If Blacks demand that non-Blacks demand revolution, it will come to pass.

**W**hites of good will don't want a white nation. Most Blacks don't really want a Black nation. Good god, who really wants *any more* nations? Any more of the religious and ethnic mania gone berserk in the Balkans, the Middle East and the fractured Soviet Union?!

No, the tormented world cries out for *internationhood*, for co-existence in a harmony of diversity and mutual aid, for an end to self-segregation along secondary or superficial or downright imbecilic lines. We can't go home again—the places of origin have changed, history has moved on, and our new homeland is called Earth. The continents are now suburbs of each other, and pan-cultural solidarity is the tie that binds.

**S**o let us now build a global revolutionary party of Blacks and the otherwise-hued, women and the otherwise-chromosomed, workers and the otherwise-employed, gays and the otherwise-oriented and all the malcontents ready to challenge the ruling sadists. And let the savvy Blacks of North America stay here, dig in, and guide us all out of the wilderness and into new life paths where beings of multiple colors and talents can balance and integrate our diversity *and* our oneness.

The world looks to America for strength. U.S. front-runners—U.S. *Blacks*—will again come to recognize and respect their own power as leaders of the human race.

Bill Cosby, Black actor/producer extraordinaire, says that Americans hate each other—but the real problem is that nobody wants to leave. Right on.

# Say NO to Shamir and NO to Zionism!

Statement addressed to the Northern California Conference of
Liberal and Progressive Jewish Intellectuals,
November 11-12, 1989, San Francisco, California

**A**s a daughter and defender of the great radical and humanist Jewish tradition, I extend greetings to this conference on behalf of myself and my organization, the Freedom Socialist Party.

We applaud your stance against Shamir and against Israel's Palestinian policy. And we urge you to go even further—to say no to the Zionist myth.

World Jewry must face the truth that Israel's horrifying treatment of Palestinian people is no aberration but the direct and inexorable product of expropriating Arab land for an exclusive Jewish state.

## A mockery of Judaism

Too many Jews, for too long, have denied the harsh underpinnings of Zionism.

How else could they be surprised by the *intifadeh*, embarrassed by Israel's iron-fisted response, or shocked by Israeli development of nuclear missiles for South Africa and provision of military training to Colombian drug dealers?

And now the Israeli army has become a brutal tax collector that forces the West Bank town of Beit Sahur to pay for its own occupation—a travesty against centuries of Jewish resistance to unjust, anti-Semitic taxes.

## Deathtrap for Jews

Israel is not, has never been, and can never be a safe refuge for Jews.

Jewish nationalism has provoked interminable war and a looming replay of the holocaust.

Indeed, how could Jewish freedom ever be gained as long as anti-Arab racism is so endemic among Zionists? This virulent racism blinds Israel's supporters to the real nature of Israel: a colonial outpost of the imperialists and an expansionist country.

Israel has leapt into the role of permanent military aggressor, a U.S. pawn in suppressing the Arab liberation struggle, and best friend to bloody dictatorships around the world.

Stubborn ethnocentric refusal to make common cause with Palestinian Arabs can only end in disaster for Jews. As our own tortured history so eloquently teaches, passion for freedom and justice cannot for long be silenced or smashed.

## For a future worthy of our past

Jews used to have a proud history of support for the dispossessed.

But ever since Israel crystallized into an exclusively Jewish state, all Jews are branded with the mark of the oppressor.

Dissent and turmoil are ballooning among Jews in Israel today, and American Jews like ourselves must intervene in the debate. We must differentiate ourselves from Jews who behave like Nazis. We must condemn both the Pentagon's agenda in the Middle East and Israel's tyrannical occupation forces.

And we must explain that the essence of the matter is not simply occupation or withdrawal from the West Bank. In the final analysis, the only salvation for Palestine is a bilateral, integrated, secular, and socialist Jewish/Arab state with full rights for Jews, Palestinians, women and non-European Jews.

This conference has an historic opportunity to unearth the vibrant roots of Jewish internationalism and humanitarianism. We believe this is the only road to Jewish survival, to the flourishing of our rich culture and creativity.

The afflicted must help each other; it is written.

# Men, Women and War

Veterans Awareness Conference,
October 27, 1972, Yakima, Washington

> When Johnny comes marching home again,
>     Hurrah! Hurrah!
> We'll give him a hearty welcome then,
>     Hurrah! Hurrah!
> The men will cheer, the boys will shout,
> The ladies they will all turn out. . .

Soldiers returning from World War I were hailed as heroes. They were even more celebrated after World War II when our boys fought the horrible fascists. Everybody hated Hitler—workers, Jews, Blacks, women, nice people, liberals. We watched the Nazis gobbling up the world with incredible brutality and we hated them and adored our brave soldiers. They were our champions and nothing was too good for them—jobs, the GI education bill, bonuses, social prestige.

But today, after Korea and Vietnam, the veteran is *not* seen as a hero. And the U.S. Army and Air Force are the enemy. How did this happen? How did the Vietnam War become the most hated and resisted of all wars in American history?

It started with the radicals. They said this was an imperialist war against a poor colonial country struggling to decide its own fate. They said the U.S. had no right to interfere. They said we were on the wrong side. They said *this is not our war.*

Then the Blacks and other racial minorities began refusing to support the war. They identified with the Vietnamese for valiantly resisting a brutal white invader. And they resented the heavy preponderance of Blacks, Chicanos, and Indians in the front lines—due to a draft system skewed against the poor and non-white. They said *this is not our war.*

Then the students began resisting the draft. They wanted to fight injustice and vicious, oppressive conditions here, rather than conquering people elsewhere.

And then a brand new group emerged on the antiwar scene: *women.* Women identified completely with the Vietnamese people, with the women and children being bombed and napalmed and raped and tortured on an unprecedented scale.

And out of women's experiences in the antiwar movement, a whole new movement was born—Woman's Liberation.

Women connected the rape of Vietnam with rape at home. They linked the plight of the Vietnamese prostitute who survives by selling sex, with their own dilemma as cheap laborers and enforced husband-hunters. Women realized that military aggression abroad was an expansion of the male domination they suffered—a sexual ascendancy propped up by economic supremacy, educational superiority, legal privilege, cultural habits, and old-fashioned brutality.

At that very moment in history when the military was training males to be *men,* to find *manhood* in war, to be *real males* by being violent, belligerent and power-hungry—at the same time, women were vehemently denouncing this concept of masculinity.

They were denying that men are intrinsically despotic, competitive and warlike and that women are biologically passive, subservient and submissive. Feminists said these sex roles—tough Tarzan versus sweet, dumb pussycat—were a bunch of nonsense. Women announced they were in no way inferior or mentally different. They traced gender variations, including body strength and size, to cultural conditioning, educational channeling, and psychological terrorism. In addition, motherhood, far from being a mark of weakness, results in greater longevity, better health, and more general adaptability. Women discovered that in the past a *matriarchy* existed, where women were the main food providers, the political leaders, and the fighting force! Scientific studies in biology, anthropology, psychology, sociology, history, and law bore out all these new findings.

**S**o—a funny thing happened to a lot of you on your way back from Vietnam. Here you were—supermen, machismo operators, conquerors—and, yet, lots of the women you were running into weren't impressed.

They refused to be dominated. They declined to be patronized. They wouldn't play an exclusive domestic, sexual, caretaker role for you. They objected to being treated like a different breed of human being. They rejected your concept of *manhood-murder* and scorned your ideal of sweet, submissive femininity. They said we are *all people*! Each of us is different, but all are equal. Tenderness, compassion, and nurturing are not just for women. And aggressiveness, responsibility and courage are not the sole province of men.

Many of you began to complain bitterly: what the hell happened to American women? It was harder to make it with the chicks. They were often insulted and repelled by your tone and approach and attitude, and you didn't know why. You'd always treated broads like that!

Sorry, pal. This is a new day and a changing country. You can't treat Blacks and Chicanos and Indians and Asians and women and children and old people and convicts and the poor like dogs any more; they won't stand for it. The wretched of the earth are standing up tall and announcing to the white American male ruler of the earth that his godliness is no longer worshipped or even accepted. The people of the world, and the women of this country, are standing up and demanding their rights: *equal rights and equal justice and equal respect and equal opportunity.*

All of you need to understand this and respect it. And learn to welcome and commend it. Because without this understanding of the basic equality and right to respect of all people, you will not be able to organize your projects or advance your goals.

In the face of this incredible new reality of women's liberation, you have a choice: You can behave like the post-Civil War slaveholder who drowned his woes in booze; or the stockbroker who jumped off a building after the Wall Street crash; or the aging movie actor who couldn't play romantic leads any more and turned to dope. Or you can do what women have always had to do: *adapt* and *adjust* to the new reality, and become a better person by learning to work with 51% of the human race in a relation of equality instead of oppression, friendship instead of shuck and jive. You will learn that love means partnership, not tyranny, and that you yourself can never be free as long as you enslave others.

**A**fter WWII, all the women went home from their jobs in the war industries and they didn't emerge as a mass until the '60s. But this time, they'll never let themselves be shut up at home again. The war blasted them out of their feminine mystique, their adjustment to second-class citizenship, and their half-human social roles.

The sisters are becoming increasingly militant and radicalized because they have become painfully aware that they are the bottom of the totem pole. Who are the poor? Women. Who are the lowest paid? Women. Who are the most needy and desperate for decent housing, medical care, transportation and education? Women. Who are the most exploited and most oppressed by everybody else? Women. Who is beaten and raped and robbed and insulted and ridiculed and hated? Women. Everybody's scapegoat, everybody's doormat, everybody's My Lai, everybody's Vietnam.

Women hate militarism because in life they are always the buck privates, the flunkies, the shit workers, the helpless victims, and the bereft mourners. As eternal underlings, women despise elites and bureaucrats and dictators and mindless discipline and the stupidities of officers and bosses and the regimentation of the human mind and human will.

When you returned from Vietnam, you found a world that was different and perplexing. But the change is good and you shouldn't be confused. Because if *you* were a woman, caught up in the effects of Vietnam and worldwide protest, you would have done the same thing—*revolt!*

In your quest for a better life, women are a tremendous source of skills and energy. But if you want to tap that well, you'll need to display a new respect for women as your comrades, not your old ladies or your chicks.

Women intend to create a new society where everybody can stop being sheep and stop being generals and start being human. You must play a part in bringing this about, because today's world of war and sexism, poverty and brutality, racism and violence cannot endure. Together, we must either change the world or be blown up by it. Together, we can win.

# The Love that Dare Not Speak Its Name in the Army

1993

I have never been able to fully grasp the hatred and terror that certain whites display toward human beings of other skin colors.

Nor have I ever really fathomed the brutishness of so many males toward women.

And I am always appalled by the hysteria of deranged straights on the matter of homosexuality.

Sure, I understand—I hope—the economic and social roots of these maladies. The cause lies in the history. Still and all, unreasoning bias continues to astound me, perhaps because nothing in my experience lends any credence to the garbage spewed by bigots.

*Most* of my best friends, for example, are gay. In 70 crowded years of meeting people, I've never encountered a group with such a high degree of creativity, talent, intelligence, wit, literacy, social sensitivity, compassion, good humor, and capacity for commitment. And all of this together spells leadership.

The differently sexualized are less wedded to the sick popular culture and more attuned to reality. They tend to be respecters of persons and easy collaborators. They warrant your trust, and I trust my life to my lesbian and gay cohorts—at home, at hostile meetings, in dangerous demonstrations and on picket line eruptions.

I would totally trust my life to them in the army.

And I would run like hell from the queer-bashers and forked-tongued demagogues that this society spawns. That is why I think that nothing less than sweeping revolution is demanded—or how else can we carve out the new cultural environment and psycho-sexual services capable of rehabilitating the Rambo-ite, fundamentalist pathologicals?

But meanwhile there is much to be learned from the tempest over gays in the armed forces. The uproar reveals three aspects of the sexual minorities issue that have nothing to do with prejudice and everything to do with establishment politics, military depravity, and the pivotal place of the traditional monogamous family in the machinery of capitalism.

**1.** *Will open gays endanger "national security"? Let's hope so.*

The generals argue that their bailiwicks were never designed to be conductors of social change. Indeed not.

The military juggernaut exists to protect the "American way of life"—which depends on *bitter feuding among workers.* What's good for General Motors is very, very bad for non-males, non-whites, non-Christians, non-citizens and other non-conventionals (like my readers). The business of big business is isms—classism, sexism, racism, ageism, heterosexism. And the business of the armed services is defending big business.

Proletarian solidarity is *verboten*. It is dangerous to officers and orders. And now that Blacks and women are entrenched in the ranks, *somebody* has to remain excluded or inferior or segregated.

What's more, expanded rights tend to make the execrated more uppity. Will lesbians and gays rest content with the magnanimous cessation of witch hunts? Will they emerge from battleship brigs and closets quietly? Or will they protest against unjust and unneeded wars? Or maybe demand the right to elect their own officers, à la Trotsky's Red Army after the 1917 Russian Revolution? And what will happen when these newly empowered vets come marching home?

The lavender menace that terrifies skittish politicos is a beautifully clear and present danger to the fraying fabric of Amerikkka.

**2.** *It's the military that's sick and perverted.*

Gay people aren't the ones with a deviant, illegitimate, immoral lifestyle. The military establishment is the body with the disease, and its name is sexual fascism.

Army culture cements a male bonding based on shared misogyny and race-hate. Basic training relies on humiliating the raw recruit by calling him a pussy or girlie. Platoon spirit is buoyed by chanting jingoistic jingles about the racial/physical traits of the enemy.

Servicemen are indoctrinated to scorn open gays who won't endorse their view of women as hunks of meat, rape objects, and practice toys for sadism. Straight male GIs are terrified that gay men will treat them the way they themselves treat women. Out lesbians are despised because they refuse to be part of the victim reservoir.

Yes, sexual marauding is intrinsic to the military, part and parcel of its climate of imperialist violence.

But if the institution is so evil, why should gays strive to be in it? Because it is their simple right not to be discriminated against. And because some of those gals and guys are equalitarians who want to be in the trenches beside their workingclass sisters and brothers in order to better challenge the Pentagon, not promote it.

Moral pollution exists—in the stance of the warmongers. And gays are the uncontaminated troops destined to clean out the stables.

**3.** *Lesbians and gays are oppressed because they threaten the forced maintenance of the fissioning nuclear family.*

It goes like this: The system extracts super-profits from the unpaid or vastly underpaid labor of women. And the patriarchal, male-headed family is the conduit for this rip-off.

A vast superstructure keeps fracturing families mortared together, despite widespread misery and repression in the home. Alternative ways of living are a Bad Influence, especially as practiced by lesbians—so bachelordom is chic, but old maidhood is always pathetic, and lesbians are kicked out of the services *six to ten times as often as gay men.* Yet the number of lesbians is growing, partly because hetero relations today are so unappetizing. The arrogance and boorishness of typical male egos eventually repel self-respecting women.

Both genders have every right to claim a sexual mode that is less dangerous and irritating and more sensually fulfilling, more democratic and supportive of integrity and activism, more respectful of motherhood and childhood, and more feminist.

Face it, globo-cops: the values of the Victorian hearth are falling into the ashbin of history. Alternate mores are filling the vacuum. Cultural pluralism on the family front is truly, delightfully subversive!

**A** new day is dawning. Homosexual rights are big-media cover stories. Gays are scaling unaccustomed heights of power. The polymorphously perverse are packing up in droves for the giant April 25 March on Washington. The gay community, with a renewed life-energy propelled by AIDS and the spectre of death, is politicized and afire. The battle against the troglodytes is joined.

But this expanded confidence needs all the *radical* vision and audacity it can muster, because our new Prez is as treacherous on civil rights as he is on the economy, stupid,* and

---

* A much publicized sign in Clinton campaign headquarters read, "It's the economy, stupid."

austerity and dashed hopes will be the sole rewards for his misguided supporters.

The message for labor and all civil rights and civil liberties movements: Insist on gay rights now. Forge a united front against the tyranny of the homophobes. Protest compromises and stalls and the "practical-politics" betrayals of the so-called liberals. And ask not for whom the presidential sellout is being prepared, for the answer is *you.*

Don't you see? Sexual liberation will never be tolerated by a market, dog eat dog, cannibalistic economy. Free love can flourish only in a caste-free and thereby a hate-free community of equal and autonomous humans, who will bypass the nature/nurture niggling and serenely proclaim their affectional *choices* free of any pressure to vindicate their delicate, personal decisions to anybody.

The only antidote to sexual fascism is socialist democracy. The only road to gay freedom is a universal, across-the-board, non-exploitative family of earthlings. Gay Pride shall ring out when the human race as a whole becomes proud of itself.

# 4

# Scoundrels,
# Sellouts
# & Wimps

# On His Majesty's Secret Service

1981

**M**y first encounter with the federal spy boys was during the Boeing strike of 1948.

I was down on my hands and knees scrubbing the living room linoleum. We lived in a housing project graced by the architectural style of Early Chicken Coop, and the front door was wide open because closing it was a near impossibility.

A stranger appeared in the doorway. "Hello, Clara," he said.

"Hi."

"I'm from the Federal Bureau of Investigation," he announced. "I'd like to talk to you about the strike. We thought that you, a strike leader, might know about the violence."

I sat back on my haunches. "Go away," I said.

"Now, Clara," he said. I glared. He turned and left.

About 20 years later, when I worked for the anti-poverty program and was deeply involved with the Black community, two FBI agents appeared on my doorstep. This time I was cooking dinner and had a pot in one hand as I opened the door.

"Good evening, Mrs. Fraser." Not so chummy this time. "We are Federal Bureau of Investigation agents. We want to talk to you about the recent bombings."

"I don't talk to the FBI," I said, and closed the door.

Yes, I've had quite a few strange encounters with the political police. So I know how my colleague Su Bondurant felt when she was besieged on the night of October 17 by two pompous minions of King Ronnie's palace guard.

Su was part of a national delegation of Radical Women and FSPers at the All People's Congress in Detroit's Cobo Hall. Su was the assigned note-taker for the delegation. Her notes were written on a tablet which she carried in a denim tote bag.

One Saturday evening, she left her bag in her hotel room and went out to dinner. She and three other delegates returned to her room after 1 a.m.

The phone rang twice. Mary answered and the party hung up. Within minutes, there came a knock on the door and a voice said, "Susan!"

She opened the door. Two men in navy blue jackets stood in the dark hallway.

"We're from the Secret Service," they said, flashing some kind of identification. "Are you Susan?"

"Yes." Mary and Laurie were now at the door, too.

"Didn't you lose something, Susan?" Su said no.

"Can we come in and talk to you?" Su said no.

"Will you come to the lobby and talk?" Su closed the door.

"Don't you want to see what we've got, Susan? We just want you to identify it."

Su opened the door. The agent was holding up her *notes*. "Are these yours? They were in the *lobby.*"

"Yes, they are mine!"

"Now will you come and talk to us, Susan?"

Again Su said no. Replied one agent, "Toodles!"—which is a word used by nobody except Laurie and which means Goodbye! And the estimable gents left—*with Su's notes.*

It took a little while for the shock to subside. Then an angry Su called the Secret Service at 2 a.m. and demanded the return of her notes. Agent Ball said he'd find out about it.

Su called Ball again early Sunday morning. He said Agent

Brush would call her. "I want my stuff back now," Su said. "You've stolen it."

"You've been watching too much TV," said Ball.

Agent Brush finally called. He wouldn't return the papers because Su had "slammed the door" in his face. The poor misunderstood gumshoe was shocked by such an unladylike breach of etiquette. Su would have to come down on Monday and *talk to them* to get her papers back.

"But I'll be out of town on Monday," she protested.

"Then get a lawyer when you return to Seattle." Su had never mentioned Seattle as her hometown.

Attorney William Sacks, representing the Steering Committee of the All People's Congress, called the SS and spoke with Agent Brush later that afternoon. Brush now claimed the papers were found in a *restaurant.* Asked how he had identified and located the owner of the tablet, since Su's name was not on it, he replied that he was a *"good investigator."* He agreed to return the papers, but only to a *lawyer,* and not before Monday.

On Monday, attorney and friend George Washington of Detroit retrieved the papers and mailed them to Su.

Why had Brush commandeered the papers? Because, he said, Su had written down the words, *"Tell Pharaoh Reagan to let our people go or face the consequences of the Red Sea"*—a direct quote from a conference speaker!

Would you believe this political parable, to the SS's witch hunting mind, constituted a *"threat against the President"* which had to be investigated? That's what Brush said.

Violations of privacy and free speech. Illegal surveillance. Unwarranted search, seizure and theft of personal property. Deceit, secrecy, harassment and intimidation. Add it all up and you've got government crime —plus the added sin of rank idiocy.

I don't know about the Red Sea, but I'm curious about the Potomac. . . Now who could *that* be knocking on my door?

# Long Arabian Nights

1991

I hate it, I hate it—I hate this war. I have never hated a war so much. It's even worse than Vietnam, than Nicaragua, which seared our vitals and consumed us with outrage and horror.

It's worse because this one is something of a shocker. We didn't really expect America's imperial decision-makers to do something so inane and self-defeating.

Yet they had to.

They have to preserve their system. They have to carve out their new world order of permanent occupation of Persian Gulf oil producers and colonialist control of the region's politics.

And who are "they"? I can imagine who advises and orders George Bush around. They are a scary assemblage of fabulously wealthy and callous white males who would blow up the planet to prevent the birth of a beautiful new world based on economic democracy and untrammeled intellectual and cultural freedom.

But why are they so bestial, so arrogant?

Well really, folks, what do you expect from the moguls of finance capital and their military and political errand boys?

The compulsive war on Iraq isn't Bush's folly. This ghastly war isn't a matter of individuals, or personal psychology, or miscalculations, or ignorance of cultural diversities, or accidents, or unpredictable quirks of fate, or sanctions versus saturation bombs.

The carnage is precisely what the U.S. government is all about. Governments reflect and express economic relations, and our economic set-up is predatory. A private-profit and profiteering economy makes for Rambo-istic militarism and an accommodating government. The state, after all, is a body of armed men.

So don't blame Bush alone. He's only a spokesman and operative for his ruling class. And he's good at his job; the years as CEO of the CIA prepared him well for executive-level deceit, chicanery and unsurpassingly cynical demagogy.

*For make no mistake about it—Desert Storm is a deliberate, long-planned, and choreographed sting. Saddam Hussein and Kuwait have been manipulated and conned into computer-predictable responses to suit our scenario.*

Imperialists always do it the sneaky way. Modern history reads like political detective fiction or the spy novel genre. The White House screams "Naked Aggression"—but the White House provoked it. Our preppy prexy demands "support" for our troops since they are there—but how did they get over there? By necessity. By the intrinsic, driving nature of an aggrandizing, money-making society. The Pentagon and the Bush leaguers manufacture both wars and guile like assembly lines produce refrigerators.

Given this social anatomy, prayers for peace and calls for sanity and restraint won't cut it. They may be comforting but they are irrelevant. The millions of appalled Americans will not get far enough with protests until they realize that "peace" isn't an answer because it isn't possible. War can't be reformed out of the system. Only revolution will count.

Bush and his cohorts resort to war because of their terror

of home-grown radicals and possible revolt. War has always been a continuation of domestic policy on another front, always launched by way of phony warnings about foreign dangers and supposed enemies, all calculated to confuse the working class and its allies, and divert the people from mushrooming evils on the home front.

And worst of all: workers and people of color, who are disproportionately found in the armed forces for want of stateside opportunity, are cruelly forced to slaughter and maim their class brothers and sisters in other lands. Internationalism—the solidarity of workers of the world against their common overlords—gives way to nationalistic patriotism and mutual extermination.

Moreover, war doesn't only stymie international consciousness but throttles dissent and resistance in the home country. War is a marvelous tactic, a magic gimmick for enforcing conformity and timidity.

The war was meant to disarm and disorient critics and potential radicals. It was meant to cancel the soaring dreams released by visions of glasnost and perestroika; it was crafted to subdue a global passion for global justice. *It was unleashed not only for Persian Gulf hegemony but to shut us all up.*

But we're incorrigible. We persist in conducting our subversive business at the same old stand. In a way, we are terrorists just like Bush—but terrorists only of the Idea. Our socialist ideals terrorize him. And that is the source of our eventual power over his ilk.

That ilk does what it has to do. But the majority of us belong to another class, a different race, the other sex, a different sexual orientation, a fresh generation, or an opposing world view. And we'll see whose ass will be kicked this time around, when all the sands of Saudi Arabia prove unable to conceal the mangled evidence of Bush's butchery. And when Bush comes to hate our war as much as we detest his.

# From the White House War Room to the Gulf Stream Waters

1991

**P**eople are often not what they seem. Not only that, people frequently don't really believe in the sentiments and ideas they claim to hold.

Which is why I cast a jaundiced eye on the supposed infallibility of public opinion polls, and why I reject the actions of even large crowds as proof of their political attitudes.

A recent article in the daily press announced that adults generally respond to inquiries into their opinions by saying what they think the other guy wants to hear, or something that conforms to an apparently conventional, safe outlook.

That's obvious. Since most of what they hear and see comes from the mass media, people regurgitate those concepts. And instead of pithy political discourse, a stale and mechanical idea-recycling process results.

We are all victimized by this dead-end, vicious-circle paralysis of public debate.

A terrible war was waged. President Burning Bush said the country overwhelmingly supported it. General Stormtroopin' Norman, in his haute couture camouflage pajamas, said the troops were all gung-ho. The soldiers said so too. TV and press reporters said what Bush and Schwarzkopf had said. Then the man and woman in the street said what all the above said. And the next thing you knew, there was vast exaltation over this super-victorious war, swiftly followed by corrosive despair and demoralization in a peace movement grown bewildered by the support-our-troops demagogues.

The country appeared to be turning ultra-right.

**B**ut don't you believe it. There are more things in heaven and earth, Horatio, than are dreamt of in your philosophy, and few workers, students or retirees in the USA are all that enamored with the philosophy that justifies the holocaust we rained down on our workingclass sisters and brothers in the Persian Gulf.

Even the frenetic welcome back parades bespeak more relief and pity than crazed jingoism. In Seattle, the parade committee split into pro- and con-militarism factions, and it's hard to tell who will produce the larger contingent—the patriots or the protesters.

**W**hat an irony. It is so gratifying on this May Day 1991 that the Moscow parade is mercifully bereft of those menacing fleets of tanks and seas of bayonets that graced Red Square in the long darkness-at-noon era. American troop parades never featured armaments—I never saw any during World War II or any other war. But Seattle's celebration will be encased in martial hardware; I fully expect to see multi-colored, sequin-studded missiles dangling from the Space Needle. Shades of old Joe Stalin!

The Reverse Vietnam/Reward Our Soldiers contagion is just that—an epidemic born of the 4th-of-July yearning to remedy past injustices against Vietnam vets and do something positive, do the right thing, show the right stuff. But how do you express sympathy for hapless kids shanghaied into incinerating the cradle of human civilization—Iraq—from whence most modern culture sprang? How can you cheer an invading force that ruthlessly murdered its own history, its own heritage, its own ancestral homeland?

You can't. You can't applaud marauders or bestiality.

What you do is befriend individuals and learn what is truly on their minds and in their hearts. For out of these innocent and misguided troops will come the new antiwar leaders, the new militants, the new revolutionaries. It was ever thus.

**D**isoriented peace activists need to take a deep breath, dig in, and peer beneath the surface of things on earth, into the hidden molecular action that reveals the contrasts and conflicts and realities of life that get obscured by misleading exterior surfaces.

War fever is not a constant. Personal demo-fatigue will pass. The Left will resurrect explosively. And a lifestyle of armchair commentary and chic-bitter resignation will pale and wither.

Indeed, many movement dropouts wither away completely—they die too young once they cut ties with their political roots and a culture that looks forward instead of nowhere.

**E**verybody knows the world is engulfed in the Gulf war's bloody afterbirth. Nobody except the Bushniks is very happy about it, no matter what pieties they may spout. Someday, sooner than you think, and this side of the rainbow, the angry, afflicted and sensitive people will embark on a voyage of self-discovery that will carry them across the whirlpool of circular logic into an undiscovered harbor swept by fresh breezes—by their recognition of their own deep-seated convictions and hopes for a brave new world.

When people start to unearth the truth about their subterranean wishes and dreams, at that point in history the planet will start becoming habitable. And the revolutionary essence of America will once again bloom.

# Camelot, Shamalot

1983

**S**ometimes, as I read the press and watch TV, I get the feeling that I don't live in the same United States as the one being described. I certainly don't live in the same country depicted in the endless sagas of Kennedyiana that inundated us in November, on the 20th anniversary of his assassination.

The Kennedy dynasty was hardly the epitome of glamour, charm, wit, wisdom, compassion, intellectual acumen, and fine art appreciation. The Kennedy clan was an intrinsic sector of America's royalists, aristocrats in much more than demeanor and style.

They were economic robber barons. They hobnobbed with the most unsavory reactionaries. They were virulently anti-labor; Bobby almost destroyed the Teamsters. Their racism provoked rivers of blood in the South. Their view of women was demeaning and exploitative. Their voracious yen to forge a global empire for the almighty dollar found us jolted and revolted at every turn.

**K**ennedy placed missiles in Turkey. He drove the Soviet Union into building the Berlin Wall. He sent Yankee-loving Cuban emigré swine to the Bay of Pigs—where an infuriated populace quickly dispatched them. And he was totally responsible for U.S. immersion in Vietnam. He was out to show up the defeated French forces at Dien Bien Phu, and the colonial worlds of Southeast Asia and Latin America were siren songs to his expansionist lust.

On one rainy day in Seattle in 1963, hundreds of University of Washington students and other antiwar protesters demonstrated as JFK's caravan drove onto campus. I saw his face as he caught sight of us, and there was no charisma there. He was icy and furious and grim; he hated us. He feared *our* vigor.

In all the retrospectives about Kennedy that were inflicted on the public, there was nothing related to the assassination theory. No analysis of the whys and wherefores of Lee Harvey Oswald or the motives of Jack Ruby, a petty hood, tavern owner and chum of the mob and the cops. The media moguls are not anxious to call attention to the vast conspiracy that cozily interlocked J. Edgar Hoover, the FBI, the CIA, the Mafia, the southern Bourbons, and all the other unsavory men who also gave us Watergate, the execution of the Rosenbergs, the murders of Malcolm X and Martin Luther King, Jr., and more.

Oswald pulled a typical Nazi-style trick after his arrest: he screamed for legal defense from the ACLU and announced that, before moving to Dallas, he had been the New Orleans chairman of the Fair Play for Cuba Committee (FPCC). He subscribed to the *Daily Worker* and the *Militant*, he said.

The press sought out Fair Play for Cuba representatives. The Seattle press, as well as the cops, duly pounced on the Seattle head of the committee, who just happened to be me.

For awhile I thought I was going to be arrested for murder, or conspiracy to murder, or evil associations, or wrongthink. I should have been scared, but I was too indignant about Oswald. I loved the Cuban Revolution and the Fair Play Committee that defended and popularized it. So I sounded off to police, to reporters, to busybodies.

Never heard of Oswald, I said; we never even had a New Orleans branch. Oswald was trying to pin the blame on Fidel, I said, when in fact his bosses were out to get Fidel. (Later, of course, we learned of all the CIA attempts to kill Castro.) It's a crude frame-up, I charged, like Hitler's Reichstag fire provocation. I'm a socialist organizer, I said, not a terrorist, and that goes for the Socialist Workers Party, the *Militant*, and FPCC.

The press carefully published my denials, along with my address, and then dropped the subject. What the cops and FBI did was to generate the usual stool pigeon operation and paperwork avalanche (which cost me hundreds of dollars 15 years later when I requested my file). For weeks after the two murders, I received threatening phone calls, and our friends patrolled the woods around our house at night.

But this was only a mild anticlimax after the Cuban missile crisis. I had given mute thanks to Khrushchev and Soviet common sense when that incident was defused. The Day After will be unthinkable, but the day before wasn't much fun, either.

The human race is still afflicted by the macho legacy of the Kennedy regime. Let's not besmirch the glowing legend of King Arthur, Guinevere, and Lancelot by comparing them to the denizens of the White House in 1963. It isn't fair to the British.

# Gerry and Golda and Eleanor. . .

1984

**W**hat do you think of Geraldine Ferraro, they want to know. Are you pleased by her nomination as vice-president? Do you think she's competent? Do you like her? Will you vote for her?

Yes; yes, probably not; and no, in that order.

I was just as surprised as everybody else by her selection as Democratic running mate. I never thought Mondale would take such a "radical" step. But in retrospect, after the enormous splash made by Jesse Jackson, it is obvious that only a female vice-presidential choice could have disconcerted and subdued the highly energized battalions who demanded that a Black be chosen.

Fritz Mondale and his wary advisers would hardly do the logical thing and designate a *Black woman* for the job, so they settled for a more muted ethnicity—a blond Italian.

Nevertheless, a truly historic step forward was accomplished. The Republicans were caught unawares and shown up. And never again will gender be an issue for the twin major parties of the ruling stratum in this country.

**T**he epic of Geraldine Ferraro is a direct and unmistakable result of the past 20 years of feminist upsurge. The women's movement achieved this breakthrough into the perennial male bastion of establishment high politics. The wonder is that it took so long. The tragedy is that this is no winged, soaring victory but a hollow, and fruitless one for women.

What good is it for a woman to gain the whole world and use her power and influence to crush the souls and bodies of millions of afflicted women throughout the world? What lofty gains has the second sex attained in the wake of the real authority wielded by the likes of Indira Gandhi, Margaret Thatcher, Golda Meir, Clara Booth Luce, Eleanor Roosevelt, and all the rest of that illustrious pantheon of female achievers? What good is status and clout if they are wielded primarily to entrench the powers that be, to glorify and whitewash the predator class, to preside over the chronic degradation of women in the name of women, to perpetuate the fiction that if one of us makes it, all of us do?!

One of my old bosses, a Black man, once said to me, "Black freedom? That's when I become president of General Motors." I take issue with this widespread confusion of personal careerism with social reform. The current swelling crop of female lieutenants of the male power structure cannot, *must not*, be identified with true leaders and serious toilers for human rights and for basic, all-encompassing, and irreversible change. What possible difference does it make to a harassed and underpaid single mother that the harassers and underpayers are themselves female?

**W**hen we resurrected feminism 20 years ago, the battle cry was that women's emancipation meant everyone's emancipation. The quest for liberation was fused with the building of a new world, a new economic system, a new sisterhood/brotherhood of global equality and fraternity. To most of us, feminism meant socialism, and success meant smashing the prevailing code of profits, imperialism, assault on the environment, repression of thought, labor exploitation, and the vicious bigotries attached to skin color and sex and sex orientation and physical handicap.

But the single-issue reformist women who yearned for immersion into the system came to dominate over those who abhorred capitalism. And the horrifying end-product of the capitulation to the lures of the merchants of death, deception and despair was precisely the climate we live in today—the Reaganesque, narcissistic, anti-social, anti-intellectual, blood and gutsy chauvinism of American culture. When the women's revolt funneled into the ancient channels and adopted the timeworn tactics of playing political wifey to the male power brokers, the huge gains of the '60s and '70s disappeared for everybody and Pharaoh ruled again.

**W**hether Ferraro is a nice lady or a bitch concerns me not one whit. Her millions don't necessarily prejudice me, nor does her real estate shark husband. What does repulse me is that she is all too patently capable of launching destroyers and activating missiles and invading Puerto Vallarta if need be and decimating what's left of our "safety net" welfare program and life-supporting social benefits.

Ferraro, to me, is one of a new legion of educated, articulate, shrewd, attractive, smartly attired, and totally unprincipled shills for the bad guys. I would no more vote for her, or any Democrat, than I would for Cleopatra if I were an Egyptian slave.

A working woman has got to draw the electoral line *somewhere!*

# The Man Who Could Be GOD

1988

A real radical is caught in a familiar quandary over the tumultuous Jesse Jackson Question.

It's outrageous and obnoxious that the politicos and the establishment media incessantly trumpet his inelectability. One is sorely tempted to run out into the streets and recruit voters for Jackson to prove it just isn't true, because it isn't.

The right-on Reverend is the best, the only non-computerized candidate in the Bushkakis (Dukabush?) electoral slumber party.

Jesse alone addresses economic, social, cultural, and foreign policy issues of vital concern to the electorate. His program and his persona increasingly lure to his side the progressives, workers, ethnic minorities, women, gays, youth and elders, and intellectuals who yearn for a different kind of America.

However, Jesse is running as a—you'll pardon the expression—*Democrat*. He dreams of leading that disgusting party. And that shows us trenchantly where he's wrong and misguided.

By playing the game of bourgeois politics, he sacrifices from the get-go the good things he says he stands for. The system cannot and will not reform itself by elevating good people to power and letting them stay good. No way. And JJ perpetuates lethal illusions when he proclaims his intention to bring about heaven on earth via clone party politics.

So what do we gain by proving we can elect a brilliant and talented Black spokesman if we and he lose our revolutionary souls and bearings in the process?

I believe there is something more important than beating the racists in an election, and that is to expose and eradicate the capitalist configuration that created and perpetuates racism—not to mention sex chauvinism, class advantage, war, famine, environmental plunder, drug epidemics, fascism and universal, enveloping ghastliness. Jackson might have chosen this better course.

If he were true to himself and his origins amidst the Southern civil rights turbulence, he would be a revolutionary figure today, committed to transforming the system. He could be a great and independent radical leader like Malcolm X or Frederick Douglass, and he could inspire the anxious masses in this country to detonate a real electoral turnaround.

But he has traded his heritage, and a universal historic role, for a place at the Democrats' tawdry table. Because he wants so badly to be a member of that shotgun wedding called the Democratic Party, because he is so concerned about winning respect and acceptance from financial titans and corrupt politicians, he *legitimizes* the establishment, despite his pious criticism.

He says nothing about socialism, or domestic revolution, or the raging need for basic structural change. So how can he draw us forward, or do anything but succumb to the tremendous undertow of capitalist realpolitik?

We'd love to go for you, Jesse. But the harsh lessons of the past, and matters of principle, and the truth about life today for the majority of humanity, make this impossible for Marxists and other clear-eyed social critics. You're admirable and superior in many respects and we wish you were one of us.

But you have retreated into becoming one of *them*, and that's your tragedy. Because they're not good enough for you.

The vital question is: what role can you play in leading America's submerged and abused millions into a thunderous challenge *against* your current political brethren?

I met Jesse Jackson once—had lunch with him at an anti-poverty/job training agency where I was the community relations coordinator. That was 18 years ago but I cannot forget the dazzling impact of his unique personality and poetic conversation. He was a spellbinder surrounded with an aura of magic. His aides regarded him with awe, and a hushed, reverent ambiance affected any group he was a part of.

He spoke of the pain he felt because of the anguish of his people, and the anger and contempt he felt for the ruling class. "You talk like a Bolshevik," I said. "Isn't socialism the only answer?" He drifted off into a kind of trance for a long moment, his eyes raised to the ceiling. "Of course," he said softly. "You and I know that. But we have to use a different vocabulary." I guess I said something related to not caring about the words if the music was right, and he said, "I will lead and the people will be free," and then we had to visit classrooms or something.

JJ could be elected god if he chose. He'd rather be president. I'd rather he were a rebel because I could never ever vote for a Democrat.

# Beware of the Arkansas Traveler

1992

Slick Willie Clinton and the Democratic Leadership Council of plutocrats and militarists pose a more sinister threat than the punctured Perotians could ever hope to. Billy Boy and his blood-and-Gore running mate should scare the blinders off every alleged radical who compulsively endorses the Democrazies on the demented grounds that independent left politics are "sectarian."

The Hollywood extravaganza that entertained us in the Madison Square Garden parody of a convention was a rude wake-up call to all populists, humanitarians, progressives, and social justice advocates, not to mention—er, ah—radicals.

Never since the halcyon days of Rooseveltian demagogy have the Democrats so blatantly telegraphed their essential nature, to wit: They are owned lock, stock, and howitzer by giant corporations and imperial special interests. The party chauffeurs are contemptuous of and insulting to the disenfranchised, the disinherited, the disenchanted, and the validly dyspeptic challengers of the world according to George and Barbara and Danny and Marilyn and Bill and Hillary and Al and Tipper and Ron and Nancy and the Kennedys and all such sainted family-value exemplars.

*Oi gevalt*, what a crew!

Clinton and his handlers brassily and crassly shlepped a menagerie of bemused, confused, and euphoria-suffused delegates right over into the ideological camp of the Republican "enemy" without so much as a perfunctory, "Sorry, kid—this hurts me more than it hurts you."

The convention circus was an excruciating exercise in routing the radicals and liberals and making them hail their oppressors. One flamboyant ethnic militant of the '60s dreamily told the press that everyone was happy because "victory" was in sight.

One can only gasp in disbelief. A victory for whom?

For Jesse Jackson and his rainbow of the disaffected, who were humiliated and rebuked by Deacon Clinton for fraternizing with a brilliant, dynamic, honest, courageous, stunningly articulate and talented young Black female artist, Sister Souljah, one of the new leadership voices to emerge from the flames of Los Angeles?

For the feminists who were powerful enough eight years ago to place Geraldine Ferraro on the ticket but have now sacrificed a *qualitative* program for women's rights to the false glamour of an expanded *quantity* of women running for office? These congressional candidates are fated to turn out little better than their male partners in legislative crime. And even the ballyhooed pro-choice plank is but another dabble in wishy-washy moderation.

A victory for the lesbian and gay politicos who had to be satisfied with a couple of impassioned pleas by people with AIDS for enlarged research-and-treatment funding, while *not one word* was heard in four endless days and nights about the terror perpetrated against sexual minorities by homophobists of both parties?

A victory for the trade-union movement, unseen and unheard at the festivities? Franklin Roosevelt at least had to "clear everything with Sidney" (Hillman, president of the Amalgamated Clothing Workers). Clinton clears things only with the engorged employers and global industrialists whose ill-gotten gains boosted him to front-runner status so early in the game.

Would a Democratic triumph bring relief to students, seniors, physical minorities, the homeless, Chicanos, Native Americans, Asian Americans, Jews? Or respite to the earth? Gore claims that his vaunted "salvage of the environment" is an investment that will *make money*—which can only mean that every cleanup will generate even more exploited and injured workers.

**W**ith such a victory, who needs defeats? Friends, trust me—this is the best time of all to desert the Democratic ship, when it has a chance to win. The shelf life of the working class grows shorter in direct proportion to the opportunities beckoning for Democratic Party chicanery.

A party that has drifted hook, line, and sinker into the still waters of suburbia has no moral or logical right to claim to represent the dispossessed. It cannot hear, much less express, the wrenching cries of pain from the volatile ghettoes and workplace pressure chambers of the inner-city tinderboxes overrun by the violent, the drugged, and the hysterical human output of a society where the decisive input into government is reserved for mercenary monsters and their opportunist or naive hangers-on.

**S**outhern-fried Billy wants a new pact between the Democrats and the "Uhmurican peepul." But one definition of "covenant" is a suit to recover damages for violation of a contract—and *that's* the kind of covenant that workers should lodge against the deceitful, duplicitous, and depraved Democrats, who have promised reform for lo these 60 years but contrived instead to entrench a vicious private-profit system.

Instead of selling its soul to the Democrat devils, the working class, which is *not* middleclass, has to form its own massive coven—an extended Labor Party whose goal is to hurl the moneylenders and their bias-mongering media groupies from our seats of government and opinion molding and our job sites and our lives. A vote for the Democrats is a vote for self-extinction, and if *that* isn't sectarian, you can have my very own recipe for chocolate chip cookies (acclaimed by the popular masses as superior to Hillary Rodham Clinton's notorious recipe).

# Betty Friedan: Exit Stage Right

## 1982

*Co-authored with Andrea Bauer*

**N**othing more starkly symbolizes the decline and fall of the respectable, middleclass wing of feminism than the latest bilge from founding mother Betty Friedan. *The Second Stage* (Summit Books, 1981) is a horrifying but highly revealing example of a mother devouring her young. Friedan gazed at what she had created and found it bad. She rested, and then she ate it all up.

This was fated to happen. The turbulent movement erupting from her 1963 blockbuster, *The Feminine Mystique*, went further than she could or would, as movements are wont do to.

Women's Liberation spawned an instant radical wing as well as a fusion with a sector of the Left, and Friedan was swiftly recognized as outflanked by *predecessor* theoreticians who were braver and more knowledgeable—Simone de Beauvoir, Frederick Engels, Susan B. Anthony, Emma Goldman, and a host of revolutionaries.

This was bad enough, but an even greater shock was in store.

The women of the '60s and '70s who evaded Karl Marx became "radical feminists," à la Shulamith Firestone, Robin "Sisterhood is Powerful" Morgan, and others. Their credo held that biology, in the form of the male's superior strength and exemption from childbearing, was the source of women's hapless destiny. Men were structurally and naturally no damn good, no matter what social system they lived in or espoused. Hence, a glandular sort of "real" revolution would have to transform *Homo sapiens* before sex equality could happen. Meanwhile, personal separatism would prevail as doctrine, if not practice.

Thus battered about by the horrifying Bolshies, man-haters, and bull dykes, and getting richer by the second from her writings, Friedan flipped. While women hotly debated whether to sauté males or capitalism, Friedan and NOW—the organization she founded—denounced both sides.

*Neither* is the enemy, they intoned. Men and the private profit system are both just dandy.

## Hail to the nutrient matrix!

In *The Second Stage*, Friedan acknowledges a few bugs in the system. Women in her world do suffer stress juggling high-powered careers, domestic chores, and the search for emotional attachments. But to a disapproving Friedan, the biggest problem is that many "best and brightest" women remain childless.

Why is this so terrible? Because the family is the "nutrient matrix of our personhood." Whatever that means.

What *she* means is that women aren't fully human unless they are mothers. And the feminist movement has denied them their birthright—the "power and the glory" of maternity. Male chauvinism, she charges, is now superseded by female machismo, and women have turned into men.

What has really happened is that Friedan has gone full circle and come home to Sigmund.

## The new redeemers

The new harried mommas will need help. Who will supply it? Would you believe the poppas and the bosses!

Once women stop trying to do it all alone, Friedan assures

us, men will share parenting and housework. It is women's fault, she says, that men don't do this now: women's self-worth depends on unilateral control of home and family affairs!

Alright. The men are now great fathers and house cleaners. But what about the *89% of households* that don't fit the old pattern of a working father, a housewife, and kids?

Enter General Motors to the rescue. Friedan insists corporations are already changing, because it is in their interest to admit that most women have to work, husbands or no husbands. After all, cars, condos, and Cuisinarts cost megabucks. The workplace, therefore, will provide flex-time, part-time, and show-and-tell time.

Friedan is shameless in her paeans to corporate progressiveness. It escaped her notice that workplace reforms cost money which would come from profits, which business will never lower to ease the lives of female workers.

## Strange bedfellows

Friedan tries to be a realist. To influence the powers-that-be to do right, she declares, women must switch strategies.

"Why," she demands, "should we let the radical right Mau-Mau us into a costly, divisive battle to the death on their terms?" Why, indeed, when we can simply *accept* their terms and join 'em. We can forge a new pro-family alliance with the right wing.

Hallelujah, sisters, a savior is born.

Now, to keep our new-found buddies, feminists must abandon "incendiary sexual issues" like abortion, gay oppression, rape, and pornography. Friedan thinks it was these controversial subjects that stalled the "first stage" of feminism.

Moreover, she avers, such a focus is caused by women's secret masochism; rape isn't men's fault anyway (rapists were denied some "tender loving mother's touch"); abortion is "selfish" and bespeaks "licentiousness"; lesbians are "exhibitionists." And *everybody* is too radical.

No wonder a backlash erupted, she whines; we created a monster.

Friedan is a great tactician. Don't organize—mourn. Don't resist—surrender. And love your enemy—love, love, love, love, love. Barf.

## Just folks

Nowhere does Friedan display sensitivity to the persecution of women of color by the very right wing she embraces. Her vision of a new coalition is impossible, immoral, unprincipled, fatal, and racist to the core.

She has always been "irritated," she writes, at the criticism that

> . . .there was something *wrong* with the women's movement because it spoke to the condition of "white, middleclass women." That was its strength, of course, in a country where all women (and men)—except for the Marxist daughters and sons of the rich—would like to think of themselves as, at least, middleclass, certainly not poor (even if they are), and, if they are a minority, would like at least the chance to enjoy what the majority take for granted.

This is evasion and double-talk. Any movement that doesn't address the *special oppression* of people of color—as well as capitalist exploitation of the working class, the *basic matrix* of this society—will not long endure. Obviously: the color-blind, class-blind sector of feminism has long been part of the problem for minorities and women workers.

## A new history, too

The one fascinating section in the book is "drawn extensively" from Dolores Hayden's *The Grand Domestic Revolution*, published by MIT Press in 1981. Hayden unearthed intriguing data about early 20th century feminist attempts to communalize domestic work, and the movement's methodical destruction by corporate powers who feared the influence of the Russian Revolution.

Friedan ignores Hayden's *socialism*. And she slanders the Bolsheviks for not seriously trying to create "new socialized housekeeping structures."

The fledgling Soviet state, beset by famine, civil war, capitalist sabotage, economic collapse, and 21 invading foreign armies, still found time to legalize divorce, abortion and homosexuality; to establish communal kitchens, childcare and laundries; to draw women into politics and to launch a far-flung and expensive campaign to liberate them from feudal bondage and to educate men. *This was feminism's shining hour!* Betty Friedan is a liar.

Her cynical rewrite of history excises the socialist alternative, leaving her free to invent "flexibility" for capitalism.

She wants to ask the support of the wealthy to help end entrenched patriarchy. And she wants to keep her own class privileges. So, with desperate polemical surgery, she tries to separate capitalism from patriarchy. But she falls flat on her sociological face.

Sexism and class society share the same vital organs; separated, they will die only seconds apart.

## The Cleaver of women's lib

*The Second Stage* expresses Friedan's Second Childhood. Or Second Coming, if you prefer. But her pages of gibberish are less sinister than her politics, which are crassly imperialist and implicitly proto-fascist.

Not content with degenerating into the Eldridge Cleaver of feminism, she has also become the Phyllis Schlafly of the Democratic Party. She is not in retreat, but in rout. She has fewer solutions than Nancy Reagan to unemployment, inflation, poverty, the wholesale annihilation of social welfare programs, political repression, war, race and sex bigotry, and all the crimes of the plutocrats.

She's even opposed to government-funded benefits, and espouses "passionate volunteerism" to cajole Big Business into private grants for childcare.

And she "feels safer" because of the coed cadets at West Point who are "sensitive and tender," yet, to humanistic values!

## A matter of choice

The turncoat Friedans of this world shrivel and shatter when the backlash comes. Yearning for popularity, conventional success, and *freedom from conflict*, these summer-soldier liberals turn into super-patriots for all seasons, and do witch hunting for the rulers.

The women's movement is much better off without them, freer to develop its innate revolutionary nature.

The lesson here is clear: turn left or turn right. In the period of the death agony of capitalism, the middle is a myth.

Bye, bye, Betty. Thanks for turning us on, but now you can go to hell. See you on the barricades—or, rather, across them.

# Showdown Time at City Light

### 1986

**W**ay, way back in olden times, when I was young and 20, I scoffed at the notion that women were maltreated.

After all, *I* had never experienced prejudice.

This sublime narcissism and arrogance of an achiever kept me from grasping the social reality.

I wonder if I was ever so far gone that I finked on a woman who needed help. I hope not, but I probably did. God knows—and she will undoubtedly punish me for transgressions against my sisters, myself.

But ignorance is one thing. Life takes care of that. Cold-blooded sellouts are something else.

And the new generation of yuppies and upwardly bound women in the trades is so replete with scabs and rank opportunists that one almost marvels at newly arrived equality advocates who actually rally 'round afflicted women.

**W**hy so many renegades? Because of *economics.*

Of course, "Economics" is an abstraction. But the people who exemplify and serve the economic system—managers, union officials, and assorted employees who join to squelch those workers who demand sexual or racial justice or their right to speak their political mind—are very concrete.

Management "teams" and labor-corporate networks

coalesce these days with a common objective: to isolate the outspoken and entrench the powers-that-be. They use workers to condemn workers, women to trash women, minorities to denounce minorities. The goody-goodies who play the game are handsomely rewarded; the rebels are hounded, crucified, fired. The economic death-penalty is the deterrent to trouble-making.

Seattle City Light, as always, hunts for witches. Sherrie Holmes, a female lineworker apprentice, was murderously attacked recently by journeyman Art Meyer on a utility pole 30 feet in the air. She survived by grabbing a crossarm, and because a second journeyman yelled Meyer off. The bruised and battered Holmes complained to management and a weeks-long investigation ensued. Meyer meanwhile stayed on the job.

Sherrie, distraught by lack of support from the union and management, turned for advice to Teri Bach, the only journey level linewoman ever produced out of 21 hires in nine years. Bach received union permission to personally represent Holmes at the hearing on her charges.

Later, a leaflet was issued by the two main civil rights groups at City Light, the Employee Committee for Equal Rights at City Light (CERCL) and the City Light Black Employees Association (CLBEA), demanding quicker action and placing responsibility for the assault on a 12-year management record of social irresponsibility.

Now Teri Bach is an upfront rebel, feminist, veteran of City Light's civil rights wars, and a leader in the struggle for job safety. She is affiliated with CERCL, Radical Women and the Freedom Socialist Party. Right on cue, therefore, the management-labor collusion team roared into action.

Sherrie Holmes was warned by male and *female* coworkers to break relations with gadfly Bach.

She was told by crew chiefs, supervisors, and female apprenticeship program officials not to associate with CERCL and RW members if she wanted a City Light career.

The union placed on the agenda of a meeting with management the issue of Bach's "unauthorized" presence at the hearing on Holmes's charges.

On September 1, the *Seattle Post-Intelligencer* featured a large photo and story on the only other female lineworker — who currently is hospitalized from a 20-foot fall. "Woman worker backs City Light. . .sees no. . .discrimination," announces the headline. Said Vicki Peterson, "Most of the women who have sued City Light have not been able to get along with the men. . . I never had any trouble working with men. I can't understand how some of these women do. . . management is not hiring the right people."

Peterson called some of the former apprentices who filed lawsuits "radical women" who only took the job in the first place because City Light "would not dare fire them."

Peterson, who faces almost four years of apprenticeship, nevertheless has "already been told she can become a crew chief after she becomes a journeyman." Remarkable!

On September 2, a female line crew helper and vociferous defender of management distributed copies of a statement she wrote which attributed the current problem to the "Freedom Socialist Gay Radical Women's movement" who are "leeches. . .ladies in drag. . .female warriors on a testicle hunt." Art Meyer is a Vietnam veteran, she boasts, and an "All-American, Heterosexual. . .[who] cannot relate to Sherry Holmes breed. . . [She is] an incompetant, beligerant [sic], flipped nose, slug. . ."

The September 2 *Seattle Times* editorialized that if the charges against Meyer are valid, he should be turned over to the police. But the editorial quotes City Light Superintendent Randy Hardy as saying that "there are legitimate questions of physical strength as well as attitudes involved." There are, he said, "only three or four female journeyman lineworker in the nation." So women are too flaccid and insubordinate to make the grade?

The shabby scenario never seems to end. The victim will be endlessly criticized, the aggressor hotly defended, Sherrie Holmes's supporters castigated, and the entire mess blamed on the bolsheviks. And turncoat women will have played a leading role in the stale melodrama.

This political trickery—so horribly evocative of Hitlerian scapegoating tactics—is an essentially fascist mechanism for self-preservation, no matter who employs it to secure their jobs and ingratiate themselves with the power structure.

When economics talks, Radical Bashing goes High Tech, and finkery obliterates worker unity against the bigots.

I won a case against City Light because of its sex and political ideology discrimination. These issues are, as ever, intertwined. Employees will learn, and management will re-learn, that *differential treatment on account of political philosophy is as much a crime as any other form of discrimination.*

Nobody is young and innocent anymore. Not even women. It's too late in history. It's too late to be in the middle, to be "moderate," to see conflicts as different "perceptions" and hence unreal, to whitewash the guilty by not taking sides. When showdown time comes, our peers—and posterity—will record indelibly what stand we took.

And the hell with vulgar economic determinism. Human beings are capable of rising above and beyond that. Principles can still overcome, even in the '80s, even in America.

# Capital's Labor Lieutenants and Socialist Sergeants: The Danger Within

1997

> The person who says it cannot be done should not interrupt the person doing it.
>
> —Chinese proverb

Radicals hear it constantly: Why don't you all just stop bickering and *get together?* Well, I'll tell you why. An omnipresent collection of leaders who refuse to lead are the obstacles to united fronts against reaction.

Here in Seattle lives a personage called Dan Savage, writer of a notorious sex advice column that catapulted him into a new career as a peculiar queer spokesperson. In the daily *Seattle Times,* he recently urged readers to *oppose* a state initiative to outlaw job discrimination against sexual minorities.

Such betrayal is typical for a species that Leon Trotsky designated as the *middle caste.* These are the opportunist power brokers in every movement who teeter on a seesaw between labor and management, between feminists and patriarchs, between people of color and the racist establishment, between gays and institutional homophobes, and like that.

When the going gets tough, these caution-purveyors search for compromise, for peaceful coexistence, for surrender. They are weary of being squeezed between the establishment and the disgruntled rank and file, on whom their livelihoods and status usually rest.

Trying to justify his astonishing stance, Savage whimpered that gays could *lose* the vote. Readers, alert! Middlecasters admonish that if we rock the boat, we'll lose everything, including the support of the masses. But what they *really* fear is being knocked off their privileged but unstable perches into the churning waters of serious revolt. And to a career reformist, even a petty perk is worth the sacrifice of a slew of principles.

Trotsky could have been painting today's global picture when he wrote in 1938:

"The economy, the state, the politics of the bourgeoisie and its international relations are completely blighted by a social crisis. . . In all countries the proletariat is wracked by a deep disquiet. The multimillioned masses again and again enter the road of revolution. But each time they are *blocked by their own conservative bureaucratic machines."* (My italics.)

One of Trotsky's case studies of this blight was the civil war in Spain. After the fall of the monarchy in 1931, rising fascism threatened the Spanish republic. To save the day and seize the state, the heroic Spanish workers needed guiding lights who would say *go for it*, who would explain that only socialism could resolve the crisis.

Instead, each of the workers' parties in some way slammed the brakes on the struggle. The Stalinists of course were the most treacherous: They idiotically defined all other left formations as just as bad as fascism. Thus they tragically divided the workers and paved the highway for Franco's iron heel.

Yet the fence-straddlers continue to try to placate capitalism, even when they hold state power and enjoy public favor after a revolution. And we see the results in disasters like the Sandinista defeat in Nicaragua, paralysis in South Africa, etc.

In the U.S., the middlecasters are the jokers in charge of ferrying the votes of their afflicted constituencies to the disgusting Democratic Party.

Within the fledgling Labor Party, top union officials kibosh running against the Dems—with the help of an entourage of onetime or sometime firebrands whose policy is to never challenge the labor elite. Race liberationists, meanwhile, are left with only a dim memory of the promising first days of the Rainbow Coalition as Jesse Jackson settles for the humiliation of a permanent seat at the rear end of the Democratic bus.

Silver-tongued misleaders are experts at swallowing the line handed down from the ruling class, no matter how foul-tasting, and regurgitating it for their audiences. First Feminists like Gloria Steinem, for instance, rationalize even the most mortal of Democrat sins, like dismantling welfare.

So how do we handle these tame tigers who make life miserable for the ranks and for serious change-seekers? We have to get them to switch their stripes, to move ahead or get out of the way, to just stop interrupting the class struggle!

Now hold it, some of you will argue; we need to defend this ilk because, after all, they represent us. *But they don't.* Objectively, the middle caste—whether operating as elected officials, ideologues and pundits, or leftish movers and shakers—are agents of the other side. They are the labor (and other) lieutenants of the big bourgeoisie, with their retinue of allegedly socialist sergeants. Unfortunately, it's easy to recognize our external enemy, but hard to realize or respond when our own standard-bearers are leading us toward defeat.

But if we build strong ranks, the leaders will change. And once a bold leadership emerges, *they* will come—the immense throngs who will climb aboard and stoke the charging locomotive delivering us to our historic destination of peace, plenty, reason—and rhyme, too.

# The Lady Vanishes: Where is the Nicole Brown Simpson Story?

1995

**W**hat does a socialist make of the O.J. Simpson story? I thought you'd never ask, and the answer depends on the defining fact that I am a socialist *feminist*. That means, in addition to seeing the world as an historic panorama of many different, evolving social systems, I see life in terms of my own vivid and traumatic experiences as a female.

Hence, the "O.J. Simpson case," in my view, is atrociously misnamed. Goddamit, it was Nicole Brown Simpson and her Jewish friend Ronald Goldman who were slaughtered—twice obliterated, in fact, first by murder and then by the media obsession with O.J. The corpses are the disposables of a culture that adulates and indulges celebrities while ignoring and defaming the women these pampered superstars torture and destroy.

We hear so little about Brown Simpson and Goldman. We are deluged with video footage of the misogynist terrorist who almost certainly dispatched them.

**I** have personal knowledge of this male type.

I have not felt the panic and helplessness of Brown Simpson as she pleaded for protection from O.J. But I have been battered, by ex-husband Richard Fraser, who assaulted me twice while I was asleep and once during a minor argument.

He also socked my son, for no reason whatever.

Those attacks were devastating. I'd never been slugged before (except by hard-core Stalinists), and I was paralyzed by confusion and disbelief.

But I had internal resources, born of feminism. Once over the shock, I discovered to my vast delight that I could hit too. And that was the end of that. Bullies are cowards.

The affront to a woman's sense of self when she is beaten by an intimate is incalculable. It can utterly shatter a personality—*or* it can engender a fightback reflex.

My counter-violent response was a private revolutionary act, yet one common to millions of women. That is why our "second sex" identifies so passionately not just with the feminist pioneers who launched a thunderous movement, but also with down-to-earth fictional heroes like Thelma and Louise who stood up for their rights and retaliated in kind when they were degraded.

Conventional sexist wisdom blames the female *victim* for the revolting behavior of ego-deficient males.

Deplorably, this bigotry is quite rampant on the Left, especially in ultra-"radical" groups like the Spartacist League. So-called socialist men, and women, too, buy the canard that "she asked for it," "she drove him to it," blah blah. Poor pugilistic man. He's the martyr after all.

This attitude is a sick denial of the essence of liberating, humanistic, anti-chauvinist Marxist thought, and a triumph of sexual fascism over socialist ethics.

And this contempt for women has carved a great gulf between leftists and feminists. Sexist revolutionaries have much to answer for: the spawning of a vast dichotomy between two movements whose logic demands integration.

Life has taught me not to expect too much from most men in parties other than my own Freedom Socialist Party. But I am particularly appalled at the *women* in feminism-impaired organizations who ape the patriarchal venom of the men.

I appeal to women radicals who sneer at feminism to let go of your psychological dependence on males as the first principle and your self-identification as "the other." Forge a rapport first of all with yourselves and your sex. If you can do *that*, you will become the best and most sensitive exponents of class militancy and inter-race solidarity.

And I appeal to honest radical men to learn to elevate the question of women's status to the top ranks of fundamental social and human issues, where it belongs.

To view reality through the bifocals of socialism and feminism is hardly schizoid. Karl Marx, Frederick Engels, August Bebel, Clara Zetkin, Rosa Luxemburg, Vladimir Lenin, Leon Trotsky, Alexandra Kollontai, George Sand, Frederick Douglass, Susan B. Anthony, Daniel DeLeon, Olive Schreiner and uncountable other feminist radicals felt deeply that to understand the nature of a given society and gauge its degree of civilization, you must study the status of women and racial minorities.

**W**omen of all ethnic groups must demand justice for and information about Nicole Brown Simpson because that is how we fight for justice for ourselves. And men must support this principled female gender-bonding. As Rabbi Hillel said, "If I am not for myself, who is for me? And when I am for myself, what am I? And if not now, when?" You can never be for others until you are for yourself.

Don't beg the cops for help, ladies. Stand and deliver. Be the master-mistress of your own fate—for self-defense is revolutionary empowerment.

# 5

# A Radical
# Yankee in
# King Capital's
# Courts

*The next five columns recount the highs and lows of Clara Fraser's eight-year-long sex and political ideology discrimination case against Seattle City Light. In 1975, the municipal utility fired Fraser from her job as Training and Education Coordinator in retaliation for her role as spokeswoman for a massive wildcat strike, coordinator and defender of a pioneer program to bring women into the electrical trades, and outspoken critic of bigoted and bureaucratic management. A monumental defense campaign won endorsements from more than 150 labor, feminist, civil rights and lesbian/gay organizations, and luminaries including Dick Gregory, Flo Kennedy, William Kunstler, Kate Millett, Joanna Russ, Crystal Lee Sutton (the Southern textile unionist whose story was told in the movie NORMA RAE), Leonard Weinglass, and many, many more. The case focused national attention on the issue of First Amendment rights on the job. Fraser's ultimate victory was reported across the country and was a triumph for the right of whistle-blowers, dissidents, and radicals to speak their minds free of reprisals.*

# Message to the Media

1977

To comfort the afflicted and afflict the comfortable.

That is the reporter's mission, as defined by Heywood Broun, the great journalist who founded the Newspaper Guild.

I have encountered dozens of newswriters who did exactly that. I have an abiding respect for the working press—their facility with language, their split-second, deadline-haunted timing, and their skillful creation of concise stories that vividly capture the flavor of a happening or viewpoint.

But I have also seen issues cynically distorted by reporters who turn the victim into the villain, and the establishment into the good guys. And many of the big time editors who trim the stories and write the heads and captions are something else!

I have never met an editor or publisher of the bourgeois press, but it is clear that their attitudes are securely anchored in their advertisers' wallets. News about social problems receives some weird and wacky treatment, and a recent experience of mine is a case in point.

I was "laid off" from Seattle City Light because the superintendent was rendered apoplectic by my philosophy and activities. My "crimes" were legion:

I joined the striking electrical workers at the utility.

I organized and tried to preserve a trainee program for female electricians.

I testified against the big boss before a public committee investigating his controversial personnel and management policies.

I helped negotiate an employee Bill of Rights that would have subdued his Napoleonic powers, had not the mayor illegally stonewalled the Bill.

I supported a recall campaign against said mayor.

I advocated career training and upgrading for Black women clerical workers.

So I was fired, and I protested. I contend that I, a socialist, have as much right to work for the government as a Republican or Prohibitionist.

I appealed to the city's Department of Human Rights, charging discrimination on account of sex and politics, and the agency found on my behalf.

This judgment was exceptionally significant because mine

was the first complaint filed under the "political ideology" section of the Fair Employment Practices Ordinance. It may well be the first such case in the country.

Since the agency cannot publicize its findings, I did—and many reporters and photographers came to my press conference.

**T**V treatment was curt and cursory. One channel flashed the item by so fast that I couldn't follow it, especially since wrong information was being transmitted.

On another channel, the anchorman "talked over" a picture of me on the screen, so my own words were not heard.

The third station let me speak. Their review was relatively extensive and correct—which may explain why the story was not rerun on the late evening time slot, when office workers and women watch the tube.

Came the dawn, and the morning paper featured a front-page capsule preview: "Clara Fraser, fired by City Light in 1975, said the Seattle Dept. of Human Rights backs her six-point discrimination complaint." The gist of the matter was not that an impartial agency upheld me—but that I *said* they did! This introductory blurb hinted that perhaps I was talking through my bonnet, even though the full story quoted the agency's attorney.

The headline was a triumph of folksiness: "Clara Fraser Isn't Through With City Light Yet." My photo was captioned "Clara Fraser—Not Through Yet." (My paranoid vibes whispered that the subliminal, missing word was "unfortunately.")

OK, no big problem, and what's wrong with humor, anyway. But this PR experience triggered an old irritation. We the afflicted, are being taken—and in my next column, I'll tell you where.

# Media Revisited

1977

In my last column, I described the product of a press conference I called to announce a victory in an employment discrimination case involving on-the-job civil liberties.

I described the shallow and rushed treatment afforded the story on television, and the personalized slant adopted by the morning paper.

I expressed my admiration for the working press, and annoyance at conservative editors who use words and pictures to afflict the afflicted and comfort the comfortable.

Even though the capitalist-owned media is a private enterprise rather than a public service, it still has no ethical right to deprive workers of the elementary information needed to survive in a world where knowledge is power and lack of it is crippling.

A case in point is the superficiality of TV news. The once-over-lightly treatment of vital affairs is so superficial that it turns frivolous and finally becomes contemptuous of news itself. The newscasters make a mockery of the news.

Nobody can object to newscasts that are clever and visually arresting—conflict, especially, can be well-portrayed. But the most dramatic confrontations—*the clash of ideas*—are handled like hot potatoes. The facts spoon-fed to the viewer are too sparse and distorted to convey the nature of an ideological dispute authentically. The lack of impact cheats the audience.

Newspaper articles lend themselves much more to in-depth analysis than do video news flashes. But stories in the press are often slanted out of perspective by the political bias or dollar sign opportunism of the editor/publisher.

The press won high public favor when it finally found the nerve, during the Watergate deluge, to admit the truth about government that most of us already knew or suspected anyway. But the lords of the press exploit this new populist glamour to perpetuate their untouchable, sacrosanct status.

There are no publicly-adopted canons of ethics to govern the press, no public tribunals to offer recourse to aggrieved readers, no legislative committees to investigate the investigators. There is no public relations person, no ombudsman, no equal rights official at any newspaper or TV office whose job it is to mediate with or represent the consumer.

Would regulation violate freedom of the press? No. Press freedom isn't the only principle around. What about fair play? Social responsibility? Truth-in-packaging? These are interlocking principles, and highly endangered ones.

The problem is that "freedom" is reserved for the owner of the medium, and *not* for the subject or person under discussion, or the reader, or the reporter. The First Amendment shelters all speech, but its prime beneficiary is the giant information industry dominated by corporate moguls who are no mean slouches at the game of intensive labor exploitation. Translated into economic terms, freedom of the press becomes sheer license for millionaire publishers and network czars to lard their own preserves and preserve their own class.

No, there is nothing sacred about their right to mold and

twist public opinion at our expense, especially when we have no equal access to their technology and pervasive influence.

The airwaves belong to the people, not the networks, and immeasurably more workers than entrepreneurs buy the dailies. We should affirm our rights to the opinion makers, those henchmen of privilege who trample the equal time ethic into the mud.

Readers and video viewers of the world, Arise! You have nothing to lose but show-biz news accounts, and the dynamic world of reality to gain!

# A Socialist on Trial

1980

I've never been raped, sexually. But I am being raped, politically and legally and psychologically, in the course of my absurdly long-running courtroom case against Seattle City Light.

It isn't a criminal case. But I'm charged with being one.

I'm not even the defendant—I'm the Charging Party, the plaintiff. Nevertheless, I'm the one who ends up on trial, with my virtue, past practices and motives subjected to a smear campaign—to the kind of slander and character assassination that routinely accompany a rape or murder hearing.

Fair players, the legally hip, and feminists have long been up in arms about the patent inequity of the courtroom process wherein a woman charges rape. It is she who finds herself on trial, not the man. The accuser becomes the accused, the victim becomes the criminal, the person affirming the law becomes the lawbreaker.

What isn't as well known is that trying to make a *discrimination* case in court is tantamount to proving that Mount St. Helens did indeed erupt last month.

Everybody knows it did, but legal proof is something else again. And if City Light's lawyers were assigned to defend the mountain against my accusation that it really did blow, their arguments would sound something like this:

1. Eruptions are a management prerogative of mountains.

2. Anyone leveling such a charge obviously hates mountains and wants to level *them*.

3. Only a subversive incompetent would be reckless enough to call wayward boulders an eruption.

4. The steam, flames and gases are a humanistic method of removing the surplus population at the foot of the mountain. (The last days of Pompeii were planned, implemented and monitored by a similarly liberal civic administration.)

5. Eruptions are more cost effective than complaining about them.

6. Mountains are scrupulously non-political, but commentators on their behavior have ulterior motives.

7. The poor mountain was only trying to protect itself from the ravages of an outside agitator. The end justifies the means, doesn't it?

**E**rgo, there was no "eruption," only self-defense against a female, radical menace. Off with her head. To the guillotine. Kill, kill, kill.

But all is not lost. The bosses and their barristers and their perjurer-witnesses are simply killing the thing they love. They don't hate me, you see, they *like* me. They say so. They all say so. They adore me, I'm a living doll.

Oh, I'm abrasive, arrogant, overbearing, disruptive, contemptuous, disloyal, disobedient, dilatory, thieving, manipulative, unproductive and hostile—but I'm nice.

Everybody in management thought I was great until I turned against them, for some mysterious reason. So they say. Actually, the top honchos were rendered apoplectic by an in-house, upfront woman socialist in middle-management who joined the striking electrical workers, tried to recall the anti-labor mayor, helped negotiated an employee Bill of Rights, testified publicly against management violations of affirmative action laws, and agreed to interviews by the media whenever they asked me.

So it's nothing *personal*, you understand. And, perish forbid, it's nothing—you'll excuse the expression—*political!* I just "ignored the chain of command" and had to be consigned to chains for suchlike *lèse majesté*.

The hell of it is, I can't even plead guilty to that charge. I'd like to, considering what I think of their brand of chain and command, but I'm shamefully innocent. Because the only way to function at all within a vast bureaucracy is to try and stagger through the tortuous channels, and I did. I tried, I staggered, I kept upright for awhile, and then I got creamed.

The commandants with their cookie-cutter politics may have *liked* me but they sure didn't want me.

There can be only one politics—theirs. Only one philosophy—theirs. One avenue of self-expression and action—theirs. One criteria for competence, efficiency, cooperation and proper demeanor—theirs. They run the government, have the power, make the rules. And woe to the critic, the whistle-blower and the unearther of skeletons in their bureaucratic closets, especially if she is a she and has been known to belittle capitalism.

If you tell the truth to a disbelieving world, you get raped.

There's no justice. Not in a courtroom, on a civil rights/ civil liberties issues. Whether you win or lose, you are ravished in the legal mill. And what kind of dollar damages does one assess for premeditated political rape in the first degree?

# The People vs. City Light

1980

**M**y marathon case against City Light is like an endless football game, with the score changing each quarter and the final tally bearing little relation to the actual yardage gained on the ground or in the air. I was leading at half-time, scored a winning touchdown in the third quarter, then came out on the wrong end of a one-point conversion.

The July 21 decision against me by two of the three hearing panelists was such a travesty of the rules of the game—and of justice—that I cannot accept it as the final score.

Hearing Examiner Sally Pasette, an attorney, found for me on the grounds of political ideology discrimination.

Elizabeth Ponder, the only Black panelist, well understands discrimination, and she ruled for me on the grounds of both sex and political discrimination.

But panelists Darlene Allison and Beverly Stanton reversed Pasette's knowledgeable decision, ignored Ponder's special expertise, and substituted their own pro-management prejudices for the objective findings of fact and conclusions of law arrived at by Pasette and Ponder. The written decision of Allison/Stanton unabashedly revealed their anti-labor bias and total lack of understanding of sex discrimination and civil liberties law. It ignored my First Amendment rights and flaunted the provisions of the Seattle Fair Employment Practices Ordinance.

Allison/Stanton attributed full credibility to all of City Light's professional-liar witnesses and no credibility to my testimony or that of my witnesses. These two Tory panelists disregarded the stacks of memos that crassly illustrated management's violations of my constitutional rights to criticize and rebel. They identified so supinely with absolute "management prerogatives" and "legitimate business reasons" for persecution that they conferred on employers a divine and tyrannical authority that far exceeds their legal—not to mention their moral!—powers.

The Terrible Two condemn me for such crimes as failure to "compromise" on affirmative action and workers' rights, and for creating "animosity" through my advocacy of fair employment practices.

They accuse me of permitting my "personal political activities and interests" to "interfere with" my job.

They denounce me for "insubordination," "vituperation," "going too far"—highly subjective value judgments that express *their* political views of management/labor relations.

So now I am being punished for persecuting poor City Light. Can you believe this?

**A**nd what is to be said about a legal process in which I am judged by two people who cannot remotely be considered my peers, who are not radicals, or feminists, or unionists, or workers, or civil libertarians, or even reasonable?

They even rejected, without explanation, my Motion for Reconsideration of their ill-considered, ill-advised and stupid decision. So now I am requesting Superior Court to review my case.

It's horrendously expensive and time consuming. But I have to keep faith with my feisty legions of endorsers and supporters from labor, civil rights, civil liberties and all the other progressive movements dedicated to preserving democratic rights in the face of swelling totalitarianism on the job. I feel ethically impelled to ride this one out so long as the tide carries me, so long as my wonderful defense committee can summon the financial resources, the personnel and the jubilant spirit of solidarity to fuel the political-legal battle.

We will carry on until free speech in the workplace is vindicated in law and in life. Otherwise, the habit of workers to speak up, to organize, to negotiate and to criticize is sorely endangered, and without these fragile liberties, not even token democracy exists. Fascism rules.

Mutual aid is the cement of resistance—and the roadway to victory. Your oppression is mine and my case is yours. Take it! Together we will make that scoreboard light up *for us!*

# Adventures among the Bureaucrats

1982

Y'all better be nice to me. I have been awarded $135,265.14 by a judge who is obviously brilliant, fair, ethical, objective, and most practical.

Of course, the money exists only on paper, I still have no job at City Light, and we have to go to court again to settle the fees for my superb and indefatigable attorneys.

The Internal Revenue Service—that eternal reviled disservice—will clutch about $30,000 of my money to its panting bosom and soon three more rivets can be drilled into a nuclear warhead. Oh, joy.

Also, about $15,000 comes off the top for Social Security and retirement benefits. I should live so long. And if I do, will these programs be solvent? Or bankrupt, as threatened?

If all this sounds like sour grapes, ingratitude, or post-partum blues, it's because I, like earlier American revolutionaries, don't like taxation without a little representation.

Anyway, I'll have about $90,000 or so after being stuck up by the feds. And do you know what? I now understand the plight—and guilt—of some white liberals. It's truly shocking, and humbling, to find yourself with a hunk of the capitalist medium of exchange when hardly anyone you know has any, and when unemployment rages.

Of course, visions of wealth dissolve when I divide those thousands by eight long years of low-paid alternative employment, perpetual job search, and legal battles. The sum of $11,000 per year isn't exactly putting on the Ritz!

**S**till, it doesn't seem right. And there is so little I can do at the moment to redress the worldwide economic imbalance. But the little I *can* do will mean a great deal to the low-income friends who sustained my body and spirit over the grueling years of jousting with the Emerald City bureaucrats.

I would like to start a modest fund for workers who suffer job discrimination and reprisals. At the top of my list is the redoubtable Merle Woo of San Francisco, with a case so achingly reminiscent of mine—and waged against my very own alma mater, the University of California!

Everyone wants referrals to lawyers "who do free job discrimination cases." But the few worker-oriented lawyers who donate services are overwhelmed, and I know of no groups that supply attorneys for employment cases. The ACLU won't. And while women, people of color, gays, handicapped, and the aged can appeal to government human rights agencies, where can a white male employee without union representation turn?

**W**hich brings me back to public officials. One of the more annoying strands in my case is the myth—the hoax—that some top-drawer politicians tried to help me. Many people believe that Mayor Charles Royer and City Attorney Doug Jewett have "long tried to settle the case," as reported by the *Weekly*, a Seattle newsmagazine.

I tried to rectify this illusion in a September 14 letter to the *Weekly*. But they weren't nice to me and didn't print it. Well, that's all right, because I just happen to have a column of my own—*nyahh*—and this is what I wrote them:

In 1979 [Royer and Jewett] insisted on terms for the conciliation agreement that I knew would be unacceptable to the City Council, i.e., a job at the Seattle Human Rights Department instead of City Light. When the Council called upon Assistant City Attorney Dona Cloud to give them the real opinion of her office, she insisted that City Light. . .could win.

And when the case went to hearing in 1980, Royer and Jewett collaborated on legal policy and launched a 5-month attack on my political, professional, and personal methods that was so exaggerated it became ludicrous, and made Joe McCarthy look like Tom Paine.

Then after I filed my court appeal, they used delaying tactics for two years before the main case came before a judge. And when Judge Goodloe ruled for me, the city promptly announced it would appeal.

Had Royer/Jewett. . .wanted to settle, they could have done it at any time. . . Instead, they put the taxpayers, and me, through the old wringer. And they're still doing it—threatening to appeal the. . .fees for my attorneys.

So I'm bemused when I read paeans of praise to this odd couple for their supposed herculean effort at diplomacy. I'm laughing with tears in my eyes.

There are many other scores to settle with the bureaucrats, but who's counting. As of now, I'm ready to take the cash and let the discredits go. Do tune in next time, however, for another chapter of Clara's endless roller coaster adventures in Imperial Ozland.

# The Four Years of Living Dangerously

1988

Only a few months after winning her case against City Light, Fraser and eight FSP leaders were slammed with a malicious lawsuit by a greedy ex-member, Richard Snedigar. Under the pretense of demanding back a donation he had made five years earlier, Snedigar launched a full-scale McCarthyite campaign aimed at smashing the FSP. He and his shameless lawyers Thomas Wampold and Michelle Pailthorp demanded that the party hand over names of members and supporters, internal meeting minutes, and financial records.

This column was written halfway into the eight year case. After a long string of negative rulings and fruitless appeals, the party had been declared in default for refusing to comply with Snedigar's demands. At the hearing where Fraser presented this statement, she and FSP attorneys Carlson and Hyde were ruled in contempt and sentenced to jail, although the sentences were stayed. It took another two years before the state Supreme Court, swayed by the arguments of acclaimed civil liberties attorney Leonard Boudin, ruled that the party's internal records were privileged information. Finally, in April 1992, the party was vindicated of Snedigar's charges. The full story of this thrilling, precedent-setting battle is told in *They Refused to Name Names: The Freeway Hall Case Victory.*

I t's Tuesday, January 12 and tomorrow I go to court to be grilled about my personal finances.

Together with my two attorneys, Valerie Carlson and Frederick W. Hyde, I've been subpoenaed to testify about my private fortune so that $50,000 or so can be seized to pay off a trio of mercenary villains named Snedigar, Wampold and Pailthorp (no, these monikers don't come out of Dickens, they're for real).

I haven't got 50 grand, and if I had I still wouldn't hand it over to this radical-baiting, witch hunting triumvirate of vengeful scoundrels.

Yet I won't take the stand and plead poverty. I'll use my assertiveness training (it's chic these days) and I'll refuse to answer any questions at all.

I'll read a statement—until they stop me—and then prepare for the wrath of a coldblooded judicial system that will not tolerate defiance of its silly, mickey-mouse rules.

This is what I will try to say to the King County Superior Court on January 13th.

> I would like to explain to the court the problem I have in answering Mr. Wampold's questions.
>
> Six years ago, in this courthouse, Judge Goodloe and I had a fascinating discussion about the importance of free-dom of belief and the Bill of Rights. He had just ruled that I could not be punished and discriminated against by City Light because of my beliefs. This upset many people in the city establishment, who have harassed me ever since.
>
> And it made Richard Snedigar envious and spiteful. Why should I have the right to my meager $85,000 net back pay award, when the Freedom Socialist Party still had the $22,500 donation he and others made to our eviction fund?
>
> Three months after my victory in 1983, he demanded the gift back, and then he sued me, my attorneys and six political leaders. He attempted to blackmail us into pay-ing him off by demanding that, in the discovery process, we disclose confidential FSP membership lists, minutes and contributor lists.
>
> I refused; people trust me to safeguard their jobs, their

anonymity perhaps, their personal privacy. I cannot betray them. It's a matter of conscience.

A default judgment was entered as punishment for our refusal to turn over the minutes. Yet no court has rendered a judgment after a fair trial on the merits of the case. Even so, I'm hauled up here like a criminal to divulge my finances. But why should I voluntarily contribute to my own impoverishment, or become a stool pigeon like Snedigar, or sell out the organizations and people I've dedicated my life to?

My financial affairs are interrelated with others, you see, and to disclose them would violate my First Amendment rights to associational privacy, because disclosure would subject me and my colleagues to further political and legal harassment. Free speech and free association are the very rights that are at issue in our appeal. Yet you force me into these proceedings before our appeal has been decided and our rights vindicated, and I believe this amounts to punitive retaliation against me for having asserted my rights in the first place. It's double jeopardy!

I never had a trial, I've not been proved guilty of anything, and I cannot give credence and legitimacy to this punishment by participating in it.

I take this position not out of disrespect to the court, but as a matter of fairness and principle. I believe that the state law or practice which allows a person to be convicted on a procedural technicality instead of the substance of a case is wrong and illegal.

I believe I have the right to question and challenge the system itself when it is screwed up, and I refuse to become a hatchet man against myself.

Snedigar, Wampold and Pailthorp know full well what my answer will be. This proceeding is unnecessary, unwarranted, unfair, and deliberately provocative, and I cannot dignify it by being an accessory to it.

I decline to testify on the grounds of the First Amendment, and I ask you to respect my convictions.

Sixty-two years ago, in 1926, the great socialist leader James P. Cannon wrote an article titled "The Cause that Passes Through a Prison." Wrote Cannon,

> The path to freedom leads through a prison. The door swings in and out and through that door passes a steady procession of "those fools too stubborn-willed to bend," who will not turn aside from the path because prisons obstruct it here and there.

The door may swing in for Fred and Val and me, but I promise you: they'll know we were there. And they'll know what cause made us pass through.

# Excerpts from an Affidavit (and a Life)

1991

In the 1991 Seattle City Council elections, FSP ran a super-powered, high-impact campaign for candidates Yolanda Alaniz, a Chicana ex-farmworker and labor/community activist, and Heidi Durham, an electrical worker and disabled rights advocate. The testimony of Fraser and others as to the long history of government and rightwing harassment of radicals won the party an exemption from disclosing information on contributors. FSP boldly went on to win matching funds as well. Alaniz made it through the primary election and garnered an historic 17.5% of the vote as an open socialist and feminist candidate.

**B**efore the Washington Public Disclosure Commission In Re: Application of FSP for Campaign Disclosure, Clara Fraser declares as follows:

**I** am the National Chairperson of the Freedom Socialist Party. I joined a socialist youth group in the 1930s and was engaged in radical and labor organizations throughout high school and college. In 1944, I joined the Socialist Workers Party and stayed with it until 1966 when I helped found the FSP.

I have firsthand experience with police, government and employers spying on, infiltrating, firing, intimidating, and discriminating against individuals and organizations. I know that public disclosure of the contributors to Advocates for Alaniz and Durham—FSP candidates for City Council—will have a seriously chilling effect on people's willingness to give money to our campaign and will result in harassment.

I can readily testify to the power of redbaiting, blacklisting, slander, threats, and enforced isolation to silence activists, send sympathizers underground, and shatter organizations.

I have been subjected to considerable personal retaliation for my beliefs, associations, and activities: job losses; antagonism from school authorities against my children; physical assaults; death threats; avoidance by certain friends, associates, co-workers, neighbors and relatives; attempted FBI invasions of my home; extensive (and absurd) police files on my beliefs and activities; arrests and jailings; character assassination on the job and in the media; punitive insurance rates; denial of credit; and frivolous lawsuits.

For 10 years after I was fired from Boeing for my views and leadership in the 1948 strike, I was unable to hold a job for more than six months before an informer or government agent notified my employer of my ideas and associations.

Only my good education and wide span of job skills enabled me to work at all.

Nor did political discrimination end with the McCarthy era, as exemplified by my political ideology and sex discrimination case against Seattle City Light (1975-82). The punitive harassment of my supportive co-workers at City Light prevails to this day.

My FBI file contains names of people who signed antiwar and other petitions. Informants stole our mailing lists and turned them over to the FBI. Names of persons who signed nominating petitions to get our candidates on the ballot were promptly turned over to the FBI by state officials. FBI agents harassed our supporters, making it extremely difficult to obtain the required signatures.

During a 1952 speech by Myra Tanner Weiss, SWP candidate for U.S. vice president, uniformed Seattle police openly photographed supporters entering and leaving her meeting, causing a number of people to turn away out of fear of being publicly identified.

**O**btaining a lawyer, or help from public agencies, continues to be difficult. Only a very few lawyers assisted us. I had to search long and hard to find an attorney to represent me in my divorce/custody trial, which featured flagrant political slander, redbaiting, and feminist-baiting by my husband.

Lacking an attorney, I had to resort in 1971 to defending myself against bogus criminal charges resulting from a police raid on a Freeway Hall fund-raiser for the Seattle Seven, a group of Seattle Liberation Front leaders on trial for their antiwar actions.

After years of search failed to locate a lawyer, I had to drop a 1971 sex and political ideology discrimination claim against Seattle Opportunities Industrialization Center (SOIC), a federally funded anti-poverty program, for wrongfully firing me.

Later the Seattle Human Rights Department (HRD) attorney handling my City Light case was pressured away from it. The replacement attorney dumped my case after the deposition process. The third attorney walked off the case at a critical juncture in the trial and had to be ordered back. Both private attorneys who represented me in Superior Court against City Light have been the target of separate harassment lawsuits that arose out of their public association with me. One HRD investigator who handled my retaliation case after I won and returned to work was fired immediately after finding in my favor, and others were pressured.

**B**ecause of the harm caused by disclosure of names of supporters and defenders, I have adamantly refused to do this for the government or courts. Recently, in the *Snedigar v. Hoddersen* "Freeway Hall" case, my commitment to this principle was tested by imposition of a $42,500 default judgment and a jail sentence for contempt of court when I refused to disclose information that would identify FSP members and supporters.

I was gratified when my right not to betray sacred confidences was upheld by the state Supreme Court in February 1990. The FSP should not and indeed cannot now be asked to violate the confidentiality of donors as a condition of participating in the electoral process as a minor party!

Bureaucratic insistence on disclosure would totally exclude us from the supposedly democratic process of electoral politics and rob the FSP and its supporters of the fundamental rights afforded to capitalist parties and mainstream candidates.

# 6

## Memoirs, Reviews & Travels

# Birth of a Column

1976

**W**e're going to have a double editorial page," said Our Editor, "and we need a column. Who can write one?"

"Oh, I can," I said airily.

Omigawd.

The beginning is the hardest, as Marx told us; it actually follows from the conclusion. So perhaps if I start from the end, I'll wind up at the beginning. I trust this is all perfectly clear.

So—the end. Well, like, the end was that I wrote a poem. Yes, that's exactly what I said—a poem. The editor doesn't know it yet, but I am already anticipating his respectful and self-restrained reflex when he discovers the awful truth.

"You wrote *what?!* We already have a poem, a real one, by a real, recognized poet, and you were supposed to do a column! Something political, about the historic significance and meaty theoretical juices and aura of excitement and high purpose of the FSP Conference! Why didn't you?"

Because it's too hard, that's why. God, she knows I tried. I sat at the picnic table in the back yard, pen in hand and typewriter adjacent, and thought and thought and thought. How to telescope into 500 words (500? It takes me 1,000 to order something from the Sears catalog!) an experience that was the absolute pinnacle, the political arch of triumph of my entire life?

The more I mused over the beautiful Tenth Anniversary Conference and the often not-so-beautiful 10 incredible years of infighting and outfighting, joy and fury, and sheer high-powered momentum of feminist rebellion and class struggle—the more I remembered, the more verbose I became in my mind. And I decided (cop-out?) that this was the stuff that books are made on, not columns.

The sun was hot, colorful flowers and shrubs were vividly etched against the white houses around me, planes were droning overhead. Analysis blended into reverie. I basked in the sunshine, staring straight ahead. And then something happened, something spontaneous and impulsive.

This poem happened.

### Centro de la Raza

silhouetted in the vista from my patio
third-dimensional against a grey-blue sky streaked with silver
almost obscured by the soaring trees, the luxuriant branches
    in three gradations of green

the building roots there, high wide solid firm—entrenched
half-encased in shadow, mysterious, commanding
a palace? a resort perhaps, a very important government
    edifice, a hospital?

white walls red roof stark chimneys and windows, windows
    windows
like a Mediterranean chateau clinging to the misty hillside
the haze envelops it in twilight,
    unutterable romance

jesus christ, clara, are you kidding? that dump?
sigh, i know what it really looks like, up front and inside. . .
    an old dilapidated ex-schoolhouse

but i view it from a distance
and as everybody knows that lends charm
and distortion too

still it has a living history, born of pain and defiance
   and the sheer imagination to DEMAND it
chicanas and chicanos won it, spoils of war,
   wrenched from the scared aghast gringo city council

the huge structure is a triumph, a beacon, a souvenir of
   struggle
a harbinger of things to come
today el centro—tomorrow el Municipal Building
why not?

there are many planes of reality
i look at it and what i see
is good and true and beautiful, like the man said

el centro de la raza
throbbing with the radiance of the revolution

And that's the way it was, Comrade Editor, one soft
summer afternoon in the life of a willing, if neophyte,
columnist. Together, we have no place to go but up.

# Valedictory for a Free Spirit

1995

According to an old Russian proverb, friendship is friendship, but politics is politics. The point, of course, is that the two should not be confused or allowed to impinge on each other in an unethical way, as happens all too often.

So how wonderful it is when no "buts" separate the two experiences, when a buddy is your close political ally, a comrade your boon companion. To be linked in this special kind of connection is a blessing of serendipity, a lovely stroke of fate that is rare and precious.

I am fascinated by long-term relationships—Marx and Engels, Susan B. Anthony and Elizabeth Cady Stanton, Emma Goldman and Alexander Berkman. My own life has been a shifting kaleidoscope of events, organizations, movements and human ties. People who have been steadfast amigos for decades are by now relatively few. And Gloria Martin was the shining star in that constellation of enduring pals.

Gloria was a historic figure in the pantheon of U.S. rebels. (I almost wrote Gloria "is" because her death is still unnerving and unreal for me.) Her accomplishments as organizer, historian, catalyst, invigorator, instructor, and popularizer of class struggle theory and practice were legion. But what was unique and particularly priceless was her extraordinary gift for friendship. I have rarely encountered anyone who surpassed her in this talent.

At every crossroads I faced, in every situation demanding a new and untraveled path, in every endeavor that was hard or tiring or discouraging, Gloria was there for 40 years, unfailingly just *there*, to encourage, support, scold, push, persuade, pressure, and impel.

I can still hear her refrain as she buoyed me up over the tumultuous years: "Clara, you can do it. . . You *must* do it. . . You can do it better than they can. . . Try it and you'll see it will work. . . Go for it, Clara. . . Just tell me what you want me to do!"

Wordsworth, the English poet, wrote of "A perfect woman, nobly planned/to warn, to comfort, and command." Yes, I knew her. Gloria.

**D**amn, we had fun together. We loved the opera and theater and movies, and we journeyed to memorable writing retreats in the mountains and at the seashore, warbling pop classics for hours en route. And since we were usually the oldest folks around, we were the most dedicated socializers; we could drink everyone under the table and outsmoke and outdance the youngsters. We were always the last to leave a party.

I could tell Gloria anything. Yet we almost never spoke of intimate, personal matters—we just intuitively respected privacy rights. The kind of let-it-all-hang-out binges prevalent these days were never in vogue with us.

We talked politics. Current events and ideologies and philosophy. Organizing. Art and books, childraising and cooking, decorating homes and headquarters, writing and gardening. And we found so much to laugh about, people especially.

**D**id we ever discuss people! Political comrades, sisters in women's liberation, friends of all colors and sexualities in the civil rights movements and anti-poverty programs, and scores of associates from our jobs and neighborhoods.

We had personality-haunted imaginations—very female! We cared about our colleagues. We analyzed them, admired them, worried about them, gloried in them, deplored their crotchets, and plotted ways and means of helping them find and express and excel themselves.

We viewed people from different angles, each of us seeing a different side of a person first. But with our once-over completed, a synthesis was usually achieved, melding what was consistent and contradictory, apparent and covert, in that individual.

After all, we were in the business of training women to be leaders in their own right. And to lead others, you must be able to lead yourself, to understand yourself, to set high standards for yourself. But it was not an easy job imparting these concepts to women emerging out of the 1950s and '60s to whom emancipation was a startling and often terrifying notion.

Gloria took on the task with relish, however, and never tired of praising the women and men who benefited from her guidance and gave back to the movement. And she always mourned a little for those who got away—the children, in effect, she had lost.

**O**ne other salient point stands out: She was that rare bird whose radicalism increased, intensified, and expanded as she aged.

She did not mellow, as in marshmallow. A detached armchair observer she never became. Indignation over injustice raged with an ever-searing flame in her soul, and her yearning for revolution became poignantly urgent and all-encompassing.

"I hate this system more than I ever have in my whole life," she told me a few months ago. "It makes me sick. I want total change!"

When some people die, they leave yawning gaps. Gloria's death has left a vast crevasse for hundreds of us who loved her, because she managed to make all of us something of what we are today. We can only fill that void by seeking to emulate her glowing, effervescent spirit of revolt.

# Sexual Economics

1979

**W**e're having dinner at her hotel and rushing the conversation because she's speaking on campus that night.

She loves to talk and question and ponder over people and ideas. She is suffused with the Iranian revolution and grateful for her opportunity to play a role in it. She is at one with the tens of thousands of women who are defying the medieval misogyny of the mullahs. She loathes the Shah and her comments on the Rockefellers are duly scatological.

This is one tough woman, resonating with quiet energy and purpose. This is Kate Millett, and she can be steely. But she also comes across as gentle and soft-spoken, with a finely tuned sensibility more reminiscent of a Southern lady than the embattled lesbian feminist, exploited artist and maligned radical that she is.

**O**n campus, an overflow audience cranes to hear her views on "International Feminism." She speaks with a unique intelligence, wit, tenderness and simplicity. Women, she announces, are the advance troops of the Iranian revolution because they came out in full force against the Shah and are in the forefront of the battle against Khomeini, who is "the worst thing to happen to Iran since the Shah."

She has as little use for national chauvinism as for the

sexual kind. "They told me I had no right to interfere in another country," she says. "Do they think my allegiance belongs to the white male ruling class of the U.S.? This country of imperialism and brutality is not what I identify with. *My people are the women and the oppressed of the world.*"

A woman criticizes her for failure to present a workingclass analysis and anticapitalist program. Millett, startled, nods at the speaker's points. "I agree with you," she says. "I'm sorry I didn't make that clear." A second floor speaker furiously disputes the first one: "That's how women always get forgotten—we're shoved into second place after the workers!" Millett says mildly, "We needn't be. I am a socialist."

After the meeting, we take her to nearby Freeway Hall to see a real workingclass and feminist headquarters. She seems pleased when Marcel, our in-house graphics genius, gifts her with one of his beautiful posters of an Iranian woman rebel.

Then we all drive to my house, where cedar logs are burning in the fireplace and refreshments are at hand. We talk about Tehran, New York City, and the flight to reformism of most feminist superstars of the '70s—and this brings us inevitably, materialists that we are, to what women always end up discussing: the bitter struggle for money.

Kate Millett is a Ph.D., a best-selling and prolific writer, a painter and sculptor, a political activist and world figure. And she is almost broke. Finding publishers is a degrading and almost impossible task, her books are not reprinted even though they sell well, her author's share of sales is minuscule, and her (surprisingly) few speaking appearances are usually low paid.

Women writers and lecturers suffer an extreme form of economic sexism, particularly when they are social rebels. Millett tries to turn her tree farm into a modestly profitable enterprise, and to that end she labors mightily with hand, sinew and muscle while the literature and visual art and the political organizing she excels at go uncreated. What has to lie fallow is her mind and her talent.

In Iran she was arrested and subjected to the terror of armed men representing the bourgeois state. "Powerless individuals shouldn't be treated like that," she says. "It just isn't fair." And neither is it fair for a Kate Millett to be underpaid and politically prevented from reaching the marketplace for her wares.

She is a pacifist; I am not. (We argued heatedly about this.) She underplays her socialism; I do not. But she is one of the bravest and most principled figures to emerge from the huge wave of radical feminism, and if the women's movement doesn't bestir itself to help shield its few real leaders from the capitalist double-cross against women's earnings, that movement will behead itself.

It was four in the morning when I deposited Millett back at the hotel, and we were still wide awake. A hard look at the economics of being female will do that to you every time.

# LaRouche: Sex Maniac & Demagogue

1986

Something salient is missing from the reams of media exposés about Lyndon LaRouche, the ultra-reactionary demonologist, millionaire entrepreneur, and terrorizer of radicals, Jews, and now Democrats.

The pundits are intrigued and puzzled by his amalgam of right and left politics, a tangled web of KKK, Freudian, encounter therapy, Populist, Ayn Rand-like, and Marxist notions. They needn't be.

His is the prototypical face of fascism, which is classically a hodgepodge of pseudo-theories crafted for mass appeal and calculated to bring about the glacial-age law'n'order coveted by imperialists and impoverished super-patriots.

As a middleclass movement designed to make the world safe for giant capital, fascism has no theories of its own. It is by nature an intellectual pillager, derivative and vulgarized, a patchwork of illusion and reality, of myth and madness, of truth and absurdity.

LaRouche is not Mussolini or Hitler or Franco—but he is all of them, in American garb and speaking the jargon of the '80s. Beneath the jargon, the commie- and Black- and Jew-baiting essence is clearly heard.

What caused his turnabout from Marxism? Mainstream analysts are ever fascinated by this phenomenon, and smug in their assumption that his was a logical jump from leftwing to rightwing "extremism." But this kind of wild jump isn't ever logical and it isn't typical. However, it happens.

LaRouche is not the first former Marxist to turn inside out. Mussolini started as a revolutionary socialist. Thousands of ex-Stalinists, of course, have become avid apostles of conservatism and witch hunts. (Whittaker Chambers comes quickly to mind.) What is interesting about LaRouche's metamorphosis is that he is a product of Trotskyism, not Stalinism, and I can think of no similar apostasy of such melodramatic proportions, although Professor James Burnham, who became William F. Buckley's right-hand man on the *National Review*, came damn close.

**I** know what hit Lyndon LaRouche. I was in the Socialist Workers Party all through his 17 years of membership, from 1949 to the mid-60s. What knocked him off his underpinnings was the good old Woman Question. Feminism undid him, and Radical Women played a role in the bizarre scenario.

He called himself Lynn Marcus back then. He never seemed to belong to any SWP branch; he was a loner. He was never active, never involved in any mass movement or internal organizational work. What he did was write—and write and write and write, until we all wished he'd be stricken by digital rheumatism.

Marcus wrote thick, dull, endless Internal Bulletins, which were dutifully distributed to the membership by the obliging National Office. (It was probably the memory of his super-prolific effusions that eventually helped destroy the vaunted internal democracy of the early SWP!) For years and years his eternal Bulletins appeared, on one of two subjects: the United Front or Economics.

I never understood any of them. Neither did anybody else. Nobody ever responded to any of them, either, but he couldn't care less. He would appear at national conventions every two years, but he wouldn't take the floor. I know he was there because I never recognized him and would ask who he was; he had that kind of non-presence, non-personality.

They said he was an economist, but nobody seemed to know where he worked or what he did. Sometimes I would feel sorry for him and go up and say hello; he never replied except in a mumble or a curt rejoinder. Once I mustered the audacity to ask him to explain his latest document. My polite interest evoked nothing but a look of utter contempt.

I gave up on Lynn Marcus. Just one of those fringie eccentrics.

I left the SWP in 1965. He left soon afterwards with Jim Robertson and the Spartacist League, but I heard nothing about him. Then in 1968, Students for a Democratic Society spawned a mammoth strike at Columbia University, and who should turn out to be one of its spokesmen but Lynn Marcus—now Lyndon LaRouche—and his group, the SDS Labor Committee. I couldn't believe it—Lynn Marcus, a popular leader?

Soon there were LaRouche people, known as the National Caucus of Labor Committees, all over the country, including the University of Washington. My older son Marc was a fervent SDSer, editor of its paper, and an editor of the *University of Washington Daily*, and he was buddies with some local NCLCers. I was in Radical Women and the FSP, and the NCLC worked harmoniously with us, because we, alone on the Left, connected our labor background and workingclass orientation with what was fresh and valid in New Left and campus politics.

And NCLC, virtually alone among New Lefties, respected trade unionists. They also enjoyed observing traditional socialist holidays like May Day and the anniversary of the Russian Revolution, so we jointly sponsored commemorations, as well as forums, fund-raisers, and mass actions against the war and racism.

And NCLC didn't oppose our feminism. They didn't support it either—they were neutrals.

**B**y 1970 the women's movement was in full sail. And the male Left, new and old, didn't like it. We were demanding that they change their ways and learn to share power with the second sex. They didn't want to change.

We were denounced: we were divisive, subjective, petty-bourgeois, off-balance, off-side, unable to differentiate between "primary" and "secondary" questions, etcetera and ad infinitum. The campus male charismatics were particularly affronted; they secretly agreed with Stokely Carmichael that the "proper position for women in the struggle is prone" (except for secretarial and organizing duties).

Some of the men got pretty hot under the collar as our movement burgeoned and theirs trembled or decomposed.

LaRouche got hot all over. Feminist radicals were competing with *him!* LaRouche developed such an acute case of political sunburn that all his Marxist skin peeled off and his quivering Napoleonic nerves were painfully exposed to an incredulous world. LaRouche went ape.

Feminism is shit, roared *New Solidarity* one day. Mothers are fuckers, the enemy, witches. Women are the Achilles heels of revolutionaries, the cause of IMPOTENCE. Women turn men into deviants, queers, and schlemiels.

And then in an explosion of Nietzscheanism that made Wagner look like a matriarchist, Lynn uncorked his *pièce de résistance:* the Leader must be Superman, Siegfried incarnate, and the Superman must be served by good girlies who appreciate the honor and know how to bow and scrape. Superman is the hope and salvation of the revolution; woman must cast off her intrinsic sinfulness and restore VIRILITY to her Master. And on and on like that.

A young Radical Women leader ran into the office waving this issue of *New Solidarity* and crying. She had never read anything like it, and she was frightened. "What are we going to do?"

I tried to explain. He's gone off his rocker. He's on a new road, to Nazism. He's a misogynist, a sex-role egomaniac. You don't dump on women and gays like *that* unless you've jumped the socialist ship and clambered aboard with the pirates to preserve your puerile penile prerogatives. The man is a menace, I said. In a few years he'll have storm troopers to beat up on workers.

She didn't quite get it and promised to study up on fascism.

**W**ithin a year, LaRouche's old guard members were gone and his newly recruited troopers were in the streets. We got some telephone threats at our headquarters, Freeway Hall. Just try it, we said, out-machoing them. They beat up Communists, and SWPers, but left us alone. Nevertheless, they caused a casualty in our ranks; one of our leading female comrades was married to an NCLC admirer (famous John Chambless of the UW Philosophy Department, who organized the first Sky River Rock Festival and became a theatrical producer for the city of Seattle Parks Department), and she was so disoriented by his growing hostility to us that she faded away from politics.

In 1973, LaRouche provided the following advice to the ladies: "Be a rat! Be a sadist! If you are a woman, find a susceptible man for your female sadism. You feel better; you are one of the rats; the rats, therefore, may not attack you, especially the gigantic, awful rat of a mother-image inside you!" And this man was still calling himself a socialist.

What better illustration of the centrality of feminism to socialism: you simply can't have one without the other.

**N**ewsweek speculates that "a romantic setback triggered a change in LaRouche's personality and a shift to a more authoritarian style." Come on. Let's don't Hollywoodize, let's not trivialize and obscure a simple law of politics: once someone starts unraveling one key thread in the complex of programmatic embroidery the whole pattern falls apart. Romantic, roshmantic—it was feminist rage and dynamic organizing that triggered Lyndon LaRouche's counter-rage and sent him hurtling pell-mell into an ideology more compatible with his comfort zone. (You'll notice I didn't say his glands or genes; some of my best friends and comrades and kids are men!)

LaRouche was sorely challenged by the anti-sexist revolution and he reacted not only wrongly, but paranoiacally. His own history and character determined that reflex, and that obsession with stereotypical gender behavior and with male sexual power as synonym for the driving force of history. The fullest expression of male-power dominance, of course, is fascism. LaRouche, like all sex maniacs, is a clear and present political danger.

Lyndon, we hardly knew you, but we learned about you and know you now, while others thrash about in the effort to decipher your "mystery" and clout. For every man whose evil fantasies you express, another man, and almost every woman is revolted by your fascism à la mode. When push comes to shove, the women and the workers, the ethnics and the gays, the anti-fascists and the Jews, and folks with a decent respect for humankind will return you to your origins—as a loner.

# Life and Death in New York Town

## 1982

And what was an ingrained West Coaster like me doing in New York last December?

Well, I'm sorry it wasn't April in Paris, or whenever it is one does the Italian Riviera. I've never been to Paris in April. I've never been to Paris. And I always manage to get to Manhattan in the dead of winter.

But it's always worth it, and this trip was fascinating, memorable, delightful—and stained by tragedy.

The good part came first. Flying on Canadian airlines, to buttress our striking air traffic controller friends in PATCO, was great. I had never seen Toronto, and the trip between the airport and the Amtrak depot permitted a panoramic view of the great city.

The train trip to New York was not a good part. Down with the evil-tempered U.S. Immigration agent who woke us up and grilled us as if we were heinous public enemies smuggling ourselves across the sacred border. I was magnanimously permitted to re-enter my own country, but travelers of color fare much worse with both Yankee and Canadian officials.

Travel tip: try not to cross the border by bus, as I did on the return trip. The baggage inspection ordeal reduces everyone to cattle.

Once in Manhattan, I was beautifully hosted by the 17th Street Kids (that street corner on 8th Avenue has got to be the noisiest all-nite marketplace in the world). Then dozens of us took off for upstate New Jersey in cars packed like covered wagons, en route to a charming country home generously lent us for the National Committee plenum of the Freedom Socialist Party.

From December 3-6 our organizers examined the shape and options of the world, awarding special attention to the Black struggle, the shattering crisis of U.S. capitalism, permanent and deepening revolution in Poland and Iran, and the status of and prospects for socialist feminism. The plenum was rich and exciting, and the lucky participants were kept fed and watered by *haute cuisine* chef Max and her culinary elves.

Next, it was back to the mean streets and the raw, driving momentum of the City. The Fraser Defense Committee there, sparked by Laurie and Nancy, is a hustling, bustling operation. They whirled me through a press conference, a half-hour interview on NBC radio, lunches and dinners with case endorsers, a public meeting on the NYU campus in Washington Square, a lovely reception in a Greenwich Village studio, and more.

It was great seeing Flo Kennedy again—she's a dream to have in your corner. And I particularly enjoyed the company of Marxist critic and literary historian Annette Rubinstein, author of one of my all-time favorites, *The Great Tradition in English Literature from Shakespeare to Shaw*. Annette chaired my public meeting superbly.

I loved the audience—old friends from the movement whom I hadn't seen in decades; transplanted Seattleites; women with discrimination cases; a bevy of youth with all that East Coast bounce. They contributed freely to the defense fund, and their warmth provided one of those shining moments when my case brings me pleasure.

**B**ut a terrible contrast to the stimulation and dynamism of New York lay in wait.

Throughout my visit, Murry Weiss was a tower of intellectual activity, physical endurance, and zest. At the plenum he led the discussion on the Political Resolution, and immersed himself in every topic and every task of clarifying policy and perspective. At the banquet finale, he presented a hilarious roast of Dr. Susan and preened himself at having finally done one of these spoofs. Back in the city, he met daily with Sam or me for literary work and planning.

He phoned me on Friday to beg off from our meeting because of a cold. By Saturday—the day of my public meeting—he still felt weak but anxious to talk, and I visited him. He bragged happily about his sale of eight tickets to my meeting, and we parted with plans to meet the next day—my last day in New York. But on Sunday he went to the hospital.

Six days later, on December 26, he was gone. And with him went an incredible saga of the role of one larger-than-life individual in history. Murry's soaring talent for revolutionary leadership and transparent joy in soil-tilling for world socialism were things of beauty. His death stings and saddens.

New York will never seem the same without him. But the fresh promise of spring is already on its way in that surging metropolis, and Murry's political heirs are there to affirm a season of renewed life and fresh hope for tomorrow.

# An Unvarnished Profile

1988

Richard Fraser, 75, originator of the theory of Revolutionary Integration, died of throat cancer on November 27, 1988 in Los Angeles. A 30-year leader of the Socialist Workers Party, he resigned from the SWP in 1966 along with the entire Seattle branch, which went on to found the Freedom Socialist Party.

Fraser's profoundly historical materialist analysis of the Black struggle illuminates the Black Question as a matter of race and class rather than nationhood; Black history is seen as key to American history, and Black leadership as central to the American revolution.

Dick was a bold and original thinker and organizer with a broad grasp of world history, economics, and politics; he was also a compelling orator, teacher, and writer, and an administrator with singular drive and energy, and a winning public persona.

But like many male revolutionaries, he was ethically contradictory. For 10 years, I was his collaborator and wife, and he appeared to champion women's emancipation. But he never actually accepted and internalized women's equality; this led him to indulge in vulgar machismo and I left him.

He refused to let me share our child and rejected a party tribunal's decision approving my right to a divorce and child custody, forcing me into a two-year-long custody case. He accused me of every bad-mother sin: I stayed out late at meetings, hired sitters, worked outside the home, neglected my family, and (gasp) was living in adultery.

But the gallant judge didn't believe that a good Jewish momma could be so depraved, and I won. (Dick retaliated by withholding his $50.00 monthly child support.)

Fraser left two legacies: Revolutionary Integration and Jon Fraser, a fine jazz musician. I am proud of my co-creativeness on both counts. For the rest, I learned a lot about the Woman-and-Man Question, so I guess he did me a favor in that regard, too. He did all of us a favor.

# The Two "Julias"

1978

The nationally syndicated gossip columns gleefully report that writer Lillian Hellman, the indomitable one, feuded with the director of *Julia* and refused to attend the premier of this film based on her memoir, *Pentimento*.

Good for you, Lillian. It's bad enough that the rest of us had to see it.

There's a screwy scene in the picture where Jane Fonda, miscast as Hellman, throws her typewriter through the window in a fit of rage. Had Hellman viewed the film, she might have thrown a typewriter at the screen. Her profound and lovely tribute to her communist friend Julia has been trivialized by Hollywood's assembly lines.

Hellman is a radical of sorts who promoted Communist Party causes for decades. Her lifelong companion was writer Dashiell Hammett, a devoted CPer who elevated detective yarns to the level of literature. He was railroaded to prison during the McCarthy era for refusing to inform on his comrades. *Scoundrel Time* is her account of their experiences with the witch hunters.

Jane Fonda was the superstar of the antiwar movement, the quintessential New Leftist—privileged, articulate and defiant. She now plays Democratic Party politics.

Vanessa Redgrave portrays Julia, the wealthy and brilliant humanitarian who is murdered by the Nazis. Redgrave, the most highly political of this female triumvirate, is a revolutionary, an active British Trotskyist.

So one would expect the film to make an authentic statement about fascism and feminism, right?

Wrong. The screenplay and direction are simply askew. The view of women is archaically romantic and patronizing, and the political insight is nowhere.

The movie is a glamorized, confusing, and ultimately sappy account of two female eccentrics.

Fonda strives mightily, via posturings, tears, chain-smoking, whisky-guzzling, and pacings on a lonely (but scenic) beach, to convey a sense of character. She fails. In her climactic scene, where she—a Jew—must smuggle $50,000 past fascist police to the underground in Nazi Germany, she behaves like a perplexed, naive imbecile, and Hellman's real-life courage is belittled.

Redgrave's Julia is more clearly defined, because Julia is a heroine of Wagnerian proportions. But Redgrave, aiming at radiance, looks glazed and transfixed instead. The problem is that Julia's motivation, her *communism* is never specified.

Neither the Nazis nor anti-Nazis make political sense.

The fascists raid Freud's psychoanalytic institute where Julia is a student—at least I think they do—and they beat and kill people with impunity until a group of students or faculty or something, headed by Julia, advances on them. This "advance" is unbelievable: Julia and her colleagues *walk*, do not *run*, to the bloody fray! Scenes like this impart a dreamlike, unreal, and puzzling quality to the entire picture.

The screenwriter and director are so edgy about the subject matter, and so ignorant about the normal behavior of strong women, that they dump the central political theme of Julia with irritating frequency, "relieving" the heavy stuff with misty flashbacks into the girls' adolescence.

The one bright note in the debacle is Jason Robards' playing of Hammett with just the right note of bemused detachment and long-suffering that the film warrants. Who Hammett is, of course, we never discover.

But you can read the book. There really *was* a Julia.

# Shadows and Substances

1979

An ice-pick slammed into the brain slew Leon Trotsky. Everybody knows that.

What everybody doesn't know is that an identical weapon was viciously used in the same way to slaughter a talented and beautiful woman radical of the '30s—Frances Farmer, once-acclaimed star of Broadway and Hollywood.

The perpetrator of the first crime was a depraved Stalinist henchman whose heinous act was a front-page sensation. But the coldblooded murderers of the outspoken and rebellious actress were never brought to justice because they were the political establishment.

The usual cabal of FBI and CIA agents, rightwing vigilantes, police, film studio moguls, Tory judges, and the power structure of the city of Seattle (Farmer's hometown) joined forces in this case with the psychiatric witch doctors, and conspired to harness the unconventional politics of a brave and brilliant feminist-before-her-time.

For the crime of dissidence, Farmer was arrested, confined to the loony bin (Western State Hospital in Steilacoom, Washington) and subjected to a snake pit regimen of torture and degradation previously reserved for recalcitrant Wobblies and Asian immigrants. She was administered incredible doses of untested drugs, electroshock and hydrotherapy, and was mass-raped by orderlies.

Yet they couldn't break her mind, her will or her indomitable revolutionary spirit. So in 1948—national witch hunt time—they plunged the "therapeutic" pick into her magnificent brain. Farmer disintegrated into passivity and died at 56, a burned-out, disoriented recluse.

This terrible tale of psychiatric abuse, of totalitarian mind control to enforce conformity, is cautiously but indignantly told by William Arnold in his stunning book *Shadowland*, a biography of Farmer—and of America.

**A**nti-communist hysteria is endemic to the Pacific Northwest.

Its lurid history is replete with the corpses of IWW labor martyrs; the radical Congressman Marion Zioncheck, hounded to death by J. Edgar Hoover and his cronies; Anna Louise Strong, revolutionary journalist without honor in her Seattle hometown; and innumerable other rebels who dared challenge the status quo and proclaim their partisanship of a better way to live and to arrange social interactions.

Of course, lots of us hell-raisers and muckrakers and social critics do manage, most of the time, to fly over the cuckoo's nest, evade the cops, outflank the neo-Nazi terrorists, and escape the prefrontal lobotomies.

Where we *do* get it is squarely in the pocketbook.

The ruling class simply exerts economic and legal sanctions against us so that we are excluded from gainful employment. *Job discrimination is the shadowy shape of organized brainwashing and political reprisal in our era.*

**I** ought to know. From the World War II loyalty oaths through the dismal days of the McCarthy purges and up until this very moment, I have been afflicted by economic harassment.

For five long, insolvent years, I have struggled to regain my job with City Light, whose management fired me because of their political and sex bias. And now, after incredible legal adventures involving the top levels of city government, my hearing is slated for September.

And it wouldn't surprise me at all if a pompous practitioner from the psychiatric establishment materializes on the witness stand to speak to *my* sanity and competence.

As author Arnold says, "It can happen to anyone." And it mostly happens to women. But experience has prepared us for these mental health medievalists, and we know how to prove that traditional psychiatry is as obsolete as the power structure that wields it against us, as absurd as the FBI informants lurking in the shadows of political cases.

We will not forget or forsake Frances Farmer. Amidst our troubles we will pay tribute to her fierce strength of character. And we will avenge her sacrifice in all our victories to come, in this new age of Aquarius.

# Dr. Zhivago: Dixiecrat of the Steppes

1958

I have read *Dr. Zhivago* and I am appalled by it.
Behind all the lyric poetry and delicate rhythms and celestial hymns to nature and tone-poem delineations of striking scenes and vistas lies a sniveling and petulant demand for middleclass security and comfort, plus an outright assertion of political and ideological support for the counterrevolution, for Christianity, for medieval logic and for capitalist individuality of the most Philistine sort.

And this is accompanied, of course, by the corollary leitmotifs of anti-Semitism and male chauvinism of a type so outrageous that they are humorous, so backward in their glaring simplicity that they pre-date by far their more sophisticated bourgeois-democratic forms.

From the point of view of technique, the book is even worse.

Boris Pasternak is a poet, dedicated to the instant, the moment of a mood, the flash of an insight, the sudden—and passing—inspiration of a symbol, the intensified and concentrated perception of a concrete idea. He is lost, technically and personally, before the structural demands of a panoramic sweep of space and history wherein human beings are meaningfully and realistically integrated. The novel is not and cannot be his *métier;* in his hands it becomes an embarrassingly awkward, cumbersome, clumsy piece of literary machinery which grinds and groans its way to final death along with the extinction of its hero, to the merciful relief of the reader.

The characters are wooden, undetermined, impossible to grasp and remember. The women aren't even characters; they are words, vague shadows. The socialists and revolutionaries are dope fiends or weaklings or crafty opportunists; the NEP men—Stalinist bureaucrat thugs—are the socialists; the criminals are the partisan leaders. Love, honor, goodness, art and beauty reside only in the counterrevolutionary doctor, an admitted weakling, but what can one person do in a world gone mad?

This book is a powerfully strong and lucid philosophical essay in anti-socialism. The story, the people, the backgrounds vanish—the author could not make them live; and indeed, they were conceived only as a device to hang the politics and philosophy on. For this book is a personal statement of belief, and nothing more; to call it a novel degrades the calling and product of novelist. This book is the twin and the opposite of the validly condemned "proletarian novel"; stripped of its ephemeral plot and people, it is a White Paper against socialism, a pamphlet dressed in lyricism, but a pamphlet essentially and purposefully.

What an exposure of Stalinism and its results it is; that is why the Kremlin hates it. But revolutionaries should hate it too, and explain its political stupidity.

Pasternak equates Stalinism with Leninism, with the revolution itself, and he hates it and wishes its destruction. If we could cut through the Cold War, Nobel Prize aspects of the hysteria about the book, and see it coldly for what it is, which nobody has yet done, we will recognize a document that is terrible and ugly and an author who is a man convulsed by searing hatred and bitter, resigned futility, a man writing with emotional wretchedness and misery.

His faint hope of progress, of thaw, expressed surprisingly

on the last page, is unreal, with that tacked-on, censor-imposed look; it fails to even dent or reorient his hammering, merciless, stunning theme that socialism, that the revolution, has corrupted and brutalized and tortured and perverted humanity.

No wonder the Nobel Prize. What a gift to the State Department, what an unexpected and unsolicited pot of political gold! Half mad with joy, they went wild and engineered the prize.

The literary critics, though embarrassed with the vulgarity and unabashed political exploitation of the book, pulled out all stops and convinced the public that doesn't read novels that this was really a great, heroic, historic and thrilling artistic achievement in itself. They even went so far as denying its anti-communist theme, so enraged were they at the crassness of the diplomat-politicians. They said it was "a-communist," i.e., above and beyond and without relationship to politics and theory. Just a beautiful book about people, they said, knowing that beautiful people would rush to devour this beautiful book and find themselves stuffed with the most beautiful arguments against socialism yet contrived in the 20th century.

And what of the non-Stalinist Left? After slapping the Cold War and the blissful literary endorsements of Secretary of State Dulles (even as did the critics), after slapping Kremlin literary standards and artist-oppressing (even as did the bourgeois critics), they fell all over themselves to show how objective and truly artistic and indulgent toward artists they were—and to a man (read *male)* decreed that *Dr. Zhivago* was a thing of beauty and a joy forever, and whosoever denied it was vulgarly mixing up politics and art. They said this was a work about individuals, about emotions, humanity, about life and truth and love and creativity. They said it must be judged by its own standards, that indeed the book was apolitical.

I contest this. Pasternak intentionally produced a political document; Pasternak, in true Stalinist style, sacrificed art in order to create a mechanical tool to espouse his manifesto, and in so doing renounced his integrity and stature as artist. Pasternak, the Kremlin and the State Department all understand each other perfectly; only the Left fails to understand. The standards, the *raison d'être*, the meaning and be-all and end-all of this book were to express a man's long suppressed but never killed defiance of the workers state.

*Zhivago* is a delayed-reaction explosion; an outburst of fantastic energy; a volcanic eruption of the vitriol and flaming hatred so long repressed within this man's soul. And it is strange this aspect of the work, its truly *heroic* character, is ignored. For Pasternak sees himself with, and is indeed akin to, the unquenchable counterrevolutionary rebels and oppositionists of all time.

Though his cause is deplorable and his outlook reactionary and historically doomed, his stand has the personal honor and the glamour and the gallantry and the pathetic courage and the romantic, reactionary, barbaric, decadent beauty of the Confederacy and the plantation house.

# Letters to a Young Relative

November 10, 1994

Dear Josh,

. . .You're an impressive nephew—one who's a fine practitioner of the dying art of letter writing. . .

Since you're thinking about life and trying to figure out how to make the world a better place, you're growing up in the right direction, with a social conscience that does you credit.

When you entered this world as a baby, you were aware of just yourself, your state of comfort—hunger, warmth, pain, fear, etc. A baby starts out as the center of its own universe. That's the nature of an infant. Mercifully, that state doesn't last in most people. As we grow up, we realize that we're on this planet with others. What we do affects them; what they do affects us.

Sadly, today many people your age take one look at the sorry state of the world and throw up their hands. They retreat into drugs, cynicism, narcissistic absorption in themselves (which is regression into infancy) or, as you put it, "are on some other trip." This is doubly tragic because not only are their own lives wasted but they waste their chance to improve society. And we all lose.

It's very fashionable today to say that the rebellious youth of the '60s were naive and that they didn't make any real difference. Nonsense! I should know; I was there.

The young people of the '60s were the driving force in the civil rights movement, the antiwar movement, the feminist movement, the environmental crusade and the fight for lesbian/gay liberation. They and their like-minded elders helped to break a brutal U.S.-style apartheid in the South, end the war in Vietnam, develop an environmental consciousness and win abortion rights and many other reforms for women and sexual minorities. Not to mention significantly altering the popular culture in terms of movies, literature, art, dance and theatre. No small potatoes in my book!

That's just more proof that determined people can have a vast impact on an apparently rigid system.

You can work to transform the system by yourself or, hopefully, with others, which is much more effective, efficient and fun. That's why I'm in the Freedom Socialist Party, and other organizations dedicated to the betterment of the human condition. I cannot accept the planet as it is and find my greatest pleasure through altering its political and economic shape. I think you might experience the same reaction.

I'm glad you're into music. It is a wonderful, expressive and powerful medium for social change. Historically it has spread ideas, influenced thinking and affected politics. The Beatles were vital in the development of the peace movement and popularizing a vision of a world that could be beautiful. And Dylan, in his good days, before he found Jesus and lost his soul, was a tremendous voice of protest.

Have you heard Pete Seegar, Holly Near, Woodie Guthrie, Sinead O'Connor and some of the less violent and sexist rappers? Of course we can't forget Beethoven, Chopin, Wagner, and others—what they created had volcanic effects on politics and revolutions.

Seattle grunge, which you like, has a two-fold aspect—it cries out in anguish against injustice, but it also dissolves in despair à la Cobain (who, incidentally, lived about a mile from me). Suffering is no substitute for organizing.

The best art is inherently subversive because you cannot reach for beauty without shaking up the present state of affairs. To compose is to rebel, and music that is humane and sensitive packs a mighty social wallop, even if it is underground and suppressed. To be a good musician and composer, you must become widely educated, well-read and experienced in activist struggles on the political front. In order to express something with your music, you must have something to say; you have to know what you believe and you have to believe passionately in your own convictions. It is the passion that reaches out, communicates, and strikes a connecting chord in others like you.

Please, Josh, understand that *there are millions of others like yourself!* I assure you, you are not alone in your feelings, yearnings and worries. There are countless Josh-like individuals out there all feeling isolated and out of the mainstream only because they haven't yet met and connected. The youth who feel like strangers on the earth right now will become comrades-in-arms in the mass movements of tomorrow.

The road isn't easy and it isn't always a rose garden, but since life is a struggle anyway, you might as well direct that struggle to worthy causes and to something larger than yourself. Involvement in a group is the highest manifestation of individuality and the greatest contributor to personal growth and development.

Where to start?

Write a letter to your school paper, daily press, radical papers or the music media (try *Rolling Stone)* and ask for like-minded people to contact you for the purpose of forming a discussion club or a support group to talk about their ideas and feelings. Or hang around clubs where musicians congregate and get to know some of them. You'll soon find kindred spirits, since musicians love to talk philosophy and concepts.

Discussion is the mother of concerted action. Decide

what issues most interest you and become an expert on them. Seek out other experts in those fields. Go to meetings of organizations dealing with issues that interest you.

Don't worry about your shyness; there are plenty of extroverts around to draw you out if they see enough of you!

I'm sending you a copy and a one-year subscription to our *Freedom Socialist* newspaper and would be delighted to know what you think of it.

I'd love to hear some of your original compositions. Do send me a tape when you can and I'll share it with my son Jonny. He is a jazz trumpeter, pianist and guitarist living in Boston.

L'Chaim to an eloquent young man who's well on his way towards making his life count by standing up to be counted.

Love,
Aunt Clara

February 21, 1996

Dearest Josh,

. . .I truly enjoy hearing from you and am delighted that you read and react to the literature I send.

You ask why afflicted and disenfranchised people do not unite, rebel and make change. The reasons have been the same throughout the ages:

1. They don't think it's possible.

2. They have no clear image of a goal, of a different kind of social structure.

3. Lacking the above, they don't want to replace the rascals with themselves and become the new stinkers.

4. They are divided by fierce internal hatreds and clashing customs. Ruling classes have always promoted disunity precisely in order to divide and conquer (through racism, sexism, homophobia, religious mania, caste distinctions and bigotries of all hues and stripes).

5. They are demoralized, despairing or just plain exhausted from the sheer effort of trying to survive. It takes energy and time for thinking and planning to achieve change.

6. There are few or no role models on hand to inspire, teach and point the way.

7. The best and brightest of the oppressed, and the most concerned among the intelligentsia, have not built a leadership based solidly on an effective program and action.

8. Corruption and seduction: enough of the oppressed are bought off and given super-status to remove possible future leaders and to tempt everybody else with the generally vain hope of stardom or success in some field. A few crumbs are flung to the hungry to keep them pacified along with dope, alcohol and artillery to turn against ourselves.

Hence, what's totally remarkable since class divisions first arose in society (they were not always there) is not that the disaffected were isolated from each other but that at decisive points they actually found the ways and means to leap over all these hurdles, achieve solidarity, engage in victorious struggles against the established order and carve out areas of power for themselves and even create totally new social structures. That's what a revolution does. And we are who we are, living the way we do, precisely because of our revolutionary forebears who won expanding freedoms for us with their brains and blood.

These peak movements in the chronicle of humanity's rise from the ocean and descent from the trees only happen at certain conjunctures of circumstances—at times when all the right elements come together, elements like the economic situation, the political scene, cultural developments, morale, and decisive current events. It's almost impossible to predict in advance what particular issues will trigger a mass uprising. The Vietnam War, Rodney King beating, Anita Hill/Clarence Thomas hearings, the Stonewall riots, assembly line factories, on-the-job brutality or low wages, slavery, colonialism, etc., etc., etc. But once something ignites large groups and they move into a resistance mode, they win adherents from sympathizers with grievances of their own who can identify. And if there is thrown into this mix, educated and trained political leaders capable of articulating a new course and persuading people to hang on and fight to the finish, great revolutions happen.

So in the final analysis the key problem is not "why don't the masses all unite," but when will the advanced thinkers organize themselves into larger radical political parties than currently exist and play their part in teaching workers that hope and transformation are eminently possible.

The road to the masses lies through the leadership. Spontaneous eruptions will fade away without long-term programs to help people maintain motivation and drive. I personally have found the life of a revolutionary committed to making things different and better to be the only way to live in a world as vicious and violent as ours. To me, the stance of the rebel makes it unnecessary for you to hate yourself in the morning and connects you indissolubly with real life all around you and globally as well. I've never been anywhere out of the country except for Canada and Tijuana and yet I feel strongly that I am a citizen of the world.

Which leads me to ask you to tell me about your trip to Israel. I'm very curious to know of your observations and conclusions. As you know I'm not a Zionist, I support the Arab liberation movement and my party has, from the outset, called for a bilateral, jointly-governed, Palestine.

On the matter of grunge, suffering and organizing: I may have confused you by what I said. Indeed suffering is no substitute for organizing, but that doesn't mean that suffering shouldn't be expressed. We're talking apples and oranges here. What I object to is making any form of culture a substitute instead of an aid and illuminator of political action. I heartily approve of Pearl Jam's battles against Ticketmaster and their appeal to Congress; I welcome all the benefits that contemporary bands perform for important political causes. I would never shoot down any art form that expresses the ideas and passions of a generation, or a particular group of people, or a country; I myself love New Orleans jazz, the blues and boogie-woogie, but I hardly expect them to change the world the way the New Left of the '60s thought rock 'n' roll would do. My comment was derived from IWW leader and poet Joe Hill's famous last remarks before a firing squad executed him in Utah in a frame-up, "Don't mourn, organize!" I have always admonished the women's movement, "Don't agonize, organize!" I believe in affirmation, not resignation, even though the self-expression of resignation and raw anger is part of the process.

. . .I want to invite you to visit me this summer, stay here as long as you want. You'll have scores of people to talk to and interesting political activities and rallies to be involved in first hand. You would have your own small room and my old car at your disposal and all the food you can eat. Seattle is a beautiful place with a rich cultural life.

I'm sending you some more subversive reading material. Please don't hesitate to tell me frankly what you think of it. . .


Love,
Clara

# Welcome to L.A.!

### 1978

From the majestic peaks and evergreens of Washington State through the rolling hills of Oregon and Northern California and the fertile valleys and desert winds of Southern California, it was a trip to remember.

The return route along the Pacific was a driver's dream: picturesque Santa Barbara, the misty towers of San Simeon, the picture-postcard ambiance of Big Sur, Monterey and the 17-Mile-Drive on the cypress-swept shores of Carmel, the Redwood Forest, the rocks that flank the wild Oregon coast, the never-ending thunder of the sea. . .

Sigh. . . But this isn't a travelogue. It's a story about people, a unique breed of folks called comrades, who were the reason and inspiration for the 3,000-mile jaunt.

Portland, the City of Roses, was in a flurry of preparation for the impending descent of born-again Jimmy Carter, slated to spend one entire evening with a middleclass family in a "typical" neighborhood. The media neglected to notice that I was concurrently ensconced not three blocks away in the spacious if older home of a Radical Women collective—an infinitely more significant occasion!

My sessions with the Portland comrades were immensely rewarding. I came away imbued once again with the awe that invariably overtakes me when I meet youthful radicals of both sexes consecrating their intelligence, thirst for knowledge, unflagging energy, and high good humor to the service of the revolutionary cause.

From the Golden Gate Bridge, the view of San Francisco in its high-rise alabaster glory has got to be one of the wonders of the world. And the comrades I talked with there vividly express the drama and dynamism of their fabled city.

These paragons of revolutionary vitality are voluble trade unionists, gifted poets, front-runners in the arenas of women's and gay rights, combatants in the minority liberation fray, and eager students and exponents of Marxist theory. And they seem to know everybody in town from Haight-Ashbury to Alcatraz.

They also know some superb restaurants, as befits healthy, red-blooded organizers. Right on, 'Frisco!

And now for the good news—for the best is yet to come.

Final destination: Los Angeles. Purpose: a national conclave of the Steering Committee of CRSP, the Committee for a Revolutionary Socialist Party founded on July 26, 1977 (fittingly the anniversary of the Cuban Revolution).

The rhythm of the three-day event veered from pounding debate to the lilt of agreement and the deep cadence of hard looks at complex issues. And throughout the alternating views and moods ran the leitmotif of proletarian democracy at work—open, candid, invigorating, and therapeutic free speech and careful listening.

Exhilarated by the productive meeting, the body joyously determined to hold the First National CRSP Conference in October, over the Columbus Day weekend. Seattle was awarded the coveted honor of host.

The Angeleno members of CRSP, who so generously provided excellent meals, transportation, shelter, meeting sites, and enthusiasm for the out-of-towners, will receive their reward for good planning and hard work in a close encounter with the impressive natural beauty of the conference site on Puget Sound. Comrades: we faithfully promise to facilitate for you, and for all the CRSP members and guests who will invade our space in the fall, a total political, social and scenic experience every bit as meaningful as my own trip to L.A.

The comradeship of revolutionists engaged in a common crusade is devoutly to be cherished. Thank you, L.A.—and onward to the forthcoming American October!

# Bread, Roses, and Heresy

1978

**D**ateline: Lincoln, Nebraska. A small airport, its contours softened by snowfall and moonlight. The car skids on the exit road. My older son, Marc Krasnowsky, drives blithely through the icy slush; his companion, Moira Ferguson, hands me a leaflet.

"We expect about 30 people," she says excitedly, "but with this snow, it's hard to tell."

The leaflet is straightforward. "Socialist Feminism: The New Wave," it announces. "A discussion by. . .Clara Fraser, a founder of Radical Women." And it quotes me: "We are *feminists* in the socialist movement and *radicals* in the women's movement." The sponsors are listed—the University of Nebraska Women Studies Program and the Women's Resource Center.

We arrive on campus, and poor Marc has to schlep my suitcase of heavy literature up the stairs. The beautiful meeting hall slowly fills with about 60 young women and men. Marc is an energetic literature salesman. "The more I sell, the less I'll have to carry out," he explains.

Moira introduces me. An associate professor of English literature and head of the Women Studies department, she offers a warm welcome and succinct account of my labor and radical activities. I speak, and then the audience takes over. The questions are fantastic!

Here on the prairie, in the middle-American conservative farm-belt, lies a rich pocket of feminism and commitment to the Left. These students, faculty, staff and young workers are intellectually alive and hungry for a reasonable theory that will fuse the scattered skeins of their interests. They want to be attached to all the anti-imperialist, pro-people mobilizations for freedom, but each contingent in the fray seems to exclude the others. The audience seeks a de-fragmenting, a synthesized programmatic focus for their energy that can validate a many-sided activism.

They speak with intensity, discussing Trotsky, Stalin, Mao, Fidel, the New Left, capitalism, Jimmy Carter, the neo-Nazis. Afterward, many of us pursue the discussion at Lincoln's most chic tavern. We meet a few nights later for more talk, and we luxuriate in the ever-novel thrill of encountering kindred spirits. We part with the understanding that they will study the *Radical Women Manifesto* and orient toward the constitution of an RW chapter.

I loved them in Lincoln. And to Moira and Marc and my new friends there, I say thank you from the bottom of my organizer's heart. You were an inspiration.

**D**ateline: *New York City.* Would you believe another unexpectedly early blizzard and another exciting meeting of radicals seeking a cohesive ideology? More dynamic women suffused with urgency to get on with the building of a socialist feminist counter-pole to the far right?

Believe it. This was a fine meeting called by a Manhattan group which includes Committee for a Revolutionary Socialist Party (CRSP) members, a meeting which once again clearly demonstrated that the new wave of socialist feminism is a living, pulsing phenomenon. Its New York adherents are highly competent technical and professional workers well-seasoned by the political wars of the last decade, and avid for theory and practice that respect history, are firmly grounded in class struggle, and can inspire women to political leadership.

Enclaves of such talented women abound here. And many women are already studying the Radical Women program and history in the course of their search for a political home that will be a viable base of operations.

The day of feminism as pure-and-simple legal reform is over. It hasn't worked, nor could it, in the very heart of Profitsland. In Nebraska, in New York, around this country, women are addressing economic issues and union problems side by side with the historic questions of family and human relations, and evaluating these subjects within the context of achieving fundamental societal change for the benefit of the exploited of every shape and hue.

Respectability and liberalism are out; heresy is in. A new army of women is a-borning. Give us bread, they cry, and give us roses—and give us revolution!

# No Place to Hide

## 1987

**W**hat are you going to do when you retire?" they asked me. "More of the same? Will you travel?"

Yes and yes, I said. First I'd recuperate from the years of forced association with City of Seattle management and lawyers. This I would accomplish by scrubbing the bathroom and excavating the recesses of my closet—good, clean, private work with no dissembling bureaucrats prying into my drawers and picking nits from my job performance.

Then, if post-traumatic stress didn't syndromize me, I would visit some powder keg countries whose agonies were a direct result of the overseer mindset and systemic military-financial arrogance of the same breed of power brokers who bring us industrial soap operas like the endless City Light story.

Well, I traveled, but not to the battlefronts. I managed to escape to utopia. The Freedom Socialist Party asked me to undertake editorial work for our national convention, and a rustic retreat setting was needed for the job.

**S**o I sailed away into the Puget Sound sunset alongside Guerry Hoddersen, the FSP's dynamic and prolific National Secretary, and we set up shop in a comparative Lifestyles of the Rich & Famous milieu on fabled Marrowstone Island, near Port Townsend. The waters murmured, the breezes caressed, the trees rustled. Name your cliché for tranquillity—we had it.

Come to find out that the serenely beautiful hills across from us—Indian Island, a naval undersea research station—was a storage dump for weapons. Shades of Chernobyl, Hanford, Three Mile Island, and all the other lethal factories and depots! Visions of atomized plutonium 239 zapping the breezes danced through our heads, along with scenes from *Dr. Strangelove* and *On the Beach*.

The plutonium didn't leak out but the news did, front page stuff. Protest meetings, of all things, were called. Real estate values plummeted. Everyone was scared. The bucolic site of our idyll was immersed in spooky, sinister miasmas.

Then the wells and the septic tank got all mixed up and the water boycotted our pipes. A polluted, arid paradise with the imminent prospect of becoming a raging inferno shed its charms. We moved our word processor and files and groceries from the inlet to a brave new wonderland—a cottage on the Olympic Peninsula, just outside Port Angeles, facing the Strait of Juan de Fuca and the mountains of Vancouver Island in Canada—and no nukes!

We loved our gorgeous grove of windswept cypresses, cedars, madronas, firs and pines. We gathered rocks and shells, saw Indians fishing the Elwah River, watched the giant containerized cargo ships of the world churn past, studied the tide charts. We reveled in the ever-changing play of light, clouds and colors, the roar and crash of the ocean, the thrill of sighting our first whale (practically on our doorstep and too huge to be considered for gefülte fish). Our productivity soared.

And then the rains came. Port Angeles hit the headlines, thanks to nature. The surging breakers surged up to our picture windows, around the house to the woodpile and patio, and *under the foundation*. Saltwater flooded the *well* and the overflow took up residence in the septic tank—and guess what couldn't flush. Once again—Toxicsland.

Why does such a primitive infrastructure afflict the waterfront estates of Washington's fabled Northwest Passages? A little matter of ideology. Too many country-dwellers up here are cantankerous, anti-social individualists, and, from the time their forebears stole the beaches from the Indians, they scorned cooperative ventures with their neighbors to build civilized water and sewage systems. So contaminated water and regurgitative toilets coexist with huge TV satellite dishes and computerized microwave ovens.

**W**eary of deluges and medieval technologies, we occasionally sought respite in Sequim, a quaint and prosperous retirement village near Dungeness and the juicy crabs. Soon the news stories broke—controversy with Indians over clam digging on Sequim Bay. Tribal harvesting of shellfish is a treaty right, but the Chamber of Commerce was in a stew over it, hungry to make chowder of the Jamestown Klallam Tribe.

**"W**eren't you lucky to find hideaways for five months?"
Yes and no. We had a taste of living amidst natural grandeur that everyone should know. But there is no fairyland, no peace, no harmony anyplace in a profit-obsessed capitalist orbit that breeds nuclear warships and warlike neo-Nazis and rural idiots. The world is too much with us, wherever.

# 7

## Socialism
## for Skeptics

# Socialism for Skeptics

1993

The '90s may not be the worst of times, but they're no picnic for radicals in the mega-capitalist countries.

We are playing to pretty tough crowds, where the hardest armor to pierce is a thick shield of cynicism. Disbelief in progress and resigned acceptance of the status quo are the intellectual high fashions that are smothering minds once open to bold visions and grand prospects.

And what with the tatters of Stalinism on one hand and newly resplendent swastikas on the other, it's not easy to persuade people that the promises of socialism can and must be for real.

A typical dialog between a Representative Skeptic (RS) and revolutionary me can last for hours, but here's a condensed version.

*R*S: World socialism? Get outta here. Face facts. Every place that used to be communist is going capitalist.

*Me:* They're going to capitalist hell is where they're going. The long-entrenched imperial countries are writhing with delirium tremens. The big shots "won" the Cold War by starving out, drive-by bombing, and CIA-ing everybody else, but the price of victory is defeat on the home front.

Our cities are dumping grounds for our radioactive problems—poverty, homelessness, joblessness, crime, illiteracy, ill-health, ecological rape, racism, sexism, homophobia, domestic and random violence, addictions, ad nauseam. There is less of everything for everybody except stress and taxes and fury. Cueball-headed Hitler wannabes menace the innocent, and bourgeois liberals give us spastic colons.

If this is the best that the U.S. Superpower can do, with its Information Highways and smart bombs and self-congratulation, somebody better call Dr. Kevorkian.

*RS:* But at least we have democracy, freedom of choice—like that sensitive sheriff from *Picket Fences* says in the bank ad. We say what we please, go where we want, and shop 'til we drop. Nobody tells me how to think! Under communism, the state makes the rules and dictates opinion—one size fits all.

*Me:* Your vaunted free will and open mind are illusions. You too are conditioned and molded, only more subtly.

Your choices run out when your money does. The goodies in the shops may be piled as high as Michael Jordan's slam dunks or as wide as Magic Johnson's field goals, but no cash, no carry.

To the homeless, choice means sleeping under a bridge or over a grate. For poor women, the right to abortion (tenuous for any female) might as well be the right to travel on the Starship Enterprise. And just try to go to Havana or Hanoi or Camp David. Or just try to be openly gay in the military. Just try to be a Marxist and still keep your job, unharassed.

Even for those whose plastic is still good, choice is a farce. *Time* or *Newsweek*. Democans or Republicrats. Letterman or Leno. Stallone or Schwarzenegger. Gimme a break, stop the insanity.

You are relentlessly bombarded with pro-establishment propaganda, images and emotional appeals all your life on every front. The narrow limits of your freedoms make you as broadly conformist as any drill team.

*RS:* But socialism has proved it can't compete.

*Me:* Not so. It's never been tested on a level playing field.

The contestants were never evenly matched.

The 1917 Russian Revolution had more stacked against it than a feminist on MTV. The country was impoverished, industrially and culturally backward, and exhausted by World War I. All the major capitalist nations swooped in for the kill, aiding and abetting the homegrown white-guard opposition.

The Soviet people repelled the invaders. But asking socialism to show its stuff in such a situation is like expecting a bullied slum kid to excel in school without breakfast, lunch, warm clothes, notebooks or defenders. The strange thing is not that a totalitarian, bureaucratic gang took over, but that the fledgling Soviet Union survived at all—and then managed to provide basic security for its inhabitants and to give the economic vampires quite a run for their money over 70 years.

But when we overthrow the super-suits in the super-economics—the U.S., Japan, and Germany—there will be no need for requisitioning, hence no need for warlords to control the dispensing of scarce consumer goods and natural resources. No foreign countries will invade anybody. Our revolution will set everybody free.

*RS:* Very pretty utopian dreams. Socialism, like the Messiah, will furnish instant peace on earth, goodwill toward all, a patched-up ozone layer and reforestation, safe sex, a two-day work week, a cure for AIDS and breast cancer, and Caribbean cruises featuring caviar and sashimi for the masses!

*Me:* Cease your snorting and scoffing. If that's what we want, that's what we'll have. And your sights are too low—one work-day a week max.

Leon Trotsky defined socialism as "shared abundance," like the economic democracy in an affluent family. We've got the abundance—we just have to transform the way we distribute it.

**T**hat was fun. I like debating. If my skeptical (and other) readers want to pitch more balls to my bat, we'll do it again.

# More Socialism for Skeptics

1994

In my last column, I inaugurated a kind of socialist catechism. A friendly reader transmitted the column via computer network and received some fascinating responses.

A man in Finland requested an *FS* subscription. A woman in California is distributing the column to a group which is producing an "FAQ" (Frequently Asked Questions) paper on socialism. A Missourian posted my words on another computerized bulletin board.

Another man hated it. He professed amazement at hearing from an open socialist—a dying breed, he said—and accused me of stacking the deck with lame questions leading to blah answers. Ouch!

His argument, condensed: "No group can know enough to centrally plan a modern economy. Capitalism isn't directed by some sinister cabal, but by millions of individual owners. The whole system is coordinated through trade and the money prices that trade generates."

OK, Mr. Free-Market Champion, let me respond to your critique.

*F*MC: Modern economy is too complex to plan.

*Me:* Stop with the mystifying and mystiquing already! With a little work, study and experience, anyone who can manage their own household economy can supervise the flow of money through a business, an entire industry, a government, banking, the stock market, and the compulsive fight of capital around the world.

Capital is simply money and commodities assigned to create a profit and be reinvested. Profit is made by the "magical" addition of *surplus value* to the value inherent in the product. The "added value," the profit, is produced by workers.

And this capital is *born to expand or die*. To be useful, the investment must result not only in a profit but in a growing rate of profit.

The outcome of capitalism is hardly the dramatic and sexy individual entrepreneurship extolled by the financial and journalistic gurus. No, the real end product is world domination (cartels, multi-nationals, international agreements) by a few huge conglomerates who each control a segment of the global market: imperialism.

The Zapatistas in Mexico today, the Chinese coolies under Chiang Kai-shek, the peasants and workers in Czarist Russia, the Black South African workers and farmers—all were smart enough to understand the private-profit system and what the hell it was doing to them.

You, too, my critic, should be sufficiently intelligent to grasp the nature and laws of the system you consider incomprehensible. Said Lenin, "Every ruler shall learn to cook and every cook shall learn to rule the state." Can you cook? Then there's hope for you.

*FMC:* Market relations aren't plotted by a group of secret schemers.

*Me:* So who said they were? Much engineering and manipulation and control through pacts does go on, but for the most part, you're right. It was Marx who pointed out the truly anarchistic nature of modern industrial capitalism—an irrational, disorganized hodgepodge operation that enormously rewards price fixers, crooks, gangsters, exploiters, con artists, gamblers, stock manipulators, and all manner of corruption. It's a crazy and ruthless economy that survives by inflicting anguish on untold billions.

So why has this stupid, hideous arrangement not been extinguished? Because sinister cabals, whose existence you dispute, use their vast power to employ violence beyond imagination against workers and whole countries, so that their investments are protected and sealed off from the very labor that produced the profit.

True, market prices and successes can't be totally plotted, *but the underlying profit system is perpetuated* by mostly unknown industrialists and financiers, and the governments they own.

*FMC:* The system is regulated through trade and the prices set by trade.

*Me:* You're confusing the system and the market. The *market* is coordinated by trade (what sells and what doesn't), but the private profit system is perpetuated by those with power and guns.

Furthermore, "trade" doesn't determine basic prices anyway. Rather than being basically dependent upon supply and demand, prices in the marketplace actually fluctuate around the *real value* inherent in a commodity.

The value of a commodity comes from the labor invested in it, including the labor that manufactured the machinery and extracted the raw materials used to create the item. And the boss's profits do not come from his smarts or his capital investment or his mark-up, but from the value created by labor—specifically, surplus-value.

Surplus value derives from unpaid wages. *The worker is never paid for the value of the product*, only for the value of her or his *labor time*, which is considerably less, and which meanders widely depending upon the historical, cultural and social conditions of a country.

Labor-power is miraculous, like the Virgin Birth. You get more out of it than you put in. Workers produce a commodity which has more value than what they get in wages to keep them functioning. This differential is *surplus value*, which is the source of capital.

You referred me to *Rules and Order* by Hayek. I'm not impressed. May I refer you to *Wage-Labor and Capital* and *Value, Price and Profit* by Marx, and to "What is Economics" by Rosa Luxemburg. Someday you may even be ready for *Capital!*

The secret of value, the *labor* theory of value, that was unearthed by the classical economists and by Marx is what the money barons fear and hate. It is the secret that will set the world free. People will learn how to control the supposedly sacred, eternal, inscrutable method of production and distribution that now controls *us*.

Socialists will produce for use according to a reasonable plan and without a thought for the odious notion of profit. And with no insatiable parasitic class to maintain, socialist society will produce abundance for all.

# Clans or Klans: Choose One

1994

Anybody who speaks up for socialism is bombarded with the objection that cooperative and mutually supportive relations among people are a fantasy.

*Homo sapiens* are intrinsically individualistic, competitive, and egotistical, claim the cynics—it's just the way we're genetically programmed. Survival of the fittest and all that jazz.

This robotic response from apparently thoughtful folk is nonsense. The overwhelming historical evidence about our *true* nature amounts to an incredible chronicle of humankind's endless struggle to make life better—for everyone.

*Confirmed Cynic (CC):* Stars in your eyes soap opera. All people care about is taking care of numero uno, by any means necessary.

That's the way it's been since we first walked erect. In the movie *Being Human*, Robin Williams' caveman feels most passionately about *"mine."* In *2001: A Space Odyssey*, Primitive Man resorts to violence instinctively before he's hardly clambered out of the primordial goop.

*Me:* That portrait of humanity is as phony as Bill Clinton's liberal image. Early humans lived in matriarchal and later patriarchal clans in which everybody contributed to the group welfare. The norm was the collective ethic.

But things changed—because *different kinds of economic and social organization create different kinds of people.* Today, in a system designed to produce profits for the few at the expense of the many, we are slugged into brutalizing each other for money, jobs, education, love, food, a place to live, recognition, self-esteem, everything.

The poor rarely understand that they lack the basics because of the way international capitalism works. They think they suffer because other cultures, races, religions and countries deprive them of what is rightfully theirs. So they resort to hysterical nationalism, unwarranted patriotism, rapacious competition, and desperate acquisitionism—convenient substitutes for revolutionary action on a global scale to remove the root cause of all the terrible infighting. When "me" replaces "we," everybody dies.

CC: Wrong. Without competition, where's incentive? We might be spared embarrassments like Tonya Harding, who went a bit too far in trying to cripple her skating rival. But then again, we'd never have seen Satchell Paige pitch a ball at 90 miles an hour. Why, the free market has brought the world to an apex of prosperity and consumer satisfaction. If men didn't have to make it or starve, why would they strain to do their best? Left to their own devices, most people are lazy bums.

Me: You can take your original sin fixation and shove it. It doesn't compute. Everybody loves winning by virtue of excellence and talent. But everybody *doesn't* love beating down others, degrading and impoverishing millions, and fomenting a host of enemies in order to be a success.

When every aspect of life becomes a virtual duel to the death, the winner generally ends up more tormented than the loser. You actually feel better if you do right.

The only proven motivator is the lure of coming up with a product or outcome or idea that will empower and raise the comfort level of the masses. Billionaires who ream the opposition may be envied, but they are never loved or immortalized in that pantheon of wonderful individuals who left the world a finer place. Who will weep for Donald Trump?

Your specious claim that dog-eats-dog is our paramount inducement to accomplishment is a calumny against history, and a vicious assault on the overwhelming global majority who make their lives meaningful by uplifting others.

*CC:* People may well be a mix of good and evil, but stop ignoring the evil part. You can't simply change human nature by writing a new software program!

*Me:* Oh, yes, you can—with hardware based on a different operating principle.

All great evils—war, poverty, selfishness, religious manias, class and caste divisions, bigotry—are produced by a *social machine* that runs on exploitation. This terrible Pandora's box poisons human nature just as inevitably as an incinerator burning toxic waste pollutes the environment with dioxin.

Given the proper social technology, we *can* write our own destinies. A shared and planned socialist world provides the material pre-conditions that impel us to do this.

**"B**ut you can't get there from here," say the skeptics. "Never mind our potential in the abstract; those living in the here-and-now are too debased, divided, and demoralized to achieve societal and personal change." *That* paradox will be lassoed next.

# Class: The Power that Heals

1994

**M**y previous column ended by posing a dilemma: The downtrodden people who need change the most seem to spend their energy sniping at each other, figuratively or for real. A Die-Hard Skeptic (DHS) takes this for granted.

**D**HS: The whole globe looks more and more like Rwanda on a bad day. The only way half of the world's citizens can exist side by side is as corpses. People this badly divided will never come together to overthrow the system, no matter how rotten it is.

*Me*: Surprise—Unity happens! Sometimes overnight, to the amazement of everybody but Marxists.

Solidarity steals onto the stage unannounced. Togetherness is provoked by too-long suppressed fury—fury at the shared whip of maltreatment, the mutual endless years of exploitation, and the common chronic dehumanization and insult.

All of a sudden, when the bosses or the government go one little step too far, an apparently spontaneous eruption occurs. All the workers previously feuding over race and sex/ sexuality and religious or national or cultural differences, and the normal menu of ego wars that rage on any job and in any community, coalesce suddenly, caught up in a euphoria of sister/brotherhood forged by a joint reaction to the guys with their heels on *everybody's* necks.

The folks in the plants and fields, in the offices and shops, may not understand this reflex themselves. But it is as inexorable as a law of nature; it is a *social* imperative. As inevitable as night following day, *class* has conquered over all.

Oppression forges resistance in spite of and across the deep chasms separating the resisters. Because when people are galvanized into fighting back, they desperately seek allies, and they sublimate previous antagonisms as they learn to work together in the upsurge against the newly identified real enemy.

This is a fact, not a utopian dream. And this fact is the engine of history.

If fusion *didn't* happen, we wouldn't be here talking about it. How do you think all our vaunted freedoms were won?

The creation of oneness out of division is what produces strikes, mass voter protests, and ultimately revolutions. The essence of human nature—its communal impulse, its fundamental habit of cooperation for survival—reasserts itself over transitory, superficial and reactionary centrifugal forces that break things apart and atomize what used to be melded. Humanity triumphs over its failures and rises to its greatest heights as it seeks justice and relief from affliction.

Note the triumphal victory over legal apartheid in South Africa. Note, even, the absolute solidarity of the baseball strike, in which players who make $5 million and players who make $50,000 are hanging tough together.

And people never forget the thrill of marching hand in hand with comrades they hated only yesterday.

*DHS*: But watch what happens after the excitement of the action wears off. Everything reverts to the status quo ante and nothing lasting is achieved. For every antiwar fighter or Black Powerite or racial or sexual liberationist who still has a shred of idealism visible, I can name you 20 who are getting rich peddling barbecue sauce or real estate or new ways to buff your bod.

*Me*: Aha! But this is precisely where the role of a party comes in. When a revolt takes place without a party or ahead of a party or behind the back of a party, you're right: the movement will not endure, huge errors of strategy and tactics will be made, key lessons will not be drawn, and front-line insurrectionists will not grow into leaders for *all* seasons.

Only the revolutionary party can ensure that activists and agitators become political professionals geared and educated for the long haul. Only the party can help the militant strike or sit-in or electoral upheaval take the next leaps forward and aim for state power. Only the party can extend isolated insurgencies into constant, concerted mobilizations for the total revamping of society.

Any putative leftist or progressive who sneers at parties and scoffs at vanguards is revealing deep-seated hostility toward revolution and socialism. A transformed reality will not be concocted out of literary documents and good intentions and dreams of paradise, but out of mortals who build an instrument that is capable of organizing the overthrow of the existing government, the creation of a new structure, and the administration of a new course.

A true humanist and visionary needs to embrace the party as the midwife who brings to birth a brave new world.

**O**kay, you non-believers out there—what stones have I left unturned? Send us your quibbles, quarrels, and questions, by mail or Internet, and let the dialectical dialogue develop!

# Hail to the Once and Future Soviet Union

1995

> Even supposing for a moment that owing to unfavorable
> circumstances and hostile blows the soviet régime should
> be temporarily overthrown, the inexpugnable impress of
> the October revolution would nevertheless remain upon
> the whole future development of mankind.
>
> —Leon Trotsky (1930)

*L*et us now pay tribute to 75 years of the Soviet Union. While idiots in academia and the media crow about its collapse, I need to express my profound respect and gratitude for its enormous attainments and unquenchable legacy.

Granted, in Moscow and environs today, all is chaos and horror. And why not? Horrendous convulsions are bound to ensue when an advanced social organism, in which production is based on need and planning rather than profit and chance, is wrenchingly replaced with the outmoded, sadistic, dog-eat-dog system of capitalism. The convulsions are history's protest; history is telling us that what is happening is wrong, regressive, and out of sync with the endless upward arc of average people struggling to improve their lives.

Yes, I weep for the Soviet Union's demise. Even more, I detest the military encirclement and CIA/mafia dirty tricks and world market pressures that finally brought it down.

I also mourn the relative passivity of its citizens, who were so traumatized by the Stalinist bureaucracy that they could not summon the hope and the energy to carry out the desperately needed *political* revolution that would have restored democracy, while still retaining the progressive economic forms and social culture.

**B**ut shedding tears for defeats is only part of the dialectic of evaluating events. In the case of the USSR, the triumph and incredibly long tenure of the revolutionary state, despite overwhelming obstacles, is the other side of the coin.

How magnificent that this daring, imaginative, and dynamic tryout of new and better ways of living together should have lasted for more than seven decades! Its own founders and theoreticians never believed that an isolated Soviet Union could persist indefinitely. They acknowledged that socialism in one country is an absurdity, and that one workers state could survive only with mounting reinforcement from more and more like-minded states exploding into being.

Similarly, they scoffed at inane bourgeois critics who whined that after 10 or 20 or 70 years the Soviet Union still hadn't reached the productive and living standards of the most developed capitalist democracies. We never promised to, said Trotsky. We have to break the stranglehold of the dead hand of the past before we can even start to come abreast of, much less surpass, nations that never had to lie fallow under centuries of insane czars, a useless nobility, crushing serfdom, and a medieval culture.

So what the Soviets *did* produce—in art, culture, industrialization, agriculture, transportation, science, space exploration, medicine, and more—is stunning.

How did the USSR endure so long and achieve so much in the face of unremitting obsession to annihilate it? Simply because of the tremendous power inherent in socialism's reasonableness, naturalness, and capacity to inspire workers and rebels the world over with its profound appeal to the ideas of justice, ethics, equality, and communalism. The Soviet Union was a dress rehearsal, humanity's first real plunge into the uncharted seas of the pursuit of happiness.

Instead of succumbing to confusion and melancholia and despair over the fall of the world's first workers state, we must commemorate it and illuminate its lessons, so that we can proceed to stage Act Two with a greater wisdom born from experience.

History never follows a straight path. Socialism will overtake the planet when its time comes, just like *capitalism* did! Many people think the current profit system is as eternal and indestructible as matter/energy, but capitalism took more than a thousand years, and innumerable false starts, to entrench itself. And it too shall pass away, when the global majority is thoroughly sick and tired of being exploited and brutalized.

We must not allow ourselves to be infected with the moaning and groaning of doomsayers who were once ready to justify Stalinism's wildest violations of Marxism-Leninism and are now ready to inter Stalinism and socialism in the same grave. We will confidently nourish our radical optimism by revering the memory of Lenin and Trotsky's Bolshevik Party, which conceived and executed one helluva revolution in a stultified, backward country, and by continuing to adapt that party's electrifying principles to the here-and-now.

We come not to bury the Union of Soviet Socialist Republics, but to praise its liberationist and humanitarian origins and aspirations. Despite the ravages of Stalinism, the good that this noble experiment accomplished lives long after it.

# The World of Tomorrow in Sound Bites

1995

A map of the world that does not include Utopia is not worth even glancing at, for it leaves out the one country at which Humanity is always landing.

—Oscar Wilde (1895)

We're taught at such an early age to be against the communists, yet most of us don't have the faintest idea what communism is. Only a fool lets somebody else tell him who his enemy is.

—Assata Shakur (1987)

P rexy Bill Clinton, speaking at a commemoration for WWII vets, grimly opined that "no generation can ever banish the forces of darkness from the future."

Are prospects really so horrible that we can expect nothing but suffering, war, destitution, and barbarism into eternity?

Thank you, President Liberal, but your bleak existentialism is wrong. Another possibility actually exists. Americans have the capability right this minute to open the door to a brand-new social landscape, to a vastly different way of life devoutly desired by the entire world.

But when it comes to transforming the profit system, the same opinion-molders who laud breakthrough products and talents and techniques as "truly revolutionary" proceed to go wild. At that touchy point, revolution becomes *bad*, its proponents viewed as virtual criminals and treated as clear and present dangers. *That* untouchable door remains locked.

Our major talking heads stigmatize communism as an untried pipe dream, a brutal dictatorship, a failed experiment. Like Hamlet, they would "rather bear those ills we have, than fly to others that we know not of." Stuff and nonsense. The Wright Brothers' first planes didn't fly. Spacecraft still blow up. And computers generate more headaches than solutions (my personal opinion!). All beginnings are rocky.

So let's shut down the fixed idea that *rightward* change is inevitable but *leftward* change unthinkable. Social revolutionaries are the authentic entrepreneurs.

Socialism (and its final stage of communism) is a wonderful goal, a beautiful and necessary vision to live and die for, a promise of a lifestyle irresistible in its harmony, workability, naturalness, passion and compassion.

It is a panorama not of Jurassic Park but of the Garden of Eden modernized and global. And some great minds have provided us with a wealth of down-to-earth definitions.

"Socialism is an opinion as to how the income of the country should be distributed. The only satisfactory plan is to give everybody an equal share no matter what sort of person she is, or how old she is, or what sort of work she does, or who or what her father was." Thus sayeth George Bernard Shaw, playwright and Fabian socialist, in *The Intelligent Woman's Guide to Socialism and Capitalism.*

"Communism, far from being an intolerable bureaucratic tyranny and individual regimentation, will be the means of greater individual liberty and shared abundance." Words from *If America Should Go Communist* by Leon Trotsky, co-leader and standard-bearer of the Russian Revolution.

"Anything that has any kind of value is made, mined, grown, produced, and processed by working people. So why shouldn't working people collectively own that wealth?"

Former Black Panther and escaped political prisoner Assata Shakur penned these lines in *Assata*.

"We visualize a social order based on the common ownership of the means of production, the elimination of private profit in the means of production, the abolition of the wage system, the abolition of the division of society into classes." Lifelong U.S. Marxist James P. Cannon furnished this capsule during his sedition trial, as recorded in *Socialism on Trial*.

"From each according to his abilities, to each according to his needs." So asserted Karl Marx in *Critique of the Gotha Programme*.

Socialism, simply, is *non*-capitalist living. Wealth is created to satisfy human needs, not inhuman greeds.

The present economic arrangement is insatiable in its avarice, unrelenting in its viciousness, rife with contradictions, and veering crazily out of control. The rule of the almighty dollar or yen or mark must and will be overthrown and supplanted by the rule of reason and justice.

I love these quotes and have only just begun to beguile you with them. Some of the rocky terrain still to be covered: How will the new system be implemented? What about small farms and businesses? What will prevent a bureaucracy from trampling on individual liberties and enforcing conformity? Tune in again to our prime-time infotainment series.

# Comes the Revolution:
# A Simple "To Do" List

1995

> We shall now proceed to construct the socialist order. . .
> The labor movement, in the name of peace and socialism,
> shall win, and fulfill its destiny.
>
> —V.I. Lenin (1917)

And *we* shall now proceed to construct a basic design for a socialist order in these not-so-United States.

Our super-pragmatic American minds have difficulty visualizing the changeover from capitalism to socialism. But to build socialism in an advanced capitalist country is not a daunting problem.

What's enormously hard is throwing the process into reverse! The backward forced march imposed upon the former Soviet Union and Eastern Europe is a ghastly shambles because it is utterly anti-historical and blindly regressive.

In moving toward socialism, however, the winds of progress impel you full speed ahead. And launching a society run by and for workers involves following a clear road map no harder to draw up and stick to than the daily task list of a mother, secretary, teacher, computer programmer, electrician, or chef.

Black poet extraordinaire Langston Hughes provided a nuts-and-bolts blueprint in "Good Morning, Revolution," 1934:

> Listen, Revolution,
>  We're buddies, see—

Together,
We can take everything:
Factories, arsenals, houses, ships,
Railroads, forests, fields, orchards,
Bus lines, telegraphs, radios,
(Jesus! Raise hell with radios!)
Steel mills, coal mines, oil wells, gas,
All the tools of production,
(Great day in the morning!)
Everything—
And turn 'em over to the people who work.
Rule and run 'em for us people who work.

Another good starting place for our journey is Elizabeth Gurley Flynn's thumbnail review in her 1955 book, *The Rebel Girl*, of a seminal 1888 work.

*Looking Backward* by. . .Edward Bellamy. . .portrayed an ideal society, due to the abolition of banks, landlords and capitalists. It was an imaginative description of what a socialist America could be like, with collective ownership of all natural resources and industries and full utilization of machinery, technical knowledge and the capacities of her people.

Another preview, from Marx and Engels in *The Communist Manifesto*, 1848:

The proletariat will use its political supremacy to wrest, by degrees, all capital from the bourgeoisie, to centralize all instruments of production in the hands of the State, i.e., of the proletariat organized as the ruling class; and to increase the total of productive forces as rapidly as possible.

And finally, James P. Cannon, founder of U.S. Trotskyism, in *America's Road to Socialism*, 1953:

> The working class. . .will take hold of society and set up
> its own government. . .and use all the concentrated
> power of this state to suppress any attempt at counter-
> revolution by the capitalists. . . The first task of the new
> government, once it has established its authority. . .will
> be to abolish private property in the means of produc-
> tion. . . Industry will be nationalized and operated
> according to a plan.

**W**e can make all this happen, you know, all of us
together. Just clip the following post-seizure-of-power menu,
memorize it, and slap it on your fridge door.

1. Restructure the government into divisions and jobs that
make sense, reflect our needs, and express our hopes and
ideals.

2. Squelch any counterrevolutionary machinations;
peaceably remove as many kvetches as possible.

3. Expropriate the expropriators. In one fell swoop,
transfer all private property from the giant capitalists to public
ownership. Nationalize the banks, great factories, natural
resources, agribusiness, communication and transportation
networks, utilities, media conglomerates, and like that.

4. Plan and reorganize these operations to create full
employment, maximum output of needed goods, and an
efficient, environment-friendly, and waste-free production
process.

5. Back to basics—complete funding for enriched
education, training, health, housing, recreation, and the general
welfare.

6. Let a million cultural flowers bloom! Spark an
explosion of rich, creative, diversified, and exciting art in all its
forms.

7. Have a nice life for a change!

# Looking Backward at the Year 2000

1996

**T**hat New Year's Day I lost my job at Boeing was the day I decided that I, Cheryl Jordan, had had enough. Standing in the unemployment line and thinking about the poor woman in Mexico now getting a dollar a day for the work that paid me $12 an hour was the last straw.

I found a job as a nurse's aide in a big new HMO. The week I started, the employees won union representation.

But contract negotiations stalled. The bosses wanted to make a mockery of patient care with low wages, long shifts or reduced hours, relentless speedup, and cuts in service.

We went on strike the same week that federal employees walked out nationally. For four years they had been yanked around at budget time, deprived for weeks of their paychecks, as people were ruthlessly cut off from vital programs.

The new Labor Party called for a general strike.

A year earlier, the idea might have given me pause, out of concern for my two children. But I couldn't support a family on HMO wages—and, by god, there had to be more to working than just managing to stay alive so you could keep on slaving away. A battle was underway for worker dignity, and I had to join it, to be true to my class, my color and my kind.

**T**he general strike was a huge success in terms of participation, but the government wouldn't budge. Radicals were saying we needed to make arrangements ourselves to provide food, electricity, heat and medical care for the public.

My union wanted to occupy the neighborhood clinics. I was on the Planning Committee.

When we proposed this to the local Labor Council, a handful of bureaucrats who had survived the shakeup a few years back were afraid we would bring the military down on our heads; the National Guard had already murdered strikers in Illinois and Mississippi.

But I saw no reason why the soldiers shouldn't be on our side, and I said so. Weren't they as mistreated as we were by a system that used them and threw them away? (It was the first time I'd spoken in front of so many people!)

After intense debate, the Labor Council approved our plan.

The army was waiting for us at the clinics. We appealed to them: "Brothers and Sisters, don't fire on us. We are your families, your neighbors, your friends. We're fighting for a better life for you, too." They didn't shoot. We embraced instead, and cheers resounded.

They were mostly kids, lots of them African American. I've never been prouder of my people than at that heart-stopping moment when the youngsters retreated from the doorway to let us pass.

And how much I learned in that first heady experience when we actually ran the clinics! How competent we became, and how thrilling it was to understand the great power that was ours to wield.

Strikers all around the country took over their job sites as well. The army was in disarray—whole groups of soldiers would break ranks and bring us their weapons.

Still the strike was deadlocked. And soon the socialists were gaining everyone's attention. They explained that the only way to end poverty and racism and sexism and war was to change the economic system so it functioned along collective lines, where nobody could exploit another for profit. They called for a massive March on Washington and advocated that we occupy key government buildings and seize state power!

**I** was one of 50 delegates sent from my union to provide first aid at the march, which turned out to be the largest ever. I am so proud to have been there among the enthusiastic millions who converged on the Potomac. Every union sent members. So did every tribal nation; every progressive organization of women, people of color, lesbians and gays, students, elders, farmers, disabled people, environmentalists, artists, and intellectuals; and every branch of the armed forces.

We saw that the power was in us, and we strode ahead to *claim* that power. When the speeches were over, we streamed into the White House, announcing that the working class was now in charge. All the bosses' hired guns had deserted them, and I never even had to take out my medical kit.

That giant March on Washington, in retrospect, had grown up to become a revolution—American's Third, this one to complete the other two.

After that, everything happened at once. A new government was formed, based on councils like the soviets in the early USSR and administered by the most popular socialist leaders. The exciting work of revamping the entire political structure began. A brand new day was dawning, a new world was about to be born. And I was one of the midwives.

But that's a tale for another time.

# The Rebellious Nature of Human Nature

1996

Is it apocalypse now? Entire societies are crashing. Disasters—natural and political, public and personal—ravage pitiful humanity from Chechnya to Liberia. The daily news is unwatchable, unreadable, unthinkable.

So, what is to be done?

Why, *nada*, according to many people. Like cancer-stricken Timothy Leary, the narcotics guru of the '60s who is preparing to make his adieus via cyberspace, the end-is-nigh crowd thinks all we can do is get on-line and scream into the existential void as that good night envelops us in nothingness.

Sorry, cynics, I do not concur.

You see, all ye who despair, I know a secret. The universal cry for freedom and a more comfortable, easier life is *genetic*. It's hard-wired into our species. And the current plague of scarcity and powerlessness for the multitudes is *against human nature*. Hence it follows as the day the night that uninterrupted revolt against repression is inevitable.

Nor are we stuck in an endless groove of fighting back, because we learn from our mistakes and successes; we *progress*. Revolutions happen. Reforms are won. And socialism, sooner than you think, will overtake world capitalism, just as surely as capitalism in its young heyday overturned feudalism.

And there's gratification to be had today as well as

*mañana.* Herewith my Top 20 List of inspiring recent events:

1. A split-off section from the British Labor Party reclaims that body's original, explicitly socialist principles.

2. Tumult amongst Gallic unionists and students holds out the prospect of another and greater French Revolution.

3. Public workers in Ontario, Canada, strike for five weeks, serving notice that austerity will not be swallowed easily.

4. The same message is driven home in the USA via walkouts and other labor actions by machinists, nurses, autoworkers, garment-sweatshoppers, and more.

5. Plans are being hatched for a Labor Party right here in the heartland of international Capital.

6. A mobilization in Mexico, sparked by the indigenous rebels of Chiapas, says *"¡Basta!"* to NAFTA.

7. The women workers in the *maquiladora* export mills of Latin America brave employer violence to form unions.

8. The UN Women's conference in Beijing and its non-governmental counterpart bring together activists from all over the globe, who protest daily about critical issues ranging from nuclear testing to the U.S. blockade against Cuba.

9. The birth-control pill for men!

10. Despite the obnoxious agenda of Million Man March orchestrator Louis Farrakhan, the tremendous response to his call bespeaks the eagerness of African Americans to *do something* about racism.

11. A grassroots movement gains a stay of execution for radical Black journalist Mumia Abu-Jamal, framed for the murder of a Philadelphia cop.

12. No more waiting to exhale for African American women. Breaking out of the traditional ghettoes of sports and entertainment, they are registering prominently in politics, law, academia and literature.

13. Not to disparage athletes and performers: the returns of Monica Seles to tennis and Michael Jordan and Magic

Johnson to basketball—for however long—testify to the irrepressibility of human striving.

14. Hawaii's nuptially minded lesbians and gays are on the way to securing the state's blessing. You may well cast a jaundiced eye on the creaky and hypocritical institution of marriage, but this still is a civil rights issue whose time has come.

15. And in Melbourne, Australia, men and women of alternative sexualities throng to the city's first gay pride march.

16. Dispelling the absurdity that evolution means bloodthirsty competition of each against all, scientists explain how sociability and cooperation became intrinsic to *Homo sapiens*.

17. After decades of Cold War space-program rivalry, the U.S. and Russia are now cooperating celestially.

18. A worldwide surge of sympathy for the Arab cause follows Israel's ghastly bombings of civilians in Lebanon.

19. U.S. voters show they are not ready to embrace reactionaries Patrick Buchanan and California Governor Pete Wilson as presidential candidates.

20. Leftist candidates enjoy a renaissance in places as disparate as Italy, Benin, Nepal, Eastern Europe and Russia. Sure, many of these politicos are just recycled Stalinists or social democrats promising a "kinder, gentler" subjection to free-marketry. Nevertheless, their popularity proves that the rumors of the demise of Marxism have been greatly exaggerated.

So fear and tremble not. The battle is not only not over—it's barely been joined. And the momentum of history, like the logic of science, is on our side.

# The Name is Karl, Friends, Not Groucho

1996

Sometimes when I tell people I'm a socialist, they think it's a joke, like that T-shirt that says, "Sure, I'm a Marxist," and features Groucho, Harpo, and Chico.

After all, socialism and its ultimate destination of communism are supposed to be absolutely, totally, unmistakably, irreparably *dead*—and buried so deeply that their remains can never be located, not even by calling in the legions of Psychic Friends in the Network for help.

But declaring Marxism forever extinguished makes as much sense as proclaiming the eternal demise of evolution or gravity or the multiplication tables. Because so long as human life persists, the earth-rooted philosophy, dynamic logic and harmonious societal goals enunciated by Karl Marx are not only highly relevant but central, *pivotal*, to the quality of that life.

The mission of Marxism is to eventually get rid of the thing that produced it: *class struggle*. This epic tug-of-war results from the hard fact that the market economy—or capitalism, if you prefer not to mince words—is an arrangement that requires two competing classes. One class *gets* and the other *gives*. One takes, the other is robbed and abused.

Neither combatant has figured out a win-win situation with any staying power—since no longterm comfy compromise can exist. So antagonism between employees and corporations simmers or rages as they joust over their respective shares of the economic pie. And the clash between them is inseparable from a system of unplanned production for private profit, marked by the mega-rich struttin' their stuff in the faces of the abysmally deprived.

This intractable conflict can be resolved only by Marxism, the sole political cuisine in town based on reality and a scientific reason for hope. All other political ideologies are recipes for accelerated disaster, and any so-called leader who does not take megaphone or E-mail in hand to sing the praises of salvation through socialism is part of the problem.

It is easy to understand apathy, cynicism, hopelessness, retreat into contemplating your own New Age navel. The collapse of the USSR under the twin battering rams of Wall Street and the White House on one side, and its own internal contradictions on the other, flung open the floodgates to a gigantic tidal wave of reaction and counterrevolution that is engulfing the planet.

As the old Soviet safety net crashes to the ground, social services are slashed everywhere—other lands need no longer compete on the benefits front. Erstwhile radicals wither into liberals, past liberals atrophy into conservatives, former conservatives petrify into fascists. Every mass movement grows increasingly rudderless. And when the unifying principle of Soviet power vanishes, countries made up of nations living side by side in relative peace and harmony (USSR, Yugoslavia) break up overnight into manic bourgeois-nationalist fragments, out for blood over issues (and a cast of characters) that are too bewildering to understand.

Yet the historical clock winds in both directions, forward and backward. Uncultured peasants turn into warriors, sullen proletarians into Communards, slaves into conductors of the Underground Railroad, Mrs.'s into Ms.'s. Reaction begets a revolutionary backlash, like in Australia right now, where protesters are slinging sledgehammers against the parliament doors of a ham-fisted new government.

It is hard to grasp this ineradicable truth about things turning into their opposites and crisis morphing into opportunity without tutoring from a knowledgeable leadership. But the Left has largely abdicated responsiblity for alerting and guiding the irate millions yearning to be free of endless strife and worry or penury. Most radicals have also succumbed to the malady of crass pragmatism, that silly notion that if something doesn't work the first time—or hasn't even been tried!—it's automatically no damn good.

Hence, once-upon-a-time Marxists accommodate themselves to the status quo, delighting the ruling moguls. A lot of folks I know sadly need to go back to nursery school and relearn that magnificent anthem about the true nature of existence and consciousness:

> The itsy-bitsy spider went up the water spout.
> Down came the rain and washed the spider out.
> Up came the sun and dried up all the rain,
> And the itsy-bitsy spider went up the spout again.

That means you, too, kids. Optimism—living today by organizing for the future—comes from exploring. And being a revolutionary is not a joke. Groucho's sardonics didn't change the world—Karl's dialectics *did*.

# 8

## Marxism: From Red Square to Main Street

# Stranger in a Strange Land

1992

The sky is falling down. The world as we've known it is ending, and not with whimpers but with very loud bangs indeed.

Everybody seems to be shootin' down everybody else. People who once were amicable family, mates, neighbors, fellow workers, colleagues, comrades, and nations are turning on each other like snarling wolves.

If friends, relatives and compatriots aren't threatening and divorcing each other, they're likely to be suing or slaughtering each other. Division, destruction and doom are the masters of the day.

Where in the world does a revolutionary, socialist, humanist—me—go to register? Did hopelessly random and unbenign cosmic forces deposit me on the wrong planet?

Is it true that there are no answers, only questions? Is ideology really dead? Are humans conceived in sin and condemned to folly? Are religious maniacs and nationalist hysterics and crass opportunists and fascist demagogues and demented damn fools the wave of a minutely Balkanized new order based on a nuclear, concentration-camp culture?

Will tomorrow never come?

I don't believe any of this claptrap—this bourgeois,

allegedly pragmatic, end-of-history, old hat crap.

I *do* believe in the scientific validity of cockeyed optimism.

I believe that the human race deserves and *will achieve* a nobler destiny than the casual brutality and chaos of a market economy and Deutschland Über Alles pop psychology.

I believe that revolution and socialism and democracy and rich personal fulfillment, within the context of a dazzling and liberating worldwide and world-class art and culture, are not only possible but *imminent.*

And I believe, above all, in true believers. Only a visionary, attempting the untried and untested, can be a practical leader. Only a politically correct radical can sow the seeds that transform scorched earth into bountiful harvests. The basic thing needed to attain devoutly wished for results is philosophy.

And finally I believe in Karl Marx. Totally. Gratefully. Admiringly. The death of his influence, like the demise of communism, has not only been greatly exaggerated, it's been contrived by venal economic warlords and their media lackeys and lickspittles, who think nothing of disinterring the remains of dead geniuses in order to misinterpret and slander them one more time.

They're going berserk over poor old Karl Marx these days. They froth and fulminate, excoriating as they exhume.

They hate him, hate him! (Where are the anti-Hate Crimes/malicious harassment liberals when we need them?) They cannot tolerate this titan among thinkers because his analysis of society is so true and trenchant—and his solutions (that dreaded S-word) are so logical and inevitable and beautiful.

Yes, Marxism and real communism and the promise of mortal happiness are beautiful goals that even today inspire and animate millions of afflicted, thoughtful workers on all continents—even, quiet as it's kept, in the USA.

**S**o my apparent strangerhood in America is only that—relative isolation in this benighted heartland of world counterrevolution. Someday soon Americans themselves will grab the helm of revolution (it's happened twice before, you know) and they will create "a land that's free for you and me and a Russian lullaby," and we'll all be strangers no more.

Keep the faith. And we'll see which class system, in the long homestretch of history, will bury the other one.

# Lenin & Liberals, Seattle Style

1997

Lenin has come to Seattle, and only his unique brand of slashing, sardonic wit could do justice to his reception here in America's Most Livable City.

Vladimir Ilyich—just call him V.I., folks—traveled to the Pacific Northwest thanks to a local art connoisseur, Lewis Carpenter, who found a superbly crafted statue of the great Soviet leader in an Eastern European junkyard, toppled on its side and bombarded by the elements and the ultrarightists.

In a wondrous impulse, Carpenter had V.I. crated and shipped to the Emerald City, where he ended up in the mildly eccentric, mildly rebellious Fremont district, a playground for hip yuppies, immutable hippies and various freewheelers.

And what did the arrival of this towering figure cause? A sensation? What else. A cascade of letters to the editor vituperated and huffed while TV anchors professed amusement.

Poor Lenin lay in the streets homeless for months until a committee finally formed to raise money for a pedestal on a bustling permanent site, next to a Mexican restaurant and in front of a hemp shop. The artwork now resides there proudly, a thing of grandeur and a thrill for some of us radical types.

Now wouldn't you think that the presence of this magnificent statue would spur a spirited debate about Lenin, Stalin, Trotsky, socialism, the USSR's collapse, and like that?

Forget it. Most liberals insist on viewing this bronze bombshell as pure art, devoid of political meaning.

The local media, predictably, aided and abetted the burial of discussion. One lone, serious editor of a neighborhood weekly honestly recognized his ignorance of Russian history, did some research, and wrote a generally insightful version of Lenin's life. Most newspapers, however, published ten lengthy letters protesting the sculpture to every tiny one written in defense and then abruptly cut short the "dialogue."

I, in contrast, see Lenin's installation as a novel opportunity for the Left to make First Contact (Trek-speak, for the uninitiated) with Fremont residents and sojourners. Whenever my comrades visit the statue to pay respects and peddle literature, people are amazed to find live, homegrown Leninists right here in Latte Land. Still, most prefer not to argue politics—sophisticated Seattle liberals consider disagreements gauche and sparring about Marxism irrelevant and tacky.

It's much more comfy for unconventional Fremont to embrace conventional politics and etiquette than to relax and acknowledge the integral link between art and social circumstances. One cannot and should not view the Seattle Lenin without musing over communism, capitalism, imperialism, nationalism, private profit and social services; it is intellectually unhealthy to resist realizing how profoundly the Soviet implosion and its horrifying aftermath affect us all. But liberals fear the actual world and see only what they want to.

So not only Gingrichites deem "liberal" to be bad; I do too.

All true revolutionaries and reformers deplore liberals. Anyone hell-bent to achieve a civilized society has got to feel utter contempt and disgust and bewilderment at chronic middle-of-the-roaders, especially those with a self-professed leftish tinge.

These fence-sitters are the non-military mercenaries for rich guys, bureaucrats and big shots. Liberals are a civilian army, paid and volunteer, with a mission to stamp out militancy, redbait rebels, butter up officials, reduce powerful programs to pablum, and get out the vote for stinkers—after which they brag sanctimoniously that they're still holding their noses!

They spatter the ranks with spurious reasons for taking the exactly wrong course, for lowering expectations, for replacing principle, truth and logic with expediency and cynicism and greed in the service of the status quo.

**A**nd why do liberals act so ghastly? All in the hope of gaining a possible wee voice in the halls of power or a bid on a cushy government job. Or simply to maintain "popularity" by going along with what, fingers in the wind, they believe to the majority/centrist/moderate/safe position.

In the process, the liberals/shliberals have infested the country with leaders who follow, with labor organizers bedded down with bosses, with movements of the oppressed yoked to the treacherous Democrats, and with sedate candlelight vigils instead of angry marches.

Liberals desperately need to be liberated from their self-imposed chains. Still, we have a few to thank for transporting Lenin's image to the USA. The *symbol* of universal revolt has arrived here from foreign parts to assist us red-white-and-blue reds to keep bringing home the ideas behind the icon—as native here as in Russia, Cuba, South Africa, anywhere.

If we do *that*, then art will once again be understood as springing from the dynamic social soil that nurtures it. And Lenin's likeness will once again inspire awe not only for its artistic form, but for its revolutionary content.

# Fighting Words
# on the Humanity of Marxism

1981

*Co-authored with Guerry Hoddersen*

Thousands of participants in the Black Hills International Survival Gathering last summer heard American Indian Movement leader Russell Means issue a twofold denunciation. In a speech titled "Fighting Words on the Future of the Earth," he denounced corporate America's establishment of "national sacrifice areas" for uranium mining on Indian land. And in the same breath, he blistered Marxism for a single-minded interest in "material gain."

Marxism, he said, is a European doctrine which "despises the American Indian spiritual tradition and culture" and advocates "national sacrifice of our homelands."

"Those who advocate and defend the realities of European culture and its industrialization are my enemies," he said. Capitalists only rape the earth "at the rate at which they can show a profit," but Marxists do it because it's "efficient," and this is due to the European, materialist origins of Marxism.

Said Means, "I do not believe that capitalism is responsible for American Indians having been declared a national sacrifice. No, it is the European tradition. . . Marxism is just the latest continuation of this tradition, not a solution to it."

## Marxism is universal

The charge that Marxists are only interested in "material gain" echoes the capitalist class itself and the anti-naturalist, idealist philosophers who deliberately confuse materialism with greed, insensitivity and disdain for "higher" values.

*Nothing could be further from the truth.*

Marxism, above all, is a creed of humanism, a call for sharing and caring, and a product of love for people, beauty and truth.

Yes, Marxism comes from Europe—and also from classical Greece, and Mideast and Arabic science, and African tribalism.

It reveres the ancient social forms and lifestyle of American Indians (Engels wrote a whole book about it: *The Origin of the Family, Private Property and the State)*. Marxists have never advocated sacrifice of Indian homelands but have always endorsed tribal sovereignty.

Marxists do not rape the earth and do not worship efficiency at the expense of people and nature.

It is not European tradition, whatever that is, but *U.S. capitalism* that commits genocide against Native Americans, Means' apologetics for Wall Street notwithstanding.

And "Indian spiritual tradition" can mean many things to different tribes. Indeed, many Indians are Christians, yet Christianity has nothing in common with the ancient culture. Too much of the original culture has been twisted and degraded and lost in the maelstrom of 400 years of capitalist oppression and the imposition of bourgeois culture. Indians, for example, were once matriarchal; descent was reckoned in the female line. Yet today sexism, and anti-gay bigotry, are often called Indian traditions!

The only universal and absolute feature of tribal culture was economic communism. It was the basis for political democracy; the high status of women, elders and youth; the advanced level of the natural sciences; and the nature-based, *materialist* outlook. *The same features that identify Marxism!*

These bold ideas make Marxism the anathema of the ruling class. It has become the powerful tool of the oppressed in the struggle to overthrow capitalism—first in Europe, where the modern industrial working class first emerged, and later around the globe, in Asia, Africa, and Latin and North America.

## Beloved enemies

Means' wholesale labeling of European thought as "genocidal" is an untrue abstraction.

He seems unaware of the actual history of Europe, with its eventual division into two warring classes. Hence, he misunderstands and distorts the struggle of antagonistic ideas which reflects the class struggle.

Surely, Means must know that it is not industrialization per se, but *privately owned and controlled* technology that destroys the earth, the working class, and indigenous peoples.

And he must know that Marxism is not a "continuation" of "European imperialism" but its sworn antithesis, with a long and honorable record of negating and expropriating the capitalist expropriator.

As for "Marxist imperialism," there is no such thing. Even the Stalinist Soviet bureaucracy is not "imperialist" because it doesn't represent finance capital, permit private investments, inherit wealth, or enrich anyone personally through its foreign or domestic policy. There is no capitalism and no capitalist class in the USSR; "imperialism" is the expansionist policy of *finance capital*, which doesn't exist in the USSR.

Means should not make identities out of differences, and buddies out of mortal enemies. This could spell disaster for AIM.

## Cultural nationalist pitfalls

The great dividing line in capitalist America is not between "spiritual" Indian and "anti-spiritual" European-Marxists, or between Indians and Europeans.

The real battle line lies between capitalists (of all colors) and the oppressed (of all colors).

By adopting the reactionary, cultural-nationalist line that secondary, "porkchop" traditions are more important than class issues, and that everything Indian is good and everything European is bad, Means seriously deflects his struggle away from the corporations and the government, and opens fire instead on his actual and natural allies, the radicals.

By trading-in revolutionary politics for narrow cultural nationalism, Means turns away from the struggle for real national sovereignty. The banks and giant industries have made it abundantly clear that only the total destruction of Indian nations will satisfy their hunger for the wealth on Indian lands. Only Marxists hold to the principle of the Native American right to self-determination—to total autonomy or alliance with other nations, as they so decide.

Only Marxists will fight to defend Indian nationalism and internationalism. Means' ill-tempered speech undermines the very international solidarity so crucial to winning political self-determination for Indian nations.

## What Marxism means

The philosophy of Marxism is called dialectical materialism. It is easy to understand. It is an ideology that knows its enemies and takes sides.

There are two paramount disputes in philosophy.

The first deals with the *nature of reality*. Is it fundamentally material or non-material? Which comes first? Which is causal?

Philosophical materialists say that basic reality is physical and natural. Philosophical idealists say it is supernatural, intangible, religious.

The second dispute is in the field of logic, the laws of thinking: are things static and separate, or are they fluid, changeable and connected?

If you believe in fixed and rigid categories, you belong to

the school of *formal logic.* If you are an evolutionist, your logic is *dialectical.*

Some materialists adhere to the formal school, some to the dialectical. Idealists, similarly, may be mechanical or dialectical.

Marxists are dialectical materialists. Means erroneously thinks they are formal, mechanical materialists.

Means places his own philosophy in the camp of formal idealism. And as we have seen, formal idealism actually contradicts Indian traditional culture, which grew out of a deep reverence for and understanding of the real, natural, ever-changing, material world.

## In the beginning

Why do Marxists call matter basic? Because it was first in time, and is the first cause of all non-material effects. Matter is *prior* to mind; existence *precedes* consciousness. Science, history and life prove this.

Matter-energy is the stuff out of which all else grows, determining in the final analysis how human beings think, feel, relate, produce, marry, create art, and so on. Marxism never dismisses the human spirit, but does place mind-feelings-ideas in their physical and historical context as effects, not as basic causes. Yes, ideas and feelings can change the world, but people must still have bodies before their minds and emotions can function.

## Matter in motion

Means decries materialists who "despiritualized the universe" and saw nature in a "mechanical mode." But Marx broke sharply from the vulgar, pre-dialectical materialists who saw nature as a giant piece of machinery.

Marx and Engels' genius was to infuse materialism with the laws of development and the dynamic of contradictions which had been so brilliantly grasped by the early Greeks and

Hegel.

Matter itself can neither be created nor destroyed, but all matter—in nature, society and the human mind—changes constantly through tension and contradiction. All things are interdependent and in a continual process of coming into being, changing and passing away.

The capitalist system itself was born, matured and will die, because of its inherently contradictory nature—*social* production (by large groups of workers assembled in one plant) on the one hand, and *private*, capitalist ownership and appropriation of profit on the other.

Means, unfortunately, pretends to see no difference between capitalism and socialism. But the two irreconcilable systems spell the difference between life and death for his people.

## Historical materialism

The application of the materialist dialectic to *history* is called historical materialism—a revolutionary science of society. It is the sociology of institutional changes caused by the interplay and conflict between the developing productive forces and the kind of world created by this technology.

Historical materialism teaches that all social life is evolutionary and revolutionary, and that human beings can learn to understand nature, production and social relations, and change them in a rational manner.

The kind of economy we live in determines the nature and level of our laws, government, culture, ideas, feelings and ethics. The competitive, jungle warfare system of capitalist production produces a destructive, anti-human science and culture. The traditional culture of Native Americans, on the other hand, came from a system of tribal communism, and is therefore infused with equality, fraternity and liberty.

Marxism is the only modern philosophy to espouse the re-creation of the pre-class and pro-human Indian world on a contemporary level of advanced science, technology and knowledge achieved by later societies.

Historical materialism promotes the synthesis of ecological balance, social harmony, personal freedom and material comfort that is the human birthright.

## The real future of the earth

The only alternative to socialist revolution that Means offers is a bleak defeatism. "I don't care if it's only a handful living high in the Andes," he announces, "American Indian people will survive [a nuclear war]. . .that's revolution."

To passively accept the inevitability of imperialist holocaust is not revolution. And nothing can be more ethnocentric or impossible than the goal of self-survival on a ruined planet.

This is defeatism, the grandiosity of despair. It is mystical pie-in-the-sky for the saved or the chosen. It is nationalism turned to acid.

But scarcity and privation need not be the Indian future. There is a better way for suffering humanity—to go forward together to reestablish the democratic collective ownership of the means of producing life's necessities.

Russell Means is not ready for this. The warrior is weary and scornful—even of his own leadership. So he bitterly lashes out at Marxists and Europeans as conventional scapegoats for his problems. Blinded by all-too-commonplace prejudices, and mistaken in his theoretical and historical analysis, he reaches a philosophical, political and spiritual blind alley.

But fresh and unsoured Indian militants, male and female, will not be hampered by retreat into a bunker mentality. They will embrace an alliance with their revolutionary comrades across racial and national lines. Means' isolationism is suicidal, but the great Indian nations, as always, will seek to live and flourish along with liberated humanity as a whole.

# How Marxists Think

Lectures from a class taught in Winter 1955-56

To many people, Marxism is a call for violent action by Crazy People. The ruling class would have it so; they claim for themselves the mantle of progress, logic, truth, beauty, and knowledge. They represent Marxists as deluded, irrational, psychotic, and hateful.

But just look at these elevated critics of Marxism: the atom-maniacs in the Pentagon; the perverted and distorted finance capitalists who would see a world plunged into barbarism before they relinquish a penny of their fabulous profits; the power-mad industrialists who calmly grind the working class to dust beneath the wheels of automation; the southern white aristocracy and their stooges in the KKK who would have every magnolia tree swaying with the strange black fruit of human bodies; the professors of knowledge who devote their lives to keeping knowledge off the campus and away from students. Are these people sane? Wise? Right? Beneficent? *Reasonable?*

Today we're going to talk about reason. Only we Marxists really take reason seriously. We are infinitely more rational than our class antagonists, because we are honest scientists, practitioners in the laboratory of society.

Science is the investigation of the motion and behavior of matter. Scientific socialism is the knowledge of the movements and behavior of *human* matter, a *social* substance.

And the basis of our science is our philosophy.

Philosophy means "first principles"—the basic laws of the world from which everything else springs. The two most important fields of philosophy are logic and ontology. Logic is *how* we think about reality; the science of the thought process. Ontology is *what* we think about reality; the study of the nature of existence.

Marxism is first and foremost a philosophy based on the highest form of logic known to humanity. Its adherents maintain more than anybody else the main principle of science: that reality and the laws governing it can be known; that we can always come closer to a complete understanding of nature, society, human thought. Indeed, Marxists are the *only* true philosophers on this earth!

You don't believe me?

Read today's philosophers. They're a joke, a headache. They've got nothing to say or are too scared to say it. The best of them see their own futility and uselessness, and say so.

Pragmatists such as John Dewey and Edmund Wilson boast about their philosophy of no philosophy, their contempt for first principles and basic questions. They're *engineers*; they make things. If the things or ideas work out right away, they're good. If they don't catch on, they're bad.

Or take the Existentialists. Upon discovering there is no God and that life is absurd and meaningless, they sent out the directive to commit suicide. After World War II, utterly despairing but lacking the guts to kill themselves, they advised, "Find the strength to live a useless life."

Bourgeois philosophy, like bourgeois economics, is dead. Marx brought world thought to a climax; afterward, bourgeois philosophy had no place to go. To understand the sources of Marxism, let's briefly trace the history of philosophy.

## The Greeks—source of Western philosophy

*Formal logic* was the crowning accomplishment of the

Greek thinkers. Aristotle, who analyzed, classified, and systematized logic, contributed the three laws of formal logic:

1. "A" equals A: the law of identity. A thing is always equal to itself.

2. "A" cannot be non-A: the law of contradiction.

3. "A" cannot be both A and non-A: the law of the excluded middle.

This manner of thinking is valid and necessary, but at the same time incomplete and limited. It is "common sense" logic—instinctive, half-conscious. Its laws are the rules of thought in the bourgeois world. They do have a material content and reflect real relations in life, but they apply only if we assume fixity—*unchanging* relations.

In *The Logic of Marxism*, George Novack identifies five basic errors in formal logic:

1. It demands a static universe. Nothing moves and develops, because motion implies self-contradiction, which formal logic cannot accommodate. Does a dollar always equal a dollar? Hardly.

2. Formal logic erects impassable barriers between things. But in reality, everything grows out of and into other things: paper into money and money into paper again; rivers into seas and seas into clouds; bacteria into animals and animals into humans.

3. Formal logic excludes difference from identity. But the working class, for example, is heterogeneous and contradictory. A worker is not a boss, but can think and act like one.

4. The laws of formal logic present themselves and the reality they describe as *absolute*, final, unconditional, eternal. But everything is really *relative*, inter-dependent. History is made up of unique, concrete, finite, related and ever-shifting circumstances.

5. Finally, formal logic can't explain *itself*: its origin, causes for being, development. Absent any other explanation, it can only be attributed to divine revelation.

### Hegel's dialectics in the Age of Revolution

The absolutism and petrification of the Middle Ages eventually produced a crisis in feudal society that brought about revolutions on all planes. The world turned upside down.

History was demanding a new method of thought to make sense of the titanic explosions detonating all stable, ancient, and honored institutions and relations. "A's" were becoming "non-A's" all over the place—feudalism was becoming capitalism, the king was being replaced by commoners, atheism was challenging God. Logic had to follow course and become more scientific, useful to humankind, reflective of the *motion* that dominated life. The inevitable reformation in logic was capped by the heroic and profound discoveries of the genius Georg Hegel (1770 - 1831).

The revolutionary thought of Hegel was the product of the French Revolution of 1789, which inspired groundbreaking ideas in politics and the arts. Hegel and other German intellectuals rebelled against the mechanical, immobile outlook dominant in science. Their theme: Everything has a history of development; nothing is absolute.

To formal logic, Hegel counterposed *dialectics*.

Dialectics holds that life is made up of concrete, changing, contradictory circumstances, and so the formulas that describe and explain life must be provisional, limited, transient.

Dialectics begins with what is real—everything that has provable existence—and says that what is real is *rational*, meaning that it is based on laws: inexorable, objective processes that can be known. These laws of reality are based on *necessity*. There is a *reason* for every phenomenon, no matter how "irrational" it may appear on the surface.

If we conclude that reality, rationality and necessity go hand in hand, then everything that exists is *justified*. Reactionaries embrace only this side of Hegel's thought. But Hegel is also revolutionary because he shows negation as well as justification: everything that exists eventually turns into its opposite and dies. And then comes a negation of the negation—a new positive. Feudalism becomes capitalism becomes socialism. Childhood develops into youth, maturity, age.

All phenomena are composed of both essence and form, and as they pass out of existence, their forms can linger long after their essences are gone. Think of a wrecked house, a lame-duck political regime, a corpse.

Hegel teaches that life is change, movement, development through contradictions. He stresses the *identity, unity and interpenetration of opposites*—like that of the working class and capitalist class, which can only exist together, though each is death to the other.

## The materialist challenge to Hegel

Hegel had his limits. He was an *idealist*, who saw thought or spirit as primary, as cause, and matter as secondary, as effect. The mind came first and created nature and society; the objective world was only a reflection, as in a mirror, of the "Absolute Idea," the fundamental reality.

He was wrong, and he was challenged. The Young Hegelians revolted against Hegel's god, returning not only to atheism, but to *materialist* atheism. In the final analysis, they said, everything has a material base or cause. There is no mind without a body; no ideas without brain cells. All ideas grow from relations of people in society, and relations of people grow from their relation with nature. So reality starts with nature—the unconscious, material universe.

Ludwig Feuerbach was the first Hegelian rebel to proclaim materialism as the only rational and scientifically demonstrable explanation of the world. He ascertained that humanity has no *innate* ideas, morals, goals. We are not cogs in a machine built by some Absolute Spirit. We are conditioned by society; environment is decisive in determining our character, personality, abilities.

But Feuerbach, too, had his limitations. He threw out dialectics along with idealism, and he was *incompletely* materialist. Like the previous Enlightenment materialists, he couldn't extend his environment thesis to *history*. What causes the social changes that transform peoples' ideas? Feuerbach believed that the motive force of society is "human nature," which lands us right back where we started from, mired in idealism.

Other breakthrough thinkers of the 18th and 19th centuries explored *property relations* as the foundation of the social environment. But what then determines property relations? Well, they said, human nature.

Utopian socialists like Charles Fourier and Robert Owen got a few steps further. They asserted that the source of property relations is found in the needs of developing production.

What you produce and how you produce it, they held, is the basis of your relation to property; what you're going to own, if anything, depends on what kind of a class set-up is demanded by the *mode of production*.

They went even further. They realized that *tools determine the growth of production*. The needs of production progress in concert with the development of new tools. But here they got stuck. What's the source of tools? They could find no material answer. Since tools are invented by human beings, they once again returned to human nature and endeavored to construct ideal societies based on romantic illusions about people's altruism.

## Marx and Engels resolve the impasse

Enter Marx and Engels. Look at the job they had before them! Young radicals, fresh out of German universities and the political struggles against the monarchy, they were feverishly studying classical German philosophy, Hegel's dialectics, Feuerbach's materialism, utopian socialism, and English political economy (the science of the production and distribution of wealth). They had before them the gigantic historical task of taking the truest kernels of all previous thought and synthesizing them into a systematic whole.

Marx's encounter with a group of workers in the League of the Just, proved crucial to achieving this synthesis. Marx was convinced of the *desirability* of socialism, but his scientific training made him ask: "Is socialism *necessary? realistic? inevitable?* Are its seeds in the present system? If so, where?" And here, before his eyes, were a handful of artisans who showed him the embryo of the tremendous social power that lay in the hands of the *organized proletariat.* The working class was growing rapidly, as were the ideas of scientific socialism; here the twain met, *the reality and the idea, the means and the end, the oppressed and the science of their liberation.*

Friedrich Engels, meanwhile, was a rich young businessman. But he was also a radical, writer, and contributor to Marx's paper. A student of English industry and political economy, he concluded that *economics* are the decisive historical force, the basis of the development of classes and the political parties representing these classes.

Reading each other's articles, Marx and Engels were thrilled to recognize in each other a kindred methodology. They entered into a lifelong collaboration.

In 1845, they authored *The Holy Family.* They contended that history is born, not in heaven, but on earth through mass interests finding expression. Socialism is the manifestation of the needs of the working class and its individual members.

The new philosophy of Marx and Engels took Hegel's dialectics, freed it from his idealism, and re-fused it with its actual, logical counterpart, materialism. They understood that the laws of motion described by Hegel, whose origin he explained by reference to the Absolute Idea, are in fact *inherent in matter itself.*

Applied to *social* development, their conclusions make up the theory of historical materialism.

This doctrine states that social structure, or the organization of classes, flows from the methods of production; that the motor force of history is class struggle between rulers and the ruled; and that these struggles have now reached a pinnacle where the exploited class, the proletariat, can't free itself from the bourgeoisie without simultaneously freeing all society from oppression forever.

In 1859, in the preface to his *Critique of Political Economy*, Marx elaborates: ". . .Legal relations [and] political forms. . .originate in the material conditions of life, the totality of which Hegel. . .embraces within the term 'civil society'; the anatomy of civil society, however, has to be sought in political economy."

And on what does political economy itself depend, if not human nature?

Marx said that human nature is an effect, caused by history; history, in turn, is caused ultimately by external nature, which supplies humankind with its means of existence. Humans must act in relation to nature. *But by acting on external nature, human beings change their own nature.* In fact, *Homo sapiens* became human precisely by acting on nature— as a tool-maker.

Tool-making is the distinctive human feature. An elephant uses a branch to sweep away flies, but this is a non-essential characteristic; elephants will be elephants whether or not they employ branches. But the boomerang of the early hunter is definitive—remove it, make him a farmer, and his nature will change.

Ancient tool-making did not result from humankind's high intelligence. Quite the contrary. Tools created the superior intellect of humans. The development of regular tool use was an accident attributable to the capabilities inherent to the unique human hand, an organ which Darwin thought probably evolved to adapt to special features in the physical environment that demanded a physiological division of labor between front and rear limbs.

Humankind continues to change as its use of tools advances. This change is *social*, because humans are social animals. Nuclear weapons affect the organization of the army, for instance. General technological leaps forward, like the Industrial Revolution, affect the whole of economic and cultural life. Ancient society, feudal society, bourgeois society—each denotes a stage of development of the forces of production.

So the determinant of political economy, including the mutual relations of people in production, is technology—the level and kind of tools used in the struggle for existence. The relations of production are expressed in laws. Social *being* therefore determines social *consciousness*. Materialism has been applied to history and history becomes illuminated.

The needs imposed upon people by nature include not only production, but also reproduction. Family structure and sexual habits, too, are an effect of the growth of productive forces. Today's patriarchal, atomized bourgeois family developed over time as the result of the historic change-over from female to male systems of kinship that accompanied the rise of private property.

In the sphere of reproduction as in the sphere of production, individual relations are determined fundamentally by the nature of the existing social system, which corresponds to the prevailing level and type of technology.

## Consciousness of necessity: the dawn of freedom

Materialist dialectics came from Hegel's idealist dialectics like astronomy from astrology and chemistry from alchemy—as its opposite, as the revolutionary negation of Hegel. Marx and Engels exposed the limits of both Hegel and Feuerbach, while explaining their historical necessity and synthesizing the valid ideas of both. The previously warring conceptions were merged into a unity on a higher level. Such is the real dialectical derivation of dialectical materialism itself.

Before Marx and Engels, logic played an insignificant part in history. Society did not develop self-consciously through thought, but through the influence of blind social and natural forces.

Our anthropoid predecessors were slaves of the physical world and its laws. People progressively triumphed over natural necessity, but as our social environment developed, with its own set of laws, humanity became enthralled to *economic* necessity. *Humankind's own unconscious creation, the social order, now dominates and crushes us.* But when we realize this, we establish the basis for the victory of reason over blind law, of consciousness over necessity. *Free humanity makes necessity the slave of reason.* We become the gods.

But we must still get with necessity, act with it, help it along.

When existing productive relations become fetters on the productive forces, when the quality of the tools has outgrown the old organization of production, when automation as it is wielded under the profit system brutally makes millions of workers jobless and unproductive—then social revolution becomes a necessity. In our time, that means capitalism demands to be replaced by socialism.

Under socialism, *logic* will become a great and dynamic power in shaping society and people, opening up limitless perspectives for the future of human thought through the use of the materialist dialectic.

The Marxist philosophy of matter in motion is the most powerful key in existence. It will unlock doors that have been locked to humanity throughout the whole course of our existence and enable us as a social species to consciously transform not just the external world, but, for the first time, ourselves.

# Suppressed Facts Behind the Khrushchev Revelations

1956

Speech to the Seattle branch of the Socialist Workers Party

C omrade Chairman and Comrades:
Sixteen years ago last Tuesday, in a quiet, book-lined study near Mexico City, a great man was sitting at his desk, writing and talking to a supposed friend, helping him with an article. He had known this man, the new husband of one of his faithful secretaries, for many months.

Suddenly, the younger man pulled an ice-axe out from under his coat and plunged it into the brain of the man at the desk. The older man toppled over in a pool of blood as his guards and secretaries rushed into the office and grabbed the assassin.

One of the guards, a young man by the name of Joseph Hansen, overcome with rage and sorrow, began to choke the murderer. But the dying man came to consciousness and said, clearly, "Don't kill him, Joe. Let him live to tell the truth; let him live to expose Stalin."

A few hours later the great man died. The titanic figure of Leon Trotsky, world revolutionary, uncompromising fighter for Marxism and Leninism, fearless opponent of all betrayers of the working class, a harried, persecuted and slandered exile—Leon Trotsky was no more.

World Stalinism rejoiced. The monster in the Kremlin, the most sinister figure in all mankind, rejoiced. And they hoped, and stated, that *Trotskyism* would be no more, because, you see, it was only a personality cult.

That was 16 years ago. Three years ago, another man died: Joseph Stalin, the instigator of Trotsky's murder. Stalin was absolute head of an absolute state machine that governed one-fifth of the world's peoples. He was also the absolute head of scores of Communist Parties around the world whose membership and supporters numbered millions of people. He was the most powerful individual in the entire world. He was never loved, but he was respected, worshipped, admired, adored, and idolized by the Communist workers and peasants whose parties he dominated. He had every reason to expect that his niche in history and in the minds and hearts of men was firmly secured; he was a God even before he died, and how much higher can anyone climb?

Yet only three years later, the legend of the man who was God lies smashed and shattered, dissolved into countless ugly fragments by the power of the realized ideas and principles represented by Trotsky. For it was the force of world revolution that produced the Khrushchev speech and that disposed of the Stalin myth once and for all.

As Trotsky tirelessly explained over the years, it was the ebb-tide of world revolution that created Stalinism and it would be the upsurge and inevitable renewal of world revolution that would sweep it aside. Stalinism rose on defeats, produced defeats, and would in its turn be defeated only by workingclass victory, by the upsurge of the masses.

So Trotskyism emerges doubly vindicated: First, as the only analysis that correctly characterized and described the terrible bureaucratic degeneration of the Soviet state, that revealed the origin of the bureaucracy and forecast its doom at the hands of the Russian masses. And second, as the ideological expression of world rebellion and revolt—a basic reality today.

The Russian proletariat is now 50 million strong, powerful, and armed with the ideas of Lenin which couldn't be completely withheld from them. But the force that gave them the impetus to move, to make demands upon the bureaucracy, to assert themselves collectively was the tremendous confidence given them by the magnificent revolution in China, the friendly workers states in Eastern Europe, the volcanic revolts of the colonial masses. From being an isolated workers state encircled by imperialism, they are now surrounded by allies and supporters, and world imperialism is on the defensive.

For 30 years Trotsky counseled the Russian working class and collective farmers to overthrow the bureaucracy. He firmly insisted that they would; that they must; that life would help them do it. Today, they are in the process of doing exactly that, and what more overwhelming triumph can there be for Trotskyism, for Bolshevism?

Trotskyism, revolutionary socialism, lives and thrives today in the aims and aspirations of the Russian working class, the mighty colonial masses, the European proletariat and the vanguard of class-conscious American workers. In every country where oppressed human beings rise against their exploiters and tread the road toward socialism, there Trotskyism lives and Stalinism, the theory of socialism in only one country, dies.

## Exhuming the truth

Frank Jacson, Trotsky's assassin, never did get around to revealing the truth, though the facts about his life as a Stalinist have been unearthed by others. Today, however, an equally sinister henchman and co-criminal of Stalin's, Communist Party First Secretary Nikita Khrushchev, has come forward with part of the truth, because the new stage of the Russian Revolution has forced him to.

Khrushchev's speech was truly a remarkable one, both for what it said and what it ignored; what it revealed, what it suppressed, and what it confused. The speech is stunning in its revelations and shattering in its implications. It is little wonder that the ranks of honest Communist Party members and sympathizers the world over are shocked, bewildered, angry, demoralized, or numb. And, though this may sound strange to some of you, we Trotskyists understand and sympathize with their reactions.

We understand only too well the confusion and stupefaction of sincere communists when they confront the hard fact that in the supposedly glorious land of socialism, the most brutal dictatorship of all time held sway. We understand how easy it is to throw up one's hands in disillusionment and disgust and say: Marx and Lenin were wrong, they never foresaw this, socialism is a delusion, the capitalists were right about the Soviet Union being a prison camp for the masses, the victorious Bolshevik revolution produced only torture chambers and dungeons for the proletariat.

We understand these reactions because we have been fighting against them, *as one-sided*, for 30 years. Only orthodox Trotskyists have consistently defended the progressive, workingclass foundations of the Soviet Union at the same time that we struggled against the corrupt, nationalist bureaucracy. Trotskyism proved that the fight for socialism is the fight *against* Stalinism and that Stalinism represents not the product and heir of Bolshevism but its betrayer and antithesis. Revolution no more produces Stalinism than unionism inevitably produces Dave Beckism. Under certain historical circumstances, however, these reversions do occur and it is our job to understand them and thus prevent them.

Stalinism is the anti-Leninist politics of the bureaucracy in Russia. The bureaucracy is a huge upper crust of millions of officials, administrators, and specialists, who live like emperors while the masses slave six days a week, live in crowded and tiny apartments, and barely earn enough for food and clothing if they can find them. This bureaucracy was the social base of the Stalinist faction in the Communist Party which finally crushed the Bolshevik faction and inaugurated a stifling dictatorship over the entire country. The Stalinist ideology justifies the bureaucracy's rule over the working class.

Only within the framework of this materialist explanation of social relations in the Soviet Union can Khrushchev's speech be understood for what it is and for what it isn't. Only Trotsky's analysis of the origin and development of the bureaucracy explains why Khrushchev left out so much. Let us review that analysis and examine Khrushchev's speech in the light of it.

## Patterns of deception

1. *The Truth:* Lenin and Trotsky together fought Stalin as the representative of a reactionary and potentially fatal ideology that was a product of Russian backwardness and hostile capitalist encirclement.

*Khrushchev:* Stresses that Stalin was too powerful as an individual and treated Lenin cavalierly. He omits Lenin's bloc with Trotsky and the existence of a growing bureaucracy. He lies in saying that Lenin's will, which repudiated Stalin, was made known to and rejected by the party, when in fact the bureaucracy suppressed it. He acknowledges Stalin's obscurity, but says untruthfully that Stalin played a great role in the revolution and civil war.

*The Pattern:* Khrushchev attempts to make Stalin a Leninist and describes Lenin's fight against him as personal and secondary. The existence of the bureaucracy and Trotsky's bloc with Lenin are hidden.

2. *The Truth:* After Lenin's death, Stalin and the bureaucracy used terror to crush the broadly supported Leninist wing of the party, the Left Opposition led by Trotsky.

*Khrushchev:* Admits mass repression of "honest, non-Trotskyist communists." (Why? Stalin's neurosis.) But he says there were no repressive measures against the Trotskyists who were "politically isolated through patient ideological explanations." He insistently calls Trotsky and others "enemies of Leninism," but gives no reasons why. He lies about the Left Opposition's program of party and government democracy, industrialization, and collectivization of agriculture, taking special pains not to mention that the bureaucracy eventually adopted the Opposition's economic platform, though their implementation was bureaucratically distorted and steeped in terror.

*The Pattern:* "Stalin is a Leninist. Trotsky was an anti-Leninist, but no political threat. No bureaucracy exists."

3. *The Truth:* By the late '20s, the Trotskyists had been smashed as an internal force. However, they continued to fight outside the USSR where their success in leading strikes and revolutions and in exposing Stalin's betrayals posed a political danger to the hegemony of the bureaucracy. In 1933, in the most criminal betrayal of all history, the Stalinists surrendered the German working class to Hitler without a fight. Trotsky declared the Third International dead as a revolutionary force and called for formation of the Fourth International. Meanwhile, opposition kept surfacing in the USSR because the people were being robbed of progress and liberty—gainsaying the claim that socialism had been established. To isolate the Trotskyists in every country and to quell internal unrest, Stalin launched the 1936-38 Moscow Trials. The trials were an abomination, an attack, not on enemies of the people, but on the people themselves by their enemy Stalin.

*Khrushchev:* He confirms that in 1934 the terror was accelerated to pave the way for the Moscow Trials: out of 139 Central Committee members elected at the 17th Congress, 70% were shot; out of 1,966 delegates to the congress, 1,108 were arrested and imprisoned. He concedes that the trials were unnecessary because Trotskyism was already defeated internally and the Trotskyists were not terrorists. He admits that the trials were frame-ups, where the only evidence was from confessions extracted by torture. He grants that the trials were contradictory to claims that socialism had been achieved.

But since socialism did indeed hold sway, the frame-ups were just an anomaly. He confirms the mass repression in 1937 in which entire peoples were deported—*for no reason!!* These fictitious anti-Soviet centers and nefarious plots were invented to make it seem that the trials had a legitimate cause.

*The Pattern:* "The terror was all a terrible mistake, since socialism was secure and there were no enemies of the people."

4. *The Truth:* The continuing oppression reflected the desperation of a regime in constant crisis, hated and unnecessary, clinging to its special interests, compelled to destroy all opposition and all potential opposition. As Trotsky observed in *The Revolution Betrayed*, written in 1936, Stalin felt persecuted because he was—ruthless terror inevitably breeds terrorism and plots. The economy and culture were advancing, giving the people confidence to resist the bureaucracy. Trotsky warned of the danger that would result from Stalin's purge of the army and sounded the alarm over the imminence of fascist attack. He attributed the Stalin cult to the bureaucracy's need for an all-wise, infallible Emperor to justify the terror that preserves their positions.

*Khrushchev:* He says the personality cult "just developed" because Stalin was vain instead of modest. He claims there was no collective leadership in place between 1935-48 because there were no party congresses. This is a lie. The bureaucracy collectively led and approved and needed the cult: it was the price of their privileges. Khrushchev discloses that the army was beheaded and that Stalin ignored repeated warnings of fascist attack. He describes Stalin's fear and cowardice, stupefaction and despair in the wake of terrible military defeats due to lack of arms and stupid and vicious tactical decisions. He shows Stalin to be a reactionary Utopian *psychologically.*

*The Pattern:* Khrushchev won't reveal that Stalin's reactionary Utopianism was expressed *politically* in peaceful co-existence with imperialism, the theory of socialism in one country, and asinine trust in pacts with fascists. Stalinist class-collaboration, the politics of the bureaucracy, is what brought the Soviet Union to the brink of collapse in World War II, to be saved only by the people fighting for their nationalized property forms—*not* for Stalin.

5. *The Truth:* The Soviet victory against Nazi Germany was a miracle of heroism by the Russian people despite unconscionable Stalinist betrayal. But while they were fighting for collectivism against capitalism, what were the Communist Parties of the West forced to do? To aid the capitalists against the militants in the working class! Stalin decreed a big patriotic whoop-de-doo, support for anti-strike pledges, and suppression of the Negro struggle. In turn, Roosevelt understood and treasured Stalinism and rewarded it: Trotsky's biography was suppressed; Hollywood glamorized the bureaucracy in *Mission to Moscow*; the Trotskyist-led teamsters union in Minnesota was smashed; and Socialist Workers Party leaders were convicted of subversion in the Smith Act trials.

*Khrushchev:* Commends the people for winning the war and confirms Stalin was an obstacle. But makes no mention of Stalin's international policies, which sucked the masses into support of the American imperialist colossus. Khrushchev never mentions Stalin's post-war sell-out pacts with the imperialists to contain world revolution. He says Stalin's maniacal egotism is what caused the rift with Yugoslavia, rather than political opposition to Yugoslavia's independent road to socialism.

*The Pattern:* Khrushchev wants us to believe that Stalin the man was going mad, but that Stalinist politics are evidently good since they are never mentioned.

In fact, it is Stalinist politics that are mad. The bureaucrats are jettisoning the man but they are desperately clinging to the only kind of politics that can maintain them.

6. *Khrushchev:* Pleads ignorance, helplessness and fear as the reasons for the collective leadership's lack of intervention against Stalin's plots. Moreover, he claims the people were hypnotized and blindly supported Stalin. Since Stalin died, however, the collective leadership has been a model of democratic and loving and tolerant stewardship. And poor Stalin believed all his crimes to have been done in the best interests of the USSR: "in this lies the whole tragedy."

*The Truth:* If the people were hypnotized, bloody repression would not have been necessary. The bureaucrats never intervened because they were hand-picked henchmen of Stalin who owed their careers and privileges and country estates to him and his regime. They knew full well what was going on. And this benevolent collective leadership has already produced tanks and corpses in East Germany; broken strikes in Poznan, Hungary; purged half the parties of Eastern Europe; continued the flagrant persecution of Jews and other minorities; and only grudgingly granted concessions on living standards, working conditions and political liberties.

There is nothing tragic about a traitor being treacherous; the only tragedy lies in the fact that so many millions of honest socialists believed the lies about Stalin by Stalin.

## The balance sheet

Let's add up the plusses and minuses of the Khrushchev speech and summarize the main pattern and purpose of his speech.

The force of the new stage of the Russian Revolution—started by the revolts in Vorkuta and other Soviet labor camps, the 1953 workers uprising in East Germany, and the mass strikes and protests in Poznan this year—has pushed Khrushchev into a terrific new concession, following the previous concessions on more and better food, more and better services, longer maternity leave, legalization of abortions, a shorter work week, higher wages, etc. To save themselves, the bureaucracy must sharply disassociate themselves from the hated tyrant Stalin. They must prove that the huge chamber of horrors was his fault alone, and that they are and will be men of a different stripe.

They seek to prove that Stalin's interests were not theirs, that they do not represent a huge parasite caste that benefited from the Stalin cult. By deliberately smashing the monster they themselves created, they hope to escape all responsibility for him.

But in replacing the hero cult with a Super-Villain cult, they expose themselves fatally. Because they can't explain why the cult arose. Or why it lasted so long. Or who it rested on.

These answers would indict all of them as a grouping alien to Marxism, born of reaction, representing the ideas of a minority caste seeking bourgeois privileges against the interests of the working class. They can't explain the why's because they would thereby confirm Trotskyism.

They can't explain the relation of Stalin's world politics to his tyranny. Because their fate rests on these same counterrevolutionary politics of class collaboration and betrayal and wholesale murder of revolutionaries. To show how Stalinism denies political reality would be Trotskyism. To show how tyranny within led to the strangulation of the Communist Parties without, replacing genuine revolutionary leaders with obedient fools, would confirm Trotskyism. To show how Stalin played with revolutions as he played with his armies, sacrificing them in his diplomatic maneuvers with imperialism, would prove the validity of Trotskyism.

So they must continue to state like idiots that the Stalin cult existed in Russia alone, and was caused by Stalin alone, and nobody else and nothing else is involved. There was no social reason, no material basis, no political results and no ideological effects. They must expose their own existence in a dream world.

Khrushchev must repeat like a parrot that Stalin played a

progressive role in the '20s, "building socialism." For if he confesses that Stalin was nothing but a terrible obstacle to socialism from the beginning, he admits that Trotsky was right. So he repeats the slanders about Trotsky, and it is on these vicious lies about Trotskyism that his whole case rests!

He cannot disclose that there *were* leaders who intervened against Stalin's policies, because they were the leaders of the Left Opposition whom Khrushchev and Co. helped murder. Every time he develops his case against Stalin, he runs smack up against the ideas of Trotskyism, and retreats in terror. This leads anybody willing to analyze the situation (in the calm and objective fashion that Khrushchev says can now be employed) to the conclusion that the present regime is merely Stalinism sans Stalin, a "bad regime of dishonest men."

He lies and ignores the first ten years, when Stalin led a political counter-revolution against the heritage of Bolshevism. He can't show how the bureaucratic waste, mismanagement, corruption and ignorance was as much an obstacle to building socialism as it was to defending the country against Hitler. Though he grants that the people won the war, he cannot admit they also are responsible for the industrial achievements and economic progress and "building socialism." Because if the people did this all by themselves, they not only don't need Stalin, they don't need the oligarchy. Khrushchev knows this, but he's damned if he's going to say it. He's not crazy!

He tells just enough to condemn Stalin explicitly, but himself only implicitly for his failure to condemn Stalinism, the internal and international class betrayal politics of the bureaucracy. He won't, because his own privileges are bound up with Stalinism.

All his other policies push the Stalinist program hard: peaceful transition and class peace, which, translated into Americanese, mean capitalist prosperity, Democratic Party control of the working class and Negro people, and Reutherite hegemony over the labor unions.

As long as the national Communist Parties are on this kind of insane line, Khrushchev is in. As long as these policies are approved by the Russian workers, Khrushchev is in. So he must prolong the frame-up of Trotsky and keep his ideas from the Russian masses, for they are Khrushchev's nemesis.

## Forward to Permanent Revolution!

The Khrushchev speech suppressed more facts than it revealed, and only the masses will finally force the whole story out of the bag, and reveal the true depths and fantastic heights of this *most gigantic hoax and frame-up in all history*.

Now that the first death blow has been dealt to Stalinism as a social phenomenon, the only way to help ease it completely off the map and at the same time to promote the socialist future, is the Trotskyist way of class struggle against Wall Street and against the agents of Wall Street in the Kremlin. For the only way real socialism can be obtained is to resist Stalinist degeneration and overthrow capitalism in its main industrial centers so that productivity can reach truly socialist heights. And conversely, the only way to fight this parasitic growth of Stalinism on the workingclass movements is to impel forward the class struggle and socialist consciousness.

Back to Lenin, is our slogan; back to Lenin up and down the line. And that means Trotskyism, international socialism, and the end of the bureaucracy.

# Women: Motor Force of Soviet Survival

1990

International Women's Day Speech, UCLA, Los Angeles, California

I t was the energy of women, the upheaval amongst women, the uninterrupted revolutionary audacity and intensity of women that caused, that impelled, that motored the new Russian and Eastern European revolution.

It was women who were the sparkplugs that created Glasnost—the movement for political openness—and Perestroika—the loosening of bureaucratic economic controls. It is women who are the active agents of all these changes. The revolution is the effect and the form of a *womanly essence.*

Let's put that in our samovar tonight and brew it!

What is the story of Soviet women? It's a horror tale—a scary saga of successive defeat and prolonged subjugation under Stalin in a degenerated workers' state. And the horror exists to this day.

But it didn't start out that way.

After the 1917 revolution in Russia, the new status of women was a beautiful and a noble and a vastly progressive phenomena. The early Soviet Union granted women more rights, more respect, more appreciation, more access to all forms of economic and political and cultural work than any other government in history. The Soviet constitution is a marvel to this day.

This is what Trotsky had to say about the status of women in the USSR in his 1937 book, *The Revolution Betrayed:*

The revolution made a heroic effort to destroy the so-called "family hearth"—that archaic, stuffy and stagnant institution in which the woman of the toiling classes performs galley labor from childhood to death.

The place of the family as a shut-in petty enterprise was to be occupied, according to the plans, by a finished system of social care and accommodation: maternity houses, crèches, kindergartens, schools, social dining rooms, social laundries, first-aid stations, hospitals, sanitoria, athletic organizations, moving-picture theaters, etc. The complete absorption of the housekeeping functions of the family by institutions of the socialist society, uniting all generations in solidarity and mutual aid, was to bring to woman, and thereby to the loving couple, a real liberation from the thousand-year-old fetters. Up to now this problem of problems has not been solved. The forty million Soviet families remain in their overwhelming majority nests of medievalism, female slavery. . .daily humiliation of children, feminine and childish superstition.

(He must be talking about adherence to the church.)

We must permit ourselves no illusions on this account. For that very reason, the consecutive changes in the approach to the problem of the family in the Soviet Union best of all characterize the actual nature of Soviet society and the evolution of its ruling strata.

## Revolution and counter-revolution in the family

At the beginning, in 1917, abortion was legalized, divorce was legalized, contraception was legalized, homosexuality was legalized. I'm talking 1917, in backward Mother Russia! The concept of illegitimacy was liquidated—the first country in the world to do that.

Prostitution was decriminalized, but only for the women. The pimps and brothel-owners were rounded up. How do you like that! The principle was to punish prostitution, but not the prostitute. The prostitute was the victim, the product of reactionary, bourgeois society and she was offered rehabilitation and training.

Women's organizations were fostered by the Communist Party and subsidized by the government. Their function was to promote and educate about women's rights throughout the enormous length and breadth of the USSR—especially reaching out to women in the Far Eastern, Asiatic cultures where women still wore the *chador*—the black veil.

Lenin, Trotsky, and all the women leaders spoke and wrote on questions of women frequently. The Bolsheviks had great women leaders including Nadezhda Krupskaya, who was Lenin's companion; Alexandra Kollontai, who was on the Central Committee of the Communist Party; and Inessa Armand, a journalist, war correspondent and feminist leader. They also had the wonderful example and role model of Rosa Luxemburg whose revolutionary work in Germany and Poland was famed in the Soviet Union. In the course of all this activity, *chadors* were trampled in the dust.

But 20 years after the 1917 revolution, abortion became a crime again. Homosexuality became a crime again. If you got a divorce, you had to pay a special tax. If you had a baby, you got a prize, a reward. Illegitimacy was restored and to advocate feminism was a kind of crime. It was "bourgeois" to do so, and uppity females were treated very harshly: fired, exiled, sometimes jailed. There wasn't one woman in the upper strata of Soviet public life, in politics, in the party, in the government. The only place a woman could shine was in the theater or the opera, as an athlete or a dancer.

Today, the plight of women is still deplorable. And the reforms of President Mikhail Gorbachev are making it even worse. In his book, *Perestroika*, he writes:

. . .Over the years of our difficult and heroic history, we failed to pay attention to women's specific rights and needs arising from their role as mother and home-maker, and their indispensable educational function as regards children. Engaged in scientific research, working on construction sites, in production and in the services, and involved in creative activities, women no longer have enough time to perform their everyday duties at home—housework, the upbringing of children and the creation of a good family atmosphere. We have discovered that many of our problems—in children's and young people's behavior, in our morals, culture and in production—are partially caused by the weakening of family ties and slack attitude to family responsibilities.

(Guess who has that slack attitude. He's talking about us, ladies! Everybody's troubles are the fault of women: youth, bad morals, bad culture, bad production.)

This is a paradoxical result of our sincere and politically justified desire to make women equal with men in everything. Now, in the course of perestroika, we have begun to overcome this shortcoming. That is why we are now holding heated debates in the press, in public organizations, at work and at ome, about the question of what we should do to make it possible for women to return to their purely womanly mission.

Gorbachev is continuing Stalin's fiction that women already have equality, or as much as they need, as much as they want. And that their real calling is to raise babies and to be good poductive little workers. He's reinforcing women's role in the home because he needs their unpaid domestic labor. This takes the onus off the state, don't you see, to provide for the upbringing of children.

The government is pushing for higher birth rates among Russians (there is a different demographic plan for the non-Russian national minorities). In Russia, you're taxed if you're childless. But you're paid 50 rubles per birth and parents get extra paid leave from work. Women with 10 or more children are honored as "Mother Heroines." If you're really good, you get a medal!

The regime's perspective on women is also revealed in an editorial in the March 1989 issue of *Socialism: Theory and Practice*, a journal printed in Moscow. The writer is talking about fulfilling the desires of women:

> There is no small number of these desires, or so feel the males who constitute the rest of the human race. Perhaps, in addition to the universal desire of women to look at least two times younger than their age, they are united to one extent or another by the idea of emancipation.

(Huh! He noticed.)

> Whereas at the start of this movement, pioneering women had to wage a selfless struggle for their rights and tear down the psychological barriers, both at home and in society, it is now different: males not only support women's emancipation to the hilt but at times they let *[let!]* women work in areas which are plainly contraindicated to them.

(Which means physically demanding work like road building, farming, logging, etc.)

> . . .Even though Soviet women do not experience social discrimination, they nevertheless are striving at this point to stay feminine. The vast majority of them are prepared to combine motherhood and married life, something na-

ture itself wills them to do, with a career and social activity. . . Devoting herself to her home and raising children is what she sees as her primary and joyous duty.

You can hardly say "All rise and sing the 'International'" after that!

## Papa Stalin's horror show

Women in the Soviet Union suffer the most from all the economic and social problems of the country. Childcare, what little there is of it, is terrible. Women put in long days at work. They spend long hours in lines trying to shop. And when they finally get home, they have to do all the cooking and the housework. And I mean all the housework. The men do not do housework. They do not raise the children. They do not cook. They do not shop.

Medicine in the USSR is dreadful. The hospitals are dirty. Childbirth is a very unhygienic process, with ill-staffed hospitals and a dearth of drugs. There is no information or education on AIDS prevention.

Contraceptives are very hard to get but abortions are frightful and cruel. Women are put through a barbaric assembly line resulting in a very high rate of staph infections. For every live birth, there are two to three legal abortions per live birth and three to five illegal abortions.

Why, you may ask, are there illegal abortions when abortion is legal? Because no anesthesia is provided for legal abortions! Women get illegal abortions for the sake of some pain killers, even though *one in five* dies. One in five women dies of illegal abortion, and there are three to five illegal abortions for every two to three legal abortions. Great country for women.

These conditions prevail and are often much worse in the rest of the Eastern Bloc.

What about the plight of older women? They're a vast

army of domestic slaves. They're generally unpaid baby-tenders or else they continue to work at very hard labor until very old ages bcause pensions are so low.

Younger women must take care of elders as well as work and raise their own family. And they all live together in a little crooked room, or maybe if they're lucky, two rooms.

The government has finally admitted that prostitution was never wiped out. And now it's rampant. The prostitutes are mostly single mothers with young children who say this is the only way they can survive.

What about family relations? We hear that the men, when not at work, are drunk or absent from the home. Alcoholism is out of control. The men are completely unsupportive and unsympathetic to the triple labors of the women. Women are the real heads of the families because the men aren't there. All observers of Soviet life remark on how independent and casual the women are with their husbands or male companions. They don't think too much of men. But at work and in politics and in unions, they have to bow down to the men because they are the bosses and have all the high-paid, top jobs.

So far as the general consciousness of Soviet women, it's undoubtedly true that while most women want to work and like their economic independence, they don't like the low wages of "female" occupations. Everybody's searching for a rich husband to support them. Western feminists are derided as man haters and the word feminism is seen as equivalent to bourgeois feminism. They know nothing of Marxist feminism. You'd think that Marx, Engels, Lenin and Trotsky opposed women's liberation.

Women have come practically full circle to where they started out in 1917. Which gives a very bad name to socialism.

### Treachery and betrayal

What happened to cause this situation?

In a nutshell, *counter-revolution* happened. We call it

Stalinism, after the person raised up by the counter-revolution to express it and reflect it.

On the heel of the 1917 revolution, Russia was invaded by 21 capitalist countries determined to smash the new Soviet state. A civil war raged for years. By the time the Bolsheviks defeated the foreign armies and the czarist White Russians, the country was in a state of exhaustion and total ruin. It was not only economically destroyed, not only did famine and disease rage, but the cream of the revolutionary leadership had been killed defending the Soviet Union.

And the country was politically isolated. No other nation had revolutions in those years.

So you have this country, still benighted with feudalism, with a heritage of terrible economic and cultural backwardness, which is isolated, its people exhausted by poverty and war, its leadership wiped out. What happened?

What happened is what *will* happen, as Lenin and Trotsky explained. When there is scarcity, lines form as people try to get what few goods are available. And as lines form, you need policemen to keep order. The police become a special caste above the masses. A whole social layer emerges—the order-keepers, the administrators, the controllers, the cops. And this caste becomes parasitic. It becomes a force for brutality. It becomes solely concerned with its own administrative activities and special privileges, and in maintaining those privileges, even if it means enforcing poverty and deprivation for everybody else.

And then Lenin dies, probably murdered by Stalin. Trotsky, who is fighting the bureaucracy and leading a huge Left Opposition against it, is exiled. The Left Opposition is slaughtered or imprisoned or driven underground. Stalin unleashes the 1936 Moscow Trials in which he frames the entire leadership of the Russian Revolution and gets rid of them—anybody that's left by that time.

In the midst of these horrors, Stalin declares that

socialism has not only been achieved, but the country's gone beyond that into pure communism! He says, "The Soviet experience has proved that it was possible and desirable to build socialism in one country."

It's neither possible or desirable. It's totally impractical and it can't happen. But he says it has. And he says it's the duty of revolutionaries everywhere to subordinate their own struggles to a defense of whatever the Soviet bureaucracy declares is in the best interest of the fatherland. Revolutions are forbidden—they're too dangerous. Just get into the Democratic Party (if you're in the U.S.), and stick with your own bourgeoisie. Fight if you must for narrow reforms, but do it quietly. Don't rock the boat and undermine the Kremlin's deals with your rulers.

On the home front, the unpaid labor of women is once again needed. So Stalin comes up with a new theory to supplant the teaching of Marx and Engels—that travesty called the "Revolutionary Nuclear Family."

The patriarchal family is triumphantly rehabilitated. Instead of Stalin admitting that the Soviets are still too poor to provide the services women need and promising to keep women's emancipation a top priority, he announces that everything is perfect for women in their happy revolutionary families. Trotsky says, "It is hard to measure with the eye the scope of this retreat."

So all the gains made by women were reversed by Stalin. The women's organizations were eliminated. Gays were forced back underground and the backlash on all the other questions took place. Counter-revolution, the regime of betrayal and treachery, solidified into a full-blown police state and a monstrous regime.

## Can't keep a good revolution down

With this background of backwardness and defeat, the current explosion is quite an uproar. But it didn't take

Trotskyists by surprise. It's what Trotsky wrote about, gave his life to, kept saying: The bureaucratic caste has got to be thrown out so that the revolution can continue, so that socialism can really be built.

You can't have socialism without democracy. And you can't have socialism unless you've reached a higher economic level than capitalism. On a low economic level, it's impossible to provide more and better social services—especially when you're still having to put a hell of a lot of money into armaments. It's silly to boast about having achieved socialism under these conditions. You can describe yourself as a workers' state or a revolutionary state, but you simply aren't socialist.

Trotsky said this revolution has to have a rebirth. The people will rise up one day and say, "I'm fed up with all this. I'm sick and tired. I'm not gonna take it anymore. And out you go, bureaucrats!"

We Trotskyists kept saying this even though everybody laughed at us. And here it is! Okay, we *were* a *little* surprised. Even though we predicted it, it's a shocker to see it happen right before your eyes. Needless to say, we're glad to see it. "Good morning, revolution!"

Russian women are armed with a long history of revolutionary struggle and a wealth of Marxist theory on women's emancipation. They're going to need these weapons for the struggles ahead, because Perestroika is bringing the threat of capitalist restoration.

A recent Marxist feminist manifesto talks about the dangers of Perestroika. With more and more independent entrepreneurs and small businessmen on the scene, a lot of factories are going to close down. Who's going to lose their jobs? Women. Young people, pensioners, handicapped people, and women will be the first to lose in connection with modernization, staff cuts, and all the other Perestroika measures.

Soviet women are angry, discontented, miserable and

defiant. It is they who are screaming that Perestroika isn't working. They are increasingly involved in strikes. They are integral to new cross-national labor unions springing up in the ethnic republics. All over Russia, women are demanding better services and better living standards. Women are going to ferociously resist the reimposition of capitalism and church control. They've had enough of the horrors of Catholic, Russian Orthodox, and Muslim dogma, as well as the horrors of Soviet bureaucracy.

I believe that women will become the major force in the new Soviet Union. They've been the power behind it all along and tomorrow they will be visible in the forefront as well.

I believe that women's emancipation depends on the forward march of Soviet democracy, and conversely that the new Russian and Eastern Bloc revolutions will grind to a halt without women's leadership.

I believe, in short and in conclusion, in Permanent Revolution—in an unstoppable, uninterruptible, worldwide revolution to solve all the burning needs and injustices and inequalities and abuses of class exploitation, political tyranny, and race, sex and sexual oppression.

Permanent Revolution is linked closely to women's liberation and women's liberation is central, pivotal, to modern politics. And why shouldn't it be? It's the oldest, the deepest, the most passionate unresolved problem of the majority of the human race. It is the unfinished struggle against the prehistoric crime of male supremacy. Women will have to free the world. And they will have to free themselves. The two things go hand in hand.

I say, with the French, *cherchez la femme.* Look for the woman. As women move, so will move the Soviet Union, the far-flung nations, the regions, the continents, the world. History will trace our path (to put it in New Age terms) from the revolution crucified to the revolution reincarnated.

# Time of the Whirlwind

### 1990

O ur house hosted a Soviet guest, a sculptor, during the Goodwill Games in August, and what a juicy tidbit that proved to be for dinner table conversation and talk show chatter.

Seattle was agog over the thousands of locals who opened their homes to the vast influx of Soviet athletes, artists and intellectuals, officials, experts, trade negotiators, and just plain workers whom Aeroflot deposited on our freshly scrubbed doorsteps.

We didn't need to go to the USSR—it came to us. Moscow-on-Puget Sound was a moveable cultural feast: the Bolshoi Ballet's *Ivan the Terrible;* Prokofiev's opera *War and Peace;* Chekhov's *The Three Sisters;* Eugenia Ginzburg's *Into the Whirlwind,* performed by Moscow's Sovremenik theatre and depicting the plight of women prisoners and their male jailers in the darkness-at-noon decades of Stalin's purges; exhibits of centuries of Russian art climaxed by the Constructivists and their "Art Into Life" creations.

All art flourished in the welcoming climate encouraged by Lenin and Trotsky after the revolution, before Lenin died.

Before the invading armies of U.S. and European capitalists drained the land.

Before the civil war provoked by imperialism exhausted

the people and drowned a huge sector of young leaders in blood.

Before the defeat of the German revolution, which the Bolsheviks utterly depended on for economic and political help.

Before the crystallizing of a caste of bureaucrats, grouped around Stalin, who exploited the ravaged country as they scrambled for power positions. (You always need functionaries to run the food banks, employment agencies, housing departments, and all the rest.)

Before Trotsky's Left Opposition to Stalin was dirty-tricked by officials intoxicated with their vodka-soaked privileges.

And before Trotsky's protest against Stalin's abandonment of revolution abroad, and democratic, commonsensical measures at home, was silenced, by exile and later by the assassin's ax.

**N**ot only Trotsky died. The counterrevolutionary hatchet men of Stalinism executed the *entire remaining leadership* of the October Revolution and killed or imprisoned millions who refused to surrender principles and humaneness.

The prime products of the bureaucracy were corpses, the death of art (suffocated in the one-size-fits-all shroud of "socialist realism"), and the cynical perversion of Marx and Lenin's ideas.

**S**o how did my discussions go with the artists and actors?

With extreme difficulty. Language differences are an impenetrable, nationalistic barrier to an exchange of thinking, and what the Goodwill Games gurus neglected—or refused? or were forced into failing to provide?—were translators. Our lives centered on competitive hunts for Russian-English translators.

You may be sure that visitors who came to talk about

trade and capital investment were accompanied by a decent contingent of translators, as were the pampered athletes. It was the artists and journalists and just-folks who suffered. Of course.

**H**appily we discovered that pantomime, sound effects and pictures are incredible lubricants to communication.

The Soviets were delighted and amazed to find socialists and lower-case "c" communists in this bucolic corner of Yankeeville.

They hated Stalin and knew little about Trotsky; what they did know about Trotsky was wrong and untrue, hardly surprising when Gorbachev, the new Bonaparte, stalls over "rehabilitating" him.

They were puzzled and divided over feminism and lesbian/gay rights, though the 1917 Soviet Constitution was the first in history to legitimize these paramount social and human interests.

Comfortable with all races and my Jewish heritage, they were as yet unscathed by recent eruptions of Soviet anti-Semitism.

They love their country, feel free to criticize it, hope for the best, fear the future, were thrilled to be here and partake of our bounty. But they deplored the seamy slums of paradise that we showed them. These people are not going to trade off their own and their children's birthrights—insured jobs, housing, education, medical care, abortion—for the terrible risks inherent in an unbridled profit system.

*The Soviet Union can never go whole-hog capitalist without a century of convulsions and turmoil.*

And we of the West, which fattened off the plunder and cheap labor of the world, will never find tranquillity either until we merge our wealth and know-how with the socialist concern for all people. Then, together, we will replace the free market—which controls us—with a free people, who control the production and division of wealth. And in the process we'll shed the bureaucrats and tycoons and moguls and emirs and tyrants.

*That* will be peaceful coexistence, real sister cityhood, for we'll be children of a common mother. Episodic goodwill exchanges will graduate to daily good-doing and good living for all.

Every person on earth has been cast into the whirlwind of change, where danger and promise collide. None of us will emerge untouched; no storm cellar will escape the tornadoes of the '90s. But after the whirlwind comes peace.

# On the Threshold of a New Epoch

1960

A speech in honor of May Day, the International Workers Holiday

Ten years ago, my May Day speech spoke of McCarthyism, the execution of the Rosenbergs, FBI terror, witch burnings and blacklistings. In those dark days, I looked to the words of Eugene Debs for a tone of courage, to Marx for an example of tenacity, to Trotsky for the comfort of his long view of history.

But today, on *this* May Day, we need not burrow among the archives to find inspiration in printed words. Those words have taken on flesh—and fresh living blood—and volcanic reality. Today we are not mourning freedom's martyrs—we are avenging them. The revolution they dreamed about is happening—in a manner they never dreamed of.

Today, millions challenge and protest. The forces of domination—in the U.S., North and South, in fascist countries, in South Africa—are trembling and hysterical under the impact of this social tidal wave. No longer are the advocates of change merely "talking on street corners to scorning men," as Bartolomeo Vanzetti wrote. Instead, enraged and determined masses are storming the citadels of entrenched power.

This is new; let's note it. From the 1920s through the end of WWII, we intoned a mournful dirge of defeat and betrayal—Stalin's bloody usurpation of power in the Soviet Union, the collapse of the general strike in England, counterrevolution in China, fascism in Germany and Spain, the genocide of the Jews.

But amid the corpses and ashes, something good remained—the Soviet Union's nationalized and planned economy, a beacon for workers everywhere even though it was repressed and strangled by the Stalinist bureaucracy. WWII weakened the Comintern's grip on its national sections and the spirit of 1917 came bursting forth in China and Yugoslavia, with rumblings all over the buffer zone. Soon, explosions were happening one after another, every day, in the British labor movement, the Arab revolutions, victories against colonialism in India, Africa, Cuba, Korea, Turkey!

We used to patiently track, over a period of years, how events in colonized countries were echoed by reactions in the imperial powers. Today, you can see the cause and effect of Permanent Revolution unfolding in a matter of days, with the newspapers freely describing how revolts are being inspired by the example of a neighbor, a former colony, a struggle halfway across the world.

Suddenly we've entered an epoch of *successful* revolutions, of daily turmoil, of an irresistible dynamic. And the source of this fabulous, new, magnificent rebellion, these victories? It's not where you might expect.

There's a widespread illusion that the road to revolution lies through the patient and systematic education of the most advanced organized workers, as a group, from a union to a political to a radical to a revolutionary consciousness. After years—decades—of this dogged tutelage, a class eventually becomes sophisticated enough to revolt.

But that's not how revolutions work. They break out suddenly—sparked by a particular issue that cannot be precisely foreseen—and they develop fast. As they progress, the goals become broader and also more concrete and revolutionary. But at the beginning, the insurrection does not produce a well-edited manifesto—not even by Dr. Castro and the Cuban intellectuals—but an outburst of resentments and anger. The initial force of this explosion depends on the depth and longevity of oppression.

That is why the early stages of revolution almost invariably feature the phenomenon of the most backward and oppressed and traditionally silent surging past the more politically sophisticated and economically secure. We have seen them: the young girls in Cuba, the women with babies on their backs in Korea and Africa. When the most oppressed in the world, the most miserable and hopeless, burst the dam holding them back, the power is fantastic. The Dark Continent erupts into freedom—and the South African miners haven't even joined the struggle yet. When they do, the die is cast.

The anti-apartheid upsurge in South Africa is being felt in the West with demonstrations in England and sit-ins in the southern United States. In the *New York Times*, Harrison E. Salisbury reports, "Some Negroes have nicknamed Birmingham, Alabama the Johannesburg of America. . .they say it's a difference of degree, that here they have not opened fire with tanks and big guns." Yes, here all they use are whips, razors, guns, bombs, torches, clubs, knives, mobs, police, dynamite, jails, blackjacks, kidnappings, and raids. If Southern Negroes ever had any illusions of the democratic nature of the state, *Johannesburg* dispelled it!

Against the brutality of the Southern police state, Negro youth and students are standing up. Uncorrupted, untempted by collaboration and "Talented Tenth"-ism and good jobs— they are audacious, enthusiastic, brave. The young do not *choose* to compromise—the antics of their elders are simply too degrading. So they electrify and stun their seniors, who are then shamed into defending them.

Not only are NAACP officials forced to mouth pious phrases of moral support, the labor bureaucrats are making similar noises. Union ranks are impressed by the indomitable civil rights activists; and germinating in their minds is the idea that what's effective against Jim Crow would be equally good against anti-labor laws, and that the best way to move your immovable leaders is to *start moving yourself*.

The American union movement has been shown up and forced to take a good look at itself by the calm demonstrations of a few thousand southern Negro students.

And how the Democrat-Republican hoax becomes increasingly exposed! Go on, Reuther, tell these southern kids whom to vote for—which phony in Truman's party to support! The wrigglings and writhings of the AFL-CIO bureaucrats are a farce, and not just to radicals. Northern students as a whole are in natural sympathy with the civil rights cause and the Cuban revolution. They are fired up and they will listen to socialists as never before.

It is a good thing that international pressures are waking up new sections of the oppressed outside the union movement.

Today's unionists are fewer and better paid, becoming privileged aristocrats in habits and thinking. The union movement as we know it is losing ground, breaking up. It is in the throes of a crisis it virtually ignores in which technological changes are throwing people out of work and dramatically increasing the number of menial, unskilled, part-time, non-union jobs.

The revolutionary impulse in America is not going to come from the unions as they are today, but from the displaced and discarded workers, from the youth, from the Negro fighters for freedom. And we radicals won't be mute spectators—in our ranks will be the new revolutionary-minded workers and youth whom capitalism and its labor lieutenants have sought to throw on the garbage heap. Their anger and resentment will be powerful.

**W**hat of the role of revolutionaries in America today? It is easier, yes, because every victory and revolt abroad gives something to us. The long period of conformity and conservatism is still with us, but it is not as strong as it was. Breaks and relaxations have appeared all over, evidencing themselves in small, even gossipy issues of popular culture which reveal elements of class struggle, of non-conformism. But still it is hard, because this country's pressures and seductions are many and insidious. We are still few and isolated, and the road ahead is uncertain and complex.

Nevertheless, we are devoted to achieving human freedom because apart from that we know there is no freedom for us.

The socialist future is clearly within the vista of our epoch, of our lives. And what better fate can a person carve out than participation in the emancipation of humanity? What better use to make of one's life than in preparing that new civilization? We look toward a time when we shall have ceased to mourn martyrs. A time when we are no longer occupied with explaining defeats and rising above betrayals. Not because we will have forgotten the past, but simply because we are so engrossed and fulfilled in the role of creating a world rich with freedom, plenty, humane relations between people, and the joy of living.

# The Meaning of May Day
# for the '70s Generation

1973

Speech at a public forum hosted by the Freedom Socialist Party

Comrades, Sisters, Brothers:
We meet this May Day to pay respects to our workingclass and revolutionary heritage by commemorating the labor martyrs of the Haymarket Massacre.

On that famous first of May 1886, an intense national movement for the eight-hour day was launched in the U.S. In the industrial jungle of Chicago, strikes and protests went on day after day and the cops reacted with murderous assaults. On May 4th, 1,200 workers gathered in Haymarket Square to denounce the violence against the 8-hour mobilizations. The rally was peaceful until, as it was ending, an agent provocateur threw a bomb into a group of police. The cops opened fire, killing several people and wounding hundreds.

In the days that followed, police and city government waged a campaign of terror against workers, immigrants and radicals. On the basis of their politics alone, eight anarchist labor leaders—Albert Parsons, August Spies, George Engel, Samuel Fielden, Louis Lingg, Adolph Fischer, Oscar Neebe, and Michael Schwab—were convicted of "inciting" the bombing. Four of the men were hanged and one committed suicide in his cell. Six years later, a powerful international defense movement freed the remaining three men and gained legal exoneration for all the frame-up victims.

On May Day, therefore, we remember labor's victories

and labor's sacrifices. We meet tonight to lend our voices to a global chorus, for May Day was proclaimed by the international socialist movement as a day of unity and solidarity with the exploited and oppressed of the entire world. The police attack on workers in Haymarket Square happened symbolically to the whole international working class of that time—and is still happening in our time. The solidarity and internationalism at the heart of May Day illuminate not only the magnificent accomplishments of the past, but also the outlines of the revolutionary future.

May Day is an integral part of *our* history as U.S. radicals. May Day is us; and our tribute to it is a decisive step in our lifelong effort to seek, discover and maintain our identity and, thereby, our political and personal course of action.

August Spies said on the gallows: "There will come a time when our silence will be more powerful than the voices you strangle today."

Their "silence," their murder, became an international *cause célèbre*, their courage a moralizing force, and their story a tremendous weapon of education for the generations that came after them. Their silence, their corpses, paid mute testimony to the monster that had destroyed them—the capitalist system of production for private profit, revealed in all its stark hideousness. If you ever start thinking that it might be possible to make peace with capitalism, just remember Haymarket and recognize its ashes in all the conflagrations and confrontations around us today. It is the same system.

Mother Jones, the great woman labor organizer, had this to say about Haymarket:

> The workers asked only for bread and a shortening of the long hours of toil. The agitators gave them visions. The police gave them clubs. . .

> The city was divided into two angry camps. The working

people on one side—hungry, cold, jobless, fighting gun-men and police clubs with bare hands. On the other side the employers...supported by the newspapers, by the police, by all the power of the great state itself.

Substitute for "working people" the word "Blacks," or "Native Americans," or "Chicanos," and this is a description of America today. Substitute for "working people" the word *"women,"* and we can see vividly the place of women in today's society. Substitute the word *"poor,"* and the spectre immediately appears of the law, the mayor, the police department, the media and the bosses arrayed against them.

But soon, we will not have to substitute any words for "working class," because one day in the very near future we women, minorities, and the poor will be marching and demonstrating together as a proud and recognized part of that class.

This will happen without the loss of anybody's special identity. On the contrary, the self-awareness and self-identification of the vanguards of today's many separate movements will lend new richness and meaning to the concept of working class.

Just as internationalism is a concept and a practice that incorporates all nations and yet rises above individual countries and narrow patriotism—just as feminism recognizes many different strata and types of women yet supplies a philosophy for them all—just so does working class express a totality of diverse parts, a totality that doesn't crush everything into an unrecognizable hodgepodge, but which brilliantly reveals the uniqueness and importance of all its components.

The prolonged sway of capitalism and imperialism, coupled with the prolonged sway of trade union corruption and conservatism, has brought about a broadened and deepened consciousness in many layers of the oppressed. And they are bringing to the fore new issues of struggle and resistance.

When for instance, a worker discovers that the union is useless in a grievance, the worker may realize this is because the union is also crippled by racism, sexism, opportunism, or political backwardness. To change the union requires a fight on many planes against all forms of prejudice and discrimination. Such experiences show the interrelations of class, sex, race, age, politics, lifestyle, and sexuality in *life*.

People forced to fight on many fronts begin to wonder about the reasons for having to struggle so often, so hard, and against so many enemies. Like American workers in the 1880s, they say, "We ask only for minimal improvements in our conditions of life and you give us jails, and insults, and threats." Something obviously must be wrong with the entire system; our separate struggles have a common enemy, and we must find a common focal point and mutual solidarity if any of us is to forge ahead, if any of us is to survive.

So we arrive at the answers: *The problem is capitalism. The solution is socialism*, the *only* antithesis to capitalist property relationships. The methodology is solidarity and internationalism. And the most dynamic forces within this entire process of creating the American Revolution are the super-oppressed—women and minorities, whose high and varied consciousness simply reflects their deep and varied victimizations.

Our beautiful, incredible, ever-reborn movements for social justice and human rights have come a long, long way since Haymarket. They were anarchists, with no concepts, plans or concerns about *how* to change the system. Today we have the stronger philosophical weapon of socialism, which stands for intervention into the class struggle, the building of a revolutionary party geared to take the power, and the transformation of society through workers power and a workers state. In addition, new human forces have emerged as participants and leaders in the social struggle—minorities, women, students and youth, sexual minorities. We have witnessed a flowering, an incredible profusion, of political awareness on dozens of fronts.

Since Vietnam, internationalism has jumped from the pages of theory into the maelstrom of daily life. In the wake, and I mean wake, of George McGovern's sound defeat as a liberal Democrat running for president, socialist instead of capitalist politics are again the order of the day for many social movements. Women's leadership and initiative in every movement, not just the women's movement itself, is spiraling upwards, and the Nixon Administration's war on the poor has revitalized the Black struggle.

The one force connecting all these movements, the one force existing in all of them, is the force of women. Oppressed as a worker, oppressed as a racial/ethnic minority, oppressed as a sex, suffering additional levels of oppression if she is a lesbian or aged—she stands objectively as the worldwide image of subjugation and in life, subjectively, she is coming to terms with the leadership role she will have to play.

As Louis XIV could say, *"L'état c'est moi,"*—the state is me—woman can truly say, "Misery and suffering and anguish, that is me." But this must be said in a political sense, not in the traditional weepy, wailing and bitching way of self-pity and boring martyrdom. Woman as Les Miserables must become Woman as Fighter, Woman as Organizer, Woman as Theoretician, Woman as Political Leader. And to the extent that she becomes this, to that extent will she avenge all the labor martyrs of the past, fulfill their dreams, and create the new society.

In 1886, there was only one Lucy Gonzalez Parsons, the fearless revolutionary orator and organizer, who was the widow of Haymarket martyr Albert Parsons. Today, millions of women around the world are fighters, radical politicians and government figures, organizers and theoreticians and spokespersons and leaders. And in this fact alone lies the potential for basic revolutionary change.

The great revolutionaries were well aware of this fact. Lenin made it clear that there could be no socialist revolution unless working women played an important part. And he also paid tribute to women's capacity for leadership:

> There is no doubt that there is far more *organising talent* among the working women and peasant women than we are aware of, people who are able to organise in a practical way and enlist large numbers of workers, and a still larger number of consumers, for this purpose without the abundance of phrases, fuss, squabbling and chatter about plans, systems, etc., which our swelled-headed "intelligentsia" or half-baked "Communists" always "suffer" from. But we do not *nurse* these new shoots with sufficient care.

Unfortunately, today we are inundated with the half-baked intelligentsia type too often.

Trotsky also looked to women for leadership:

> Opportunist organizations by their very nature concentrate their chief attention on the top layers of the working class and therefore ignore both the youth and the woman worker. The decay of capitalism, however, deals its heaviest blows to the woman as a wage earner and as a housewife. The sections of the Fourth International should seek bases of support among the most exploited layers of the working class, consequently among the women workers. Here they will find inexhaustible stores of devotion, selflessness and readiness to sacrifice.

> *Down with the bureaucracy and careerism! Open the road to the youth! Turn to the woman worker!* These slogans are

emblazoned on the banner of the Fourth International.

The problem is that women still underestimate their own potential, their own capabilities, their own *responsibility* for leadership. And it is kind of scary to some women to be informed that *they* are the *key* to social change, the key to socialism, the key to revolutionary internationalism, the thread and connecting link to the masses of impoverished and desperate and angry all over the world.

The new, bold woman leader will find that the hardest burden of all she will have to bear will not be hatred and contempt from threatened men, because she expects that. It will not be persecution from the system, because what else is new? It will not be the furious and sometimes vicious political disputes within the radical movement, because ideological debate is meat and drink for a living radical. No, the hardest burden will be imposed by some of her "sisters" who expect single-issue reforms for women to be won within this system as a result of practicing ladylike and feminine tactics.

But it was ever thus. Rosa Luxemburg was considered "not a feminist" because she was always debating and writing and organizing with and against men at the pinnacles of party leadership. Nonsense. Susan B. Anthony and Elizabeth Cady Stanton were constantly criticized for their involvements in "other" issues—"male oriented" is the epithet today—which is nonsense. War, racism, poverty, police brutality, and class struggle are indeed women's issues, they're just not middleclass ladies' issues.

The indefatigable Emma Goldman took on everybody over her right to address any and every question of human liberation:

My [1915] tour. . .met with no police interference. . . although the subjects I treated were anything but tame: anti-war topics. . .freedom in love, birth-control, and the problem most tabooed in polite society, homosexuality. . .

Censorship came from some of my own comrades because I was treating such "unnatural" themes as homosexuality. . .

In Los Angeles I was invited by the Women's City Club. Five hundred members of my sex, from the deepest red to the dullest grey, came to hear me speak on "Feminism." They could not excuse my critical attitude towards the bombastic and impossible claims of the suffragists as to the wonderful things they would do when they got political power. They branded me as an enemy of woman's freedom, and. . .stood up and denounced me

The incident reminded me of a similar occasion when I had lectured on woman's inhumanity to man. Always on the side of the underdog, I resented my sex's placing every evil at the door of the male. I pointed out that if he were really as great a sinner as he was being painted by the ladies, woman shared the responsibility with him. . . She idolizes in him the very traits that help to enslave her—his strength, his egotism, and his exaggerated vanity. . . When she has learned to be as self-centred and as determined as he, when she gains the courage to delve into life as he does. . .she will achieve her liberation, and incidentally also help him become free. Whereupon my women hearers would rise up against me and cry: "You're a man's woman and not one of us."

Yes, we need to be a "man's woman," if that means being strong and aggressive and outspoken. We need to be a woman's woman, to be sensitive and compassionate. We need to be *feminist* women, to seek freedom for all women. We need to be *socialist* women, because until we change the institution of private property ownership and the transmission of that property through the bourgeois family, no woman will be free. We need to be *internationalist* women, because this is one world and sexual oppression has no national boundary lines.

We need, in short, to be the kind of women who are the kind of *people* who will firmly establish as their lifetime purpose and practice the emancipation of humanity.

And brothers—you are cordially invited to join us. Feminism, socialism, and internationalism should be the qualities of men as well as women. Let us struggle together as equals, co-leaders and comrades in this most rewarding and fulfilling of battles.

Happy May Day!

# Fourth of July Oration

1982

Current fashions in world leftism decree that our very own, home-brew, red-white-and-blue working class be regarded with lofty arrogance. No full-blooded anti-imperialist can pass the course in Revolution II without sneering and sniping at U.S. workers.

Indeed, my sisters and brothers in the shops and offices and mines and mills of the USA have been endowed with a new and hyphenated moniker—the "backward-Americans."

We're retarded. Furthermore, we're no damn good at all. The fate of the world is in other, older and better hands, and made-in-USA radicals should shut up. What do we know, anyway? What insurrections and guerrilla operations have we ever mounted? Besides, even if Yankee radicals gave a revolution, none of the workers would come. They're too dumb.

U.S. toilers, it seems, have yet to shed their diapers. We haven't got mass socialist or communist parties. We've never made it to the little leagues of a Labor Party. We're even short on syndicalists, anarchists, and other such trade unionists who hate Marxism and political parties but expect The Workers to lead an anti-capitalist revolution for non-socialism. Or something.

Anyway, we're abjectly bereft of Europe's perennial kvetches, revisionists, opportunists, accommodationists, ritual radicals, social democrat bureaucrats, and Stalinist hatchet men.

*THIS IS BAD????*

**S**uch backwardness, you might demur, might not be such a bad thing. Thinking *dialectically*, it could even be a boon and a benefit. You might say this. Please do.

What's so great about the "advanced" radical movements in other countries that never get anywhere or that go haywire?

Who needs the world-weary compromisers in the mass reformist parties who have mouthed off about *socialismo* for a hundred years and never got close to making a revolution? Or to making one that didn't end up degenerated, deformed, aborted, diseased, distorted, sexist, racist, homophobic, cruel to oppressed nationalities and hellishly undemocratic?

Call me an American chauvinist if you like. But I infinitely prefer the tumult of my own working class, a class that *leaps* into battle when it finally decides to fight and makes up most dramatically for its late start. This conservative-minded class has the startling habit of suddenly erupting into militance and brilliant innovativeness. It moves further and more swiftly on the strike front than faster-than-a-speeding-bullet you know who. On strategy and tactics it is a world leader.

Ours is an historically youthful class, a self-confident, even smug class, a practical and pragmatic and yet refreshingly romantic class. And it is an *undefeated* class.

Let's give credit where credit is due. North American employees have won some of the best conditions, benefits, and pay scales on the face of the earth—wrested them from slavers, robber barons, giant monopolies, and assorted plutocrats in command of the flagship of imperialism. No small feat, that. Attention must be paid. And respect, too.

**T**he first American Revolution of 1776 inspired soaring hopes among huddled masses everywhere yearning to be free.

The second American Revolution, the Civil War, further electrified the exploited millions of the earth; the determination of the workers in the northern and western United States to smash the "peculiar institution" of slavery wove a unique and glorious chapter in human history.

The saga of U.S. labor—from its thrusts at organization even before the Colonial Revolution, through its thunderous development into the National Labor Union of the 19th century, then the AFL, later the IWW, and finally the audacious and irresistible CIO—is a thrilling story of heroism.

Workers of North America, who are of all races and stem from widely diversified nations and cultures, have nothing to be ashamed of and much to be proud of.

But my working class, of course, is really no better or worse than anybody else's working class. My class is equally the product of its own particular history, geography, and culture, and equally the victim of its own lieutenants who labor for the generals instead of the privates and non-coms.

Nevertheless, our revolution can and must be made, with a little help, and a little less intolerance, from our friends abroad. Every revolution today flounders and sours because the U.S. colossus co-opts, encircles, starves, bombs or subverts it. That is why the North American revolution is everybody's revolution. Don't sell it short.

# 9

# The Socialist Feminist Future

# Approaching the Final Conflict

Excerpt from a Political Resolution adopted at the
Freedom Socialist Party National Convention, September 1988

*Co-authored with Guerry Hoddersen*

T he human race is closer than it has ever been to driving the usurpers and exploiters off the face of the earth.

Humanity is also closer to annihilation—but that in itself is a powerfully compelling reason to vanquish the ruling class!

In the race against time, we have every historical and logical reason to put our confidence in humanity. The people have always struggled against odds for survival. And won! And, in the process, a limitless diversity of culture, art, beauty and knowledge has been created. To save all this from destruction, and to preserve the potential for far greater achievements, is worth fighting for. And people do. Everywhere. All the time.

The FSP can take great pride in being a part of this colossal struggle for survival and freedom. We have kept the faith, as the Black Panthers used to say; we have not caved in to the pessimists, doomsayers, defeatists and cynics, ever ready to give up on humankind because *they* have no will to fight. We have helped create in theory and practice the foundations for a truly egalitarian socialist society where both sexes and people of all colors, cultures, nations, sexual orientations, ages and physical capabilities can learn from each other and share a life that is richer and more meaningful due to the interaction. We have courageously taught others to fight and have stood fast with them. We have evinced the sheer audacity to think that revolution in the heartland of imperialism is not only necessary but possible and indicated!

Socialist feminism is for now. But it's also ahead of its time. And that's the way it should be, because the party is the advance guard of the future. And with every passing day, the future rushes forward to meet us.

All around the world, a multi-hued assembly of the planet's forgotten, put-down, and excluded is moving to the fore. And what the party has always maintained—that the most oppressed will lead the way to a world fit for human habitation—is actually unfolding:

From the jungles and mountains of Central America to the high plateaus of the arid southwestern United States, where indigenous peoples are fighting the giant multi-nationals which poison our life and the environment.

From the shantytowns of South Africa to the college towns of the U.S., where Blacks are grinding apartheid into the dust.

From the sun-drenched Philippine islands to the dark sweatshops of tenements in Chinatown, where Asian/Pacific workers combat tyranny and exploitation.

From the U.S./Mexico border towns to the kangaroo courts of the Immigration and Naturalization Service, where Chicanos and Mexicanos fight for their right to earn a living without regard to borders.

From the battle fronts of the disabled and elderly who demand that all humans be judged by what they *can* do, not by what they can't, to the front lines of the struggle against the worldwide AIDS plague, where lesbians and gay men tackle fear-engendered prejudiced and hatred.

In these and many, many more struggles, the most afflicted are out in front. And interwoven with each and every one of these struggles is the dynamic role played by the women of the world, the second sex which is taking first place in the Survival of Humanity Sweepstakes.

To rephrase Pogo, we have met the future and the future is us. As an earlier FSP Political Resolution so beautifully and powerfully declared: "The world belongs to the class that draws from it the means of survival for the race. And the future belongs to those who envision, prepare and fight for it."

# Clara Fraser:
# A Passion for Politics

I n my mind's eye, I see Clara Fraser focused on some task: a commanding presence, yet totally at your service—if your goal is to free the wretched of the earth.

I picture Clara in her garden on a sunny day. Dressed in shorts, soaking up the rays, she is ensconced at a picnic table control center, surrounded by papers, pencils, phones, a typewriter, pets, iced tea and flowers.

Or I think of her entertaining a boisterous crowd in that same back yard, serving up gourmet barbecue and captivating conversation. She's dissecting movies and TV shows, recounting hilarious political escapades, defending the revolutionary potential of the U.S. working class: "a self-confident, even smug class, practical, pragmatic, refreshingly romantic—and *undefeated*."

Another characteristic view of Clara: in her element speaking from a podium. She holds the audience in the palm of her hand. With her gravelly voice and gleeful chuckle, she makes sense of the hard issues of the day and enlightens listeners about Bolshevism, dialectics, history, class struggle, literature, culture and contemporary philosophy.

For me, fresh out of the sexist and anti-authoritarian New Left, Clara was a revelation: an inspiring teacher who trained women to be leaders and men to be feminists—and vice versa! Her boldness and radicalism far exceeded that of the yippies and hippies of the "don't trust anyone over 30" generation, though she was already 20 years beyond the pale. This Jewish woman also was afforded enormous respect by Black and Native American militants because of her decades on the front lines and unwavering support for the unsung women stalwarts of these movements.

After experiences with double-talking, sanctimonious politicians, I was riveted by Clara's honesty and profound understanding of society. She was a breath of fresh air—a godless communist and troublemaking, truth-telling Trotskyist. I discovered that was exactly what I wanted to be, too!

## A star of her class

Clara's background suggests she was destined to be a defender of the downtrodden.

A "red diaper baby," she was born in 1923 to a Russian social democratic mother and a Latvian anarchist father. She grew up steeped in the vibrant radical culture of East Los Angeles, a multi-ethnic, workingclass ghetto. Like other children in her community, she attended socialist summer camps and after-hours Jewish schools. In junior high school, she and her friends joined the Young People's Socialist League, the youth organization of the Socialist Party.

As a young woman, Clara dreamed of breaking out of poverty by becoming a rich and famous Hollywood writer. But after dabbling with screenwriting, she discovered that revolutionary politics satisfied her need for expanded horizons and personal, creative and intellectual fulfillment. At age 22, amidst the mayhem of World War II, she joined the Los Angeles branch of the Socialist Workers Party. Soon after, she transferred to Chicago to join her first husband, stationed there in the Navy. She was an activist in the Chicago SWP and participated in a campaign to unionize the large department store where she worked as a copywriter. In 1946, Clara agreed to the party's request that she assist the Seattle branch for an unspecified period—and there she remains to this day.

Her life has been happily consumed with strikes, labor activity, civil rights mobilizations and defense committees; coalitions against imperialist wars, police brutality and job discrimination; aid to revolutions and liberation struggles around the globe; campaigns for welfare rights, legalized abortion and affirmative action; and voracious study of Marxist economic theory, Black history and the daily newspaper. Meanwhile she has earned her living at a myriad of jobs, including secretary, office manager, taxi driver, bus cleaner, typographer, and assembly line electrician at the Boeing aircraft behemoth.

When Boeing workers struck in 1948, Clara helped engineer an innovative picket line of mothers and babies—a stroller brigade—to defy an anti-picketing injunction. Following the strike's defeat, Clara was one of a hundred leaders prohibited from re-entering the plant—the first of many blacklistings she encountered during the anti-communist witch hunts of the McCarthy era.

Despite being hounded from job to job, Clara kept on working and organizing and raising two talented sons, the products of her marriages to two political co-thinkers. Her oldest son, Marc Krasnowsky, became a journalist and the younger, Jon Fraser, is a jazz musician.

From the late '50s onward, the Seattle branch of the SWP grew increasingly at odds with the Farrell Dobbs-Tom Kerry leadership of the party. At issue was whether radicals should follow or lead—whether they should dissemble in the mass movements or use transitional slogans to educate for socialism.

The national SWP adulated the reactionary, non-workingclass separatism of the Black Muslims. The party smugly ignored the burgeoning surge of women for liberation. And it curried popularity among anti-Vietnam War ranks by drastically diluting down its program to the simplistic, single-issue demand of "Bring the Boys Home."

In contrast, the Seattle SWP, with some support nationwide, advocated the class solidarity of Black and white workers, called for a greatly expanded understanding of and attention to women's emancipation, and urged the antiwar movement to support the socialist, anti-colonial aims of the Vietnamese revolution.

The branch was truly a model minority. For a long decade, it was loyal, active, extremely disciplined, and successful in its work, with growing local influence and impact. But as it attempted to change the course of the national SWP, the branch was subjected to virulent harassment, slander and duplicity. Finally, in 1966, when the SWP banned all dissident groupings, threw Clara off the party's National Committee, and unleashed a lynch-spirit against Seattle, the branch had to break free or die. Driven out of the SWP, it proceeded to form the Freedom Socialist Party.

It was a courageous step to leave an organization to which she'd given 20 years of her life. I was even more awed when I learned of Clara's next move. She would not countenance the abusive sexism of her second husband, Richard Fraser, even though the ensuing battle split the fledgling Freedom Socialist Party.

In divorce proceedings, Fraser, a party leader, viciously depicted Clara as an unfit mother, offering as "proof" her political activism, dedication, and late night meetings. He spiced up his charges with accusations of adultery—a patriarchal concept that is unacceptable to radicals.

Clara called on the party to repudiate this treachery and walk its talk on the Woman Question. It is not acceptable, she argued, to espouse revolutionary feminism in public but expect one's mate to be a hausfrau. Nor is it permissible for a socialist leader to resort to bourgeois, sexist ideology to attack a political colleague in the hostile environment of the courts.

Clara asked the membership to pass a resolution

demanding that Fraser drop his courtroom smears or be expelled. The motion carried. . .by one vote. The minority— all but one of whom were male—stormed out, deserting the party. That split created the FSP as it exists today: a Leninist party in which both men and women are expected to be feminists and defenders of all the oppressed.

After two years of bitter legal struggle, Clara won her divorce and custody of her child.

## Times a-changin'

In the '60s and '70s, U.S. politics finally began to catch up to Clara.

The women's liberation movement roared onto the scene. And in 1967, Clara, Gloria Martin and others founded Radical Women, which ever since has been the revolutionary wing of the women's movement and the feminist wing of the socialist movement. Clara's programmatic anchoring, tactical brilliance and roll-up-your-sleeves activism were instrumental in creating a unique and powerful brand of multi-racial, workingclass feminism.

Radical Women and FSP were always where the action was. Clara and her comrades collaborated with Black women from the anti-poverty program to lead Washington State's first abortion rights demonstration. They encircled the Black Panther headquarters to prevent a police attack, aided Native American fish-ins and Chicano building takeovers, and protested the destruction of low-income housing in the Asian American community. They campaigned for employer-funded childcare. They helped organize the first lesbian/gay pride marches and won groundbreaking protections for sexual and political minorities in Seattle's open housing and fair employment ordinances. Many RW members found entrée to the labor movement through non-traditional trades.

Clara was arrested in 1969 on a strike picket line and again in 1971 when police raided a benefit for antiwar defendants in the Seattle Seven conspiracy trial. She beat the rap both times, skillfully representing herself in court in the second case. She continued to deflate the legal mystique in a series of pioneering classes on "Women and the Law: Courtroom Self-Defense," which gave a generation of women the confidence to enter law school and handle their own legal affairs. Many other activists embraced revolutionary politics after taking Clara's popular classes on *Capital* and the history of philosophy.

Social unrest had reached such a pitch that, in order to maintain control, the federal government was forced into some palliative measures. The "War on Poverty"—first suggested by socialist Michael Harrington in *The Other America*—was initiated by President Kennedy and sustained by Johnson. To staff it, the government resorted to hiring some radicals and social activists—only they had the organizing skills, the community standing and the commitment to mobilize the inner-city ghettos and impoverished rural hinterlands.

In the brief period before these innovative programs were dismantled by the Nixon Administration (which feared their potentially incendiary effect), Clara and many other radicals leaped at this unprecedented chance to actually get *paid* to help the poor and disadvantaged better their conditions through job training, basic and advanced education, lobbying, neighborhood organizing, and a host of actions that enhanced political consciousness, community involvement, and grassroots leadership.

Clara was right at home working with welfare mothers, parolees, prostitutes, youth, and unskilled women workers from Black, Chicano, Native American, Asian American, Gypsy and poor white communities. She and her colleagues initiated highly successful campaigns for liberalized state and local policies on a broad range of social issues, including abortion rights. As Coordinator of Community Relations at the Seattle Opportunities Industrialization Center and a labor market analyst for the Concentrated Employment Program of the Seattle-King County Economic Opportunity Board, Clara deftly coordinated the participation of labor, media, educators, and government in projects benefiting the poor without ever obscuring her political background and identity. She also helped her lifelong colleague, Gloria Martin, create an anti-poverty workers union.

In 1973, Clara's broad-based employment history, administrative skills, and status as a feminist led to her being hired as Training and Education Coordinator at Seattle City Light, a publicly owned power company. One of her assignments was to promote and implement a trailblazing program to hire and train women utility electricians. This she achieved despite the continuous sabotage of management which intended the program to be a short-lived publicity stunt.

When an 11-day wildcat strike erupted at the utility, Clara became one of its leaders. Although she was only a "provisional" employee, without civil service or union protection, Clara's sense of solidarity was immovable. As always, she boldly wove together class, gender and race issues. She helped inspire female employees and workers of color to join the strike. She was elected to represent the workforce on a committee negotiating an Employee Bill of Rights and Responsibilities. And she was a frontrunner in a campaign by city workers to recall the mayor because of his support for the tyrannical, anti-labor practices of City Light Superintendent Vickery.

After a year-and-a-half of thorny negotiations, the Employee Bill of Rights was completed—and Vickery abruptly fired Clara. She immediately filed a discrimination complaint against City Light, documenting countless examples of rank political bias and sexism, typified by Vickery's public boast: "If Clara were as loyal to me as she is to Karl Marx, I'd hire her back in a minute."

Clara's seven-year battle against City Light's blatant

political retaliation and sex discrimination roused international support. And ultimately, she beat the Seattle city fathers on all fronts: in the media, on the witness stand and in the court of public opinion. City Light was forced to rehire her into her old job, pay back wages and damages amounting to $135,000, and cover her attorneys' fees. This triumph set a tremendous precedent for workers' rights to free speech on the job.

Virtually as soon as Clara returned to work at City Light, she and the FSP were targeted in another lawsuit—a McCarthyite attempt to destroy the party. Known as the Freeway Hall Case, the suit was launched in 1984 by Richard Snedigar, a vindictive ex-member who sought to regain a $22,500 donation given years before to the party's new headquarters fund. He demanded FSP minutes, membership lists, and contributors' names—which the party refused to hand over despite ruling after ruling in Snedigar's favor. At one point, Clara and the party's attorneys were sentenced to jail for refusing to divulge financial information. (The sentences were stayed and eventually overturned.)

FSP pursued the case to the Washington State Supreme Court, where Leonard Boudin, the renowned civil liberties attorney, eloquently described how privacy is the lifeblood of the right to dissent. The party was ultimately vindicated in 1992. *They Refused to Name Names: The Freeway Hall Case Victory*, published by Red Letter Press, tells the story of this momentous case and the invaluable contribution it made to the rights of all activist organizations.

## Revolutionary mentor

Clara, now National Chair of the FSP, has taught me to fight back and never shrink from doing what is needed, no matter how difficult.

From a one-city outpost, she has nurtured an international party with branches on both coasts and affiliates in Canada and Australia.

She is one of the few American Jews to take a courageous, outspoken stand against the oppressive Zionist state of Israel (helping lead me back to my Jewish workingclass roots).

She accords her comrades and political allies the courtesy and respect of telling them when they are off-track, and provides tremendous support for all people and movements heading in a positive direction.

She embodies the fact that the struggle for a decent life for working people is worth living and dying for. She is gloriously optimistic and can pulverize the most determined doomsayer.

I continue to learn perseverance and the long view of history from Clara. She teaches us that the best kept secret is the power of the working class in all its diversity. She inspires us to have the confidence to go for the power so that workers can run society for the benefit of all.

"All we need is one short but good revolution," Clara likes to say. And this grande dame of socialism, as the *Seattle Post-Intelligencer* once dubbed her, is the one to show us how to do it with style, and to have fun along the way!

ADRIENNE WELLER
Portland, Oregon

# Resources

Alaniz, Yolanda. *The Indian-Sandinista War in Nicaragua.* Seattle: Freedom Socialist Publications, 1986.

Alaniz, Yolanda, and Megan Cornish. *The Chicano Struggle: A Racial or a National Movement?* Seattle: Freedom Socialist Reprints, 1986.

Arnold, William. *Shadowland.* New York: McGraw-Hill, 1978.

Ashbaugh, Carolyn. *Lucy Parsons: American Revolutionary.* Chicago: Charles H. Kerr, 1976.

Bebel, August. *Woman Under Socialism.* Translated by Daniel DeLeon. New York: Schocken Books, 1971.

Bellamy, Edward. *Looking Backward, 2000-1887.* New York: Penguin Books, 1982.

Boot, Tom. *Revolutionary Integration: Yesterday and Today.* Seattle: Freedom Socialist Reprints, 1983.

Cannon, James P. *America's Road to Socialism.* New York: Pioneer Publishers, 1953.

Cannon, James P. *The First Ten Years of American Communism: Report of a Participant.* New York: Pathfinder Press, 1973.

Cannon, James P. *The History of American Trotskyism: Report of a Participant.* New York: Pathfinder Press, 1944.

Cannon, James P. *Notebook of an Agitator.* New York: Pathfinder Press, 1958.

Cannon, James P. *Socialism on Trial.* New York: Pathfinder Press, 1970.

Cannon, James P. *The Struggle for a Proletarian Party.* New York: Pathfinder Press, 1972.

Chambless, Dorothy Mejia. *Race and Sex, 1972: Collision or Comradeship?* Revised Edition. Seattle: Radical Women Publications, 1976.

Crisman, Robert, Stephen Durham, Monica Hill, and Merle Woo. *Permanent Revolution in the U.S. Today.* Seattle: Freedom Socialist Publications, 1985.

Deaderick, Sam, and Tamara Turner. *Gay Resistance: The Hidden History.* Revised Edition. Seattle: Red Letter Press, 1997.

Durham, Heidi. *The War on the Disabled: Adding Insult to Injury.* Seattle: Freedom Socialist Publications, 1982.

Durham, Heidi, and Megan Cornish. *Women Workers: Sparkplugs of Labor.* Seattle: Radical Women Publications, 1990.

Durham, Stephen, and Susan Williams. *AIDS Hysteria: A Marxist Analysis.* Seattle: Freedom Socialist Publications, 1986.

Durham, Stephen, and Susan Williams. *The Nature of the Nicaraguan State.* Seattle: Freedom Socialist Reprints, 1988.

Engels, Frederick. *The Origin of the Family, Private Property, and the State.* New York: Pathfinder Press, 1972.

Engels, Frederick. *Socialism: Utopian and Scientific.* Chicago: Charles H. Kerr, 1918.

Flexner, Eleanor. *Century of Struggle: The Women's Rights Movement in the United States.* Cambridge: Harvard University Press, Belknap Press, 1975.

Flynn, Elizabeth Gurley. *The Rebel Girl: An Autobiography, My First Life (1906-1926).* New York: International Publishers, 1973.

Fraser [Kirk], Richard, and Clara Fraser [Kaye]. *Revolutionary Integration: The Dialectics of Black Liberation.* Seattle: Freedom Socialist Reprints, 1977.

Friedan, Betty. *The Feminine Mystique.* New York: Norton, 1963.

Goldman, Emma. *Living My Life: An Autobiography of Emma Goldman.* Salt Lake City: G.M. Smith, 1982.

Hellman, Lillian. *Pentimento: A Book of Portraits.* Boston: Little, Brown, 1973.

Hellman, Lillian. *Scoundrel Time.* Boston: Little, Brown, 1976.

Hoddersen, Guerry, and Clara Fraser. *Towards the '90s: Approaching the Final Conflict.* Seattle: Freedom Socialist Reprints, 1990.

Hughes, Langston. *Good Morning, Revolution: Uncollected Social Protest Writings.* New York: L. Hill, 1973.

Jones, Mother. *The Autobiography of Mother Jones.* Chicago: Charles H. Kerr, 1980.

Kapp, Yvonne. *Eleanor Marx.* 2 vols. New York: Pantheon Books, 1977.

Kato, Nancy Reiko. *Women of Color: Front-runners for Freedom.* Seattle: Radical Women Publications, 1990.

Kollontai, Alexandra. *The Autobiography of a Sexually Emancipated Communist Woman.* New York: Herder & Herder, 1971.

Lenin, V.I. *The Emancipation of Women.* With an appendix, "Lenin on the Woman Question," by Clara Zetkin. New York:

International Publishers, 1969.

Lenin, V.I. *"Left-wing" Communism: An Infantile Disorder.* New York: International Publishers, 1934.

Lenin, V.I. *State and Revolution.* New York: International Publishers, 1932.

Lenin, V.I. *The Suppressed Testament of Lenin.* New York: Pioneer Publishers, 1935.

Luxemburg, Rosa. *Reform or Revolution.* New York: Pathfinder Press, 1973.

Luxemburg, Rosa. *Rosa Luxemburg Speaks.* New York: Pathfinder Press, 1970. (Includes "What is Economics?")

Martin, Gloria. *Socialist Feminism: The First Decade, 1966-1976.* Seattle: Freedom Socialist Publications, 1986.

Marx, Karl. *Capital: A Critique of Political Economy.* Vol. 1, *The Process of Capitalist Production.* Edited by Frederick Engels. Translated from the 3rd German edition by Samuel Moore and Edward Aveling. New York: International Publishers, 1967.

Marx, Karl. *Critique of the Gotha Programme.* New York: International Publishers, 1938.

Marx, Karl. *The Living Thoughts of Karl Marx, Based on Capital: A Critique of Political Economy, Presented by Leon Trotsky.* New York: Longmans, Green, & Co., 1939.

Marx, Karl. *The Poverty of Philosophy.* New York: International Publishers, 1963.

Marx, Karl. *Wage-Labour and Capital & Value, Price, and Profit.* New York: International Publishers, 1976.

Marx, Karl, and Frederick Engels. *The Communist Manifesto.* New York: Pathfinder Press, 1985.

Marx, Karl, and Frederick Engels. *The Holy Family: Or, Critique of Critical Critique.* Moscow: Foreign Languages Publishing House, 1956.

Millett, Kate. *Sexual Politics.* New York: Simon & Schuster, 1990.

Novack, George. *An Introduction to the Logic of Marxism.* New York: Merit Publishers, 1969.

*Radical Women Manifesto.* Revised Edition. Seattle: Radical Women Publications, 1996.

Rubinstein, Annette T. *The Great Tradition in English Literature from Shakespeare to Shaw.* New York: Citadel Press, 1953.

Schreiner, Olive. *The Story of an African Farm.* Gloucester, MA: Peter Smith, 1976.

Schreiner, Olive. *Woman and Labor.* New York: Johnson Reprint, 1972.

Shakur, Assata. *Assata: An Autobiography.* Westport, CT: L. Hill, 1987.

Shaw, Bernard. *The Intelligent Woman's Guide to Socialism and Capitalism.* New York: W.H. Wise, 1931.

Smith, Lillian. *Killers of the Dream.* New York: Norton, 1978.

Strong, Anna Louise. *I Change Worlds: The Remaking of an American.* Garden City, NY: Garden City Publishing, 1937.

*They Refused to Name Names: The Freeway Hall Case Victory.* Seattle: Red Letter Press, 1995.

Trotsky, Leon. *The Transitional Program for Socialist Revolution.* New York: Pathfinder Press, 1977.

Trotsky, Leon. *Fascism: What It Is and How to Fight It.* New York: Pathfinder Press, 1969.

Trotsky, Leon. *The History of the Russian Revolution.* London: Pluto Press, 1977.

Trotsky, Leon. *My Life* New York: Pathfinder Press, 1970.

Trotsky, Leon. *The Permanent Revolution, and Results and Prospects.* New York: Merit Publishers, 1969.

Trotsky, Leon. *The Revolution Betrayed: What Is the Soviet Union and Where Is It Going?* New York: Pioneer Publishers, 1957.

Trotsky, Leon. *The Third International After Lenin.* New York: Pioneer Publishers, 1936.

Wallace, Michele. *Black Macho and the Myth of the Superwoman.* New York: Verso, 1990.

Weiss, Murry, and Robert Crisman. *Permanent Revolution and Women's Emancipation.* Seattle: Freedom Socialist Reprints, 1982.

Wilde, Oscar. *The Soul of Man Under Socialism and Other Essays.* Garden City, NY: Doubleday, 1923.

Williams, Susan. *Lesbianism: A Socialist Feminist Perspective.* Seattle: Radical Women Publications, 1973.

Williams, Susan. *Women's Psychology: Mental Illness as a Social Disease.* Seattle: Radical Women Publications, 1975.

Wollstonecraft, Mary. *Vindication of the Rights of Woman.* New York: Penguin, 1992.

*A Victory for Socialist Feminism: Organizer's Report.* Seattle: Freedom Socialist Publications, 1969.

# Index

Logic 327; dialectical 76, 315, 321–322; formal 76, 315, 319–320; idealist 314, 322, 323; materialist 312, 314–316, 322–323. *See also* Dialectical materialism; Marxist philosophy

Luxemburg, Rosa 47, 192, 277, 342, 366

# M

Malcolm X 165, 171, 391

Male dominance, origins of 33

Male supremacy 33, 42–43, 51, 93, 135, 143, 149, 236, 248, 350

Marcus, Lynn. *See* LaRouche, Lyndon

Martin, Gloria *104*, *110*, 224–227, 383, 385

Marx, Karl 79, 86, 224, 275, 277, 289, 291, 299, 306, 323–327, 348, 352, 355, 385; on women 42, 192

Marxism 87, 191, 298, 299–301, 306, 311–317, 318–327

Marxist economic analysis of capitalism 40–41, 117, 275–277; commodities 60, 116. *See also* Labor theory of value; Surplus value

Marxist philosophy 67, 311–317, 318–327. *See also* Dialectical materialism; Historical materialism

Matriarchy 33, 59–61, 71, 133, 144, 278, 312

May Day: origins of 360–362

McCarthy era 215, 242, 246, 381

McCarthyism 210, 355, 386

Means, Russell 124, 311–317

Middle caste 187–189

Militarism 143, 146, 159

Millett, Kate 195, 228–230

Morales, Rosa *107*

Moscow Trials 333, 347

Multi-issue politics 53, 122, 363

# N

National Association for the Advancement of Colored People (NAACP) 357

National Caucus of Labor Committees 233–234, 235

National Organization for Women (NOW) 36, 88, 178

Nationalism 37, 136–138, 228–229, 279, 300, 317; Black 37, 48–49, 136–138; Jewish 17, 121, 140. *See also* Cultural nationalism

Native Americans 92, 106, 120, 124, 131–133, 143, 144, 175, 267, 311–317, 362, 380, 383, 384

New Left 51, 67–68, 72, 74, 88, 233, 242, 258

News media 195–197, 198–200

Nicaragua 158, 188

# O

Old Left 88

Older women 345–346, 364

Opportunism 47, 88, 187

Oswald, Lee Harvey 165–166

# P

Pailthorp, Michelle 210, 213

Palestine 17, 121, 139–141, 257

Parks, Rosa 38

Parsons, Lucy Gonzalez 364

Pasternak, Boris 248–251

Patriarchy 35, 60, 63, 89, 181

People of color 32, 95, 122, 143, 174, 180

People's front 56

Perestroika. *See* Union of Soviet Socialist Republics: Glasnost & Perestroika

Truman, Harry  128
Unity  14, 94–95, 281–282
Utopian socialists  89, 323

**V**

Vanzetti, Bartolomeo  355
Vietnam War  48, 88, 142–143,
  146, 158, 162, 164–165, 253,
  257, 364, 382

**W**

Wallace, Michele  134–135
Wampold, Thomas  210–211,
  213
War, role under capitalism  34,
  158–160
Weiss, Murry  *109*, 239
Weiss, Myra Tanner  *109*, 215
Welfare  36, 69, 181–182, 189,
  384
Weller, Adrienne  379–387
White supremacy  39. *See also*
  Racism
Wilde, Oscar  287
Williams, Dr. Susan  86
Windoffer, Melba  *104*
Wobblies. *See* Industrial Workers
  of the World (IWW)
Wollstonecraft, Mary  59, 86
Women  362; conditions for
  emancipation  42, 52–53, 367;
  exclusion from social production  40–41; leadership of
  54–55, 59–71, 72–79, 92, 94,
  132, 228, 350; origins of
  oppression  33–34, 54, 59–61,
  116; psychology of oppression
  13, 63; social role under
  capitalism  40–41, 52, 61, 89;
  violence against  31, 190–192
Women of color  14, 15, 52–53,
  54, 65–66, 90, 92–93, 180
Women workers  15, 45–46, 52,
  54, 90, 365
Women's liberation  15,
  132–133, 143–146, 167,

177–178, 234, 253, 382, 383;
  connection to class struggle
  13, 39–42, 53–54, 66, 86,
  88–90, 115–122; connection
  to race liberation  13, 39–40,
  44–45, 53, 54, 90, 115–122,
  132–133; revolutionary nature
  of  41–42, 50, 53, 55, 67,
  70–71, 86–88, 168, 182, 264,
  350. *See also* Feminism;
  Socialist feminism
Woo, Merle  125, 208
Working class  116, 119, 123,
  180, 324; composition of
  119–120, 362
Working class, U.S.  369–371,
  379
World War II  142, 145, 246,
  335, 355–356

**Y**

Yugoslavia  335, 356

**Z**

Zetkin, Clara  90, 192
Zionism  121–122, 139–141,
  257, 387. *See also* Nationalism: Jewish

Available from

# RED LETTER PRESS

## Gay Resistance: The Hidden History
by Sam Deaderick and Tamara Turner

A lively and impassioned survey of the origins of
sexual oppression and the thousand-year struggle
for lesbian/gay freedom.
$7.00 • 56 pages

## Socialist Feminism: The First Decade, 1966-76
by Gloria Martin

"Argues forcibly that socialist feminism was not just a fad
but is a visionary politics of tomorrow."
—MITSUYE YAMADA, poet and human rights activist
$8.95 • 244 pages, bibliography, index

## Woman Sitting at the Machine, Thinking
Poems by Karen Brodine

"A posthumous gem from one of America's finest
avant garde/political poets."
—POETRY FLASH
$8.95 • 120 pages

## They Refused to Name Names: The Freeway Hall Case Victory
The record of an inspiring fight for justice—and a
guide to defeating harassment lawsuits.
$4.00 • 48 pages

Order from **RED LETTER PRESS**
409 Maynard Ave. S., Suite 201, Seattle, WA 98104
Add $1.50 per book for shipping

*For a complete list of publications:*
Phone: (206)682-0990 • Fax: (206)682-8120
E-mail: redletterpress@juno.com • http://www.socialism.com